P1

1815

STEPHEN BATES read Modern History at Oxford before working as a journalist for the BBC, *Daily Telegraph*, *Daily Mail* and the *Guardian* where he was in turn education editor, a political correspondent, European Affairs editor and latterly religious affairs and royal correspondent. He is now a full-time author. His previous books include: *A Church at War: Anglicans and Homosexuality*, *God's Own Country: Religion and Politics in the US*, a biography of Herbert Asquith; *The Poisoner: the Life and Crimes of Victorian England's Most Notorious Doctor*; and *Two Nations: Britain in 1846*.

1815

Regency Britain in the Year of Waterloo

STEPHEN BATES

HEAD
of ZEUS

First published in 2015 by Head of Zeus Ltd

1 3 5 7 9 10 8 6 4 2

A CIP catalogue record for this book is available
from the British Library.

ISBN (HB) 9781781858219
(E) 9781781858202

Text design and typesetting by Lindsay Nash
Printed and bound in Germany by GGP Media GmbH, Pössneck

Head of Zeus Ltd
Clerkenwell House
45–47 Clerkenwell Green
London EC1R 0HT

www.headofzeus.com

For my brother Colonel Christopher Bates and sister Felicity Rickard

Contents

'A change in life itself'

— ROBERT SOUTHEY

At about nine o'clock in the evening on Sunday 18 June 1815, Arthur Wellesley, the Duke of Wellington, commander of the British, Dutch and Belgian forces in that day's battle, rode forward to meet Field Marshal Gebhard von Blücher, the Prussian general whose troops had arrived a few hours earlier, in time to drive the French army of Napoleon Bonaparte finally from the field and from waging war in Europe.

They met, surrounded by piles of dead and dying troops, the wounded and the exhausted survivors of the great, climactic conflict, as cannon smoke and the smell of gunpowder wafted acridly across the trampled, muddy, debris-strewn cornfields of the rolling farmland south of Brussels. Around them lay nearly 50,000 casualties from the 180,000 troops estimated to have taken part in the battle. There were men killed outright by musket-balls large and sluggish enough to punch huge mortal wounds in chests and stomachs and by cannon-balls which, bounding through the air and visibly bouncing off the ground like footballs, could decapitate a soldier or knock over a line of men. Those who had been wounded, if they were lucky, might survive the ministrations of sawbone surgeons and, if they were not, would die agonizingly slowly of gangrene, shock and exposure, or at the hands of the local and military scavengers who were already beginning to creep across the battlefield to see what they could pillage.

'*Mein lieber Kamerad!*' exclaimed the septuagenarian Marshal Blücher, before resorting to the one language he and Wellington had in common, that of their enemy: '*Quelle affaire!*' It was, the duke supposed – unfairly – the only French the old man had; but it did not stop Blücher apparently pointing to the propitious name of the farmhouse near where they were meeting: La Belle Alliance. What a name for the battle, he suggested. No, the duke thought better of the idea. In the British tradition, it would be named after the nearest small town, a couple of miles further north on the road back to Brussels: Waterloo.

It had been a battle so enormous, so terrible and so decisive that the great powers of Europe did not go to war with each other again for nearly forty years, until the Crimean War in 1854. Waterloo was also, at the time and for nearly a century afterwards, *the* battle of the nineteenth century as far as Britain was concerned. All its other battles were distant affairs on a much smaller scale, in the Crimea or far away on colonial frontiers. Decades later Waterloo's wizened survivors would be pointed out, celebrated and eventually even photographed as veterans and heroes all, as if, like Shakespeare's warriors, gentlemen in England then a-bed, or even unborn, still held their manhoods cheap they were not there. So great was the honour that some, most notably the Prince Regent, would later claim they had indeed been present at such a famous British triumph of arms. The fat, gout-ridden, rouge-smeared prince came to believe he had even led a cavalry charge. When he said so in front of Wellington, the duke replied dryly: 'I have heard you Sir say so before, but I did not witness this marvellous charge.' Then and ever since, the fact that most of the duke's army – even before the Prussians arrived – were not actually British has often been forgotten, not least by Wellington himself. But what was of even greater significance for the country was that the defeat of Napoleon not only brought to an end a continental conflict that had lasted for nearly a quarter of a century, throughout the adult life of most of the troops taking part, but that it ushered in almost a century before British troops would again be engaged in Europe. Not for another ninety-nine years and sixty-six days would British soldiers open fire on a western European enemy. When they did so, on 23 August 1914, it would be thirty miles down the road from Waterloo, at Mons.

The battle of Waterloo was therefore a decisive culmination of a period in British history, but also a hinge point in it: a short, sharp break between the distant worlds of the eighteenth century and the modern, scientific, technological age, as contemporaries saw it, of the nineteenth. A single day's battle (the preliminary skirmishes two days before, serious though they were, tended to be overlooked) had changed Britain irrevocably. Above all, Waterloo created a sense of national pride and a sentiment, not entirely unlike the warm glow that infuses modern memories of the Second World War 130 years later. Wellington famously described the battle as a close-run thing and so it was: it might very well have ended differently, but the victory, however achieved, helped shape the nation's identity and self-esteem across the coming century.

What sort of country, though, was Britain in 1815? It was not one filled with martial ardour, not a country in which there was any sense of being all in it together. The long-running war imposed a considerable financial burden on the nation. It had cost the equivalent of six times the national income of the 1790s by the time it finished in 1815: the astonishingly precise figure cited was £1,657,854,518. The national debt almost quadrupled from £228 million to £876 million, and the interest on that debt at the end of the war was more than the entire government spending had been at its start. But the cost did not overwhelm the country and the income tax which had been introduced to fund the war was abolished in 1816. Indeed, Britain could afford to fight an entirely separate war on another continent, against the United States, at the same time – that cost another £25 million – a war which had ended in one of the British army's most humiliating defeats only six months before Waterloo (see Chapter 1).

The British soldiers who fought on that June day were in many ways separate from the country and the society they were defending. Britain did not use conscription for its soldiers, though it still seized and impressed sailors for its navy. It was not a 'people's war', as the major conflicts of the twentieth century would be. The troops were regulars, mostly drawn from the labouring and unemployed classes, many of them from Ireland and Scotland, the majority of whom had not fought in the previous battles of the Napoleonic wars and so were raw in combat. Many of those who survived would not see their homes and families again for years and, in the days before photography and easy contact, might not be recognized when they did return. There were some who suspected it was a deliberate government policy; in the words of the short-lived radical broadsheet *Black Dwarf* in 1817: 'The army and the people are therefore separated from each other altogether and no intercourse must be allowed where it can be prevented lest the soldier should begin to remember that he is a man.' Their officers were usually members of the aristocracy and gentry who had bought their commissions and were scarcely chosen for their military abilities. Quite the reverse, they were united only by the belief that their place was to command.

Yet that did not mean that the effects of the wars were not experienced indirectly by the wider population. Although Britain itself had not been invaded – scattered landings in Ireland and Wales in the winter of 1796–7 had been easily repulsed – many of the country's young men, particularly those living near the Channel coast, had signed up for local militia units. These tended to be derided by cartoonists as full of gormless toy soldiers in ill-fitting fancy uniforms, bumpkins employable only to defend their local districts. But many had been tradesmen or were from the professional classes – 40 per cent of Edinburgh's volunteers were lawyers in 1797: men with something to lose, defending home and hearth, recruited earlier in the war when there was a real fear of a French invasion. Their presence, drilling and parading, formed a constant background to country life – and, in the absence of a regular police force, they would be called in to keep order and put down disturbances such as those that sprang up in the years after 1815. As the war ended, there were perhaps 600,000 men in uniform in the army and navy: a huge number in a country of maybe 13 million people.* By 1815 the country was having difficulties recruiting enough men of the right age and aptitude for soldiering.

By the time of Waterloo, the Napoleonic wars had been going on, with only a brief outbreak of peace, for twenty-two years. They had become a distant rumbling for most of those back home without access to vivid and immediate depictions of far-away fighting in foreign lands. In the words of G. M. Trevelyan: 'the war was in the newspapers, but it scarcely entered the lives of the enjoying classes.' Or, as Jane Austen wrote to her sister Cassandra in May 1811 after news of the Spanish Peninsular War battle of Albuera reached home: 'How horrible it is to have so many people killed! And what a blessing that one cares for none of them!' Even the news of the battle of Waterloo, fought scarcely 200 miles from London, took four days to reach the pages of *The Times*.

* The 1811 census counted 12.6 million people in England, Scotland and Wales: a population that had increased by more than 13 per cent in the previous decade.

The war impinged surprisingly little on contemporary art and literature, perhaps because it had been dragging on for so long. There are no active soldiers or battlefield casualties in the works of Jane Austen, even though she had two brothers serving in the Royal Navy and clearly admired the service. George Wickham in *Pride and Prejudice* is in the militia, and a couple of Fanny Price's relatives in *Mansfield Park* – fringe characters – are Royal Navy men. The character of Frederick Wentworth, a successful naval commander, is central to the plot of *Persuasion*, but his purpose is to be representative of a 'new' sort of non-aristocratic Regency gentleman. Wentworth is a veteran of the Napoleonic wars, a self-made man who ends up marrying the book's heroine Anne Eliot after she had broken off her earlier engagement with him, on the advice of her godmother, on the grounds that he lacked fortune and connections. The war was a raw backdrop to national life, followed in the newspapers and prayed for in church. Its victories when news came through were celebrated, but even its apparent ending in 1814 had not finally brought peace. There was no outpouring of national mourning, grief or regret, but the celebrations were short-lived. Over twenty-two years about a million British men, it is thought, had fought in the wars; a third of them had died – many from fever and disease rather than in battle – and many of the survivors had lost limbs.

There was indeed a degree of ambivalence about the battle in some quarters. Some progressives, in the face of everything, still saw Napoleon and the legacy of the French Revolution as beacons of liberty, somehow more vibrant and dynamic than Britain's staid political system and bureaucratic ministers. On hearing the news of Waterloo, the essayist William Hazlitt tied a crêpe mourning band around his hat and wandered about, drunk, unwashed and unshaven for several weeks, while the poet and journalist Leigh Hunt bemoaned the death of what he called 'cosmopolite philosophy' – a sense of internationalism.

Within a very short time indeed the government would be petrified that the labouring underclass might rise up just as their French counterparts had done in 1789 and overthrow the established order. Some of those working-class leaders thought they might do so too and spoke of sticking ministers' heads on poles, though in the end it was they who would be hanged and vengefully decapitated by the state. It was a febrile period: an age of economic upheaval and technological change. Bad harvests caused high prices and food shortages. The proximate cause of this seems to have been an enormous volcanic eruption far away in the Indonesian archipelago, which disrupted the climate of the northern hemisphere (see Chapter 12). This was unrecognized at the time, but its effects were devastating and exacerbated in Britain as laid-off men – including 300,000 returning soldiers – faced unemployment, poverty and starvation. Skilled craftsmen also discovered that their work was being undercut by new machinery and they lost their living too, especially as the dividends of peace meant reduced orders. Now increasingly one man might supervise the working of a loom that could do the work of ten; factories could produce stockings of inferior quality but much more cheaply, quickly and plentifully than a trained stockinger could. You might go a long way before finding revolutionary sentiments being openly expressed, but they did bubble up unexpectedly in places such as rural Derbyshire and Nottinghamshire, among labourers and skilled artisans, sometimes provoked by hunger and want, sometimes incited by undercover agents and spies of the state, and occasionally motivated by an ill-focused fervour for political change (see Chapter 13). Their pathetic uprisings – mere cries of pain, ill-formed and diffuse – would be put down with savagery and frequent incompetence by the authorities.

The old days and the old ways were going. The conservative Poet Laureate Robert Southey described the changes brought by the end of the war as 'a change in life itself'. In the countryside the old common lands were being enclosed and the game laws tightened against poachers. There was new machinery there too; threshing machines and seed drills were limiting the independence of the peasant class. They too would rise up periodically against their oppressors, their employers and landlords, when food was short and harvests bad, burning their hay ricks, stealing their potatoes and turnips, and breaking the machines.

Britain was the beneficiary of a burgeoning empire stretching from Canada to Australia, from the Caribbean to the East Indies. The country was changing rapidly as raw industrialization took hold in towns that would soon become cities. Its new factories and their owners were working out ways of marshalling and maximizing the efforts of their labour forces, including children. The new mills and factories needed to be kept going at regular hours and for as long as possible, so it was no longer possible to allow spinners and weavers to work at their own pace, from home as they once had: there could be no more 'St Mondays' – unofficial holidays after an order was finished and no work was to be done. Employers could not afford such unpredictable idleness and saw no need for days of cakes and ale among their workforces. Now, too, farmers were cushioning themselves against foreign competition by ensuring that agriculture was protected by high tariffs, whatever effect that had on their labourers' wages – even if it reduced them to starvation. A majority of the population still worked in agriculture, following the annual routines of the seasons, their days governed by daylight rather than the clock and factory bells or whistles. Many, perhaps most, people never travelled more than a few miles from their homes and, if they did, they had to walk. This was a man's only alternative if he could not afford another means of transport.

Even so, those who had the means and opportunity to travel further would be able to go no faster than a horse's pace: either riding or by stagecoach. There was a certain romance and excitement to such a journey, though the road would be bumpy and occasionally dangerous – and cold and wet if one had to sit on a cheaper outside seat. As the polemicist William Cobbett wrote in his *Political Register* in March 1816: 'Next after a fox hunt the finest sight in England is a stage coach just ready to start. A great sheep or a cattle fair is a beautiful sight; but in the stage coach you see more of what man is capable of performing.' A thousand Christmas card designs still attest to that romance. However, change was coming. Richard Trevithick had run his first steam-driven locomotive at an ironworks in Wales in 1804 and George Stephenson had just built his first engine for a colliery in Northumberland, but the idea that these might one day be used for transporting people was still more than a decade away. In the mean-time, canals to transport goods more cheaply and in greater bulk than carts and horses could manage were being built across the country: the Regent's Canal across north London, the Kennet and Avon linking Reading and Bath (see page 88). Now materials – coal and iron, bricks, even Mr Wedgwood's crockery – could be carried across the country, if not at great pace, then still faster and more smoothly than ever before, and finished goods could find new, more distant markets.

In this mix of old and new, the country's landowners and country squires were building themselves elegant mansions and creating landscaped parks. Cobbett hated aspects of this too, especially the incomers: the men whose wealth did not derive from the land and whose bond with the countryside's inhabitants was mercenary, not paternalistic. It was disconcerting:

the difference between a resident *native* gentry, attached to the soil, known to every farmer and labourer from their childhood, frequently mixing with them in those pursuits where all artificial distinctions are lost, practising hospitality without ceremony, from habit and not on calculation; and a gentry only now-and-then resident at all, having no relish for country delights, foreign in their manners, distant and haughty in their behaviour, looking to the soil only for its rents, viewing it as a mere object of speculation, unacquainted with its cultivators, despising them and their pursuits, and relying for influence, not upon the good will of the vicinage, but upon the dread of their power.

Cobbett, the old romantic imagining an England that never quite was, might almost have been thinking of Mr Darcy. He would also have thought the same of the incomers and weekend cottagers two hundred years on.

Where the Mr Darcys of the world made their money of course was in London, a city which was itself undergoing dramatic changes in its appearance. The Prince Regent had commissioned the architect John Nash to design a park for the northern edge of the city, whose surrounding houses would be linked to the centre through a curving and elegant boulevard of shops also named after the heir to the throne (see pages 134–5). Within a few years the Regent's Park would have a boating lake and a menagerie for the London Zoological Society and would be framed by imposing stuccoed and pillared houses and meeting rooms, crescents and churches. Regent Street itself would sweep all the way down to Pall Mall, past the Athenaeum Club before culminating in Waterloo Place, Carlton House Terrace and the monument to the Regent's brother, the Grand Old Duke of York, overlooking St James's Park. The prince was also at this time having built for himself a modest little pavilion in Brighton in the Indian style. Nor was the prince alone in his *grands projets*: the Cavendishes were building the Burlington Arcade as a covered corridor of shops just down Piccadilly; and in the middle of south London, at Dulwich, Sir John Soane was designing the first purpose-built public art gallery in the country. This was the handsome aspect of London life, rather than its bustling, crowded, noisy, money-making and chaotic side: Cobbett's 'Great Wen', Southey's 'fungoid excrescence from the body politic', the city of corruption and temptation, without redeeming virtues. To them it was a place to despise, for precisely the reason that Mary Crawford gives in *Mansfield Park*, published in 1814, when she speaks of 'the true London maxim' whereby 'everything is to be got with money'. As Edmund Bertram, *Mansfield Park*'s would-be clergyman, remarks later in the novel: 'We do not look in great cities for our best morality.'

The country's philosophers were at this time devising a philosophy, utilitarianism, that was intended to take no account of sentiment or choice: people were themselves to be engines, drones working for the larger good and better purposes of the state – efficient, mechanical and uniform. Under this influence the local parish systems of outdoor relief for the rural poor, subsidizing them from the poor rates when times were hard and bread prices high,* would soon be abandoned in favour of a new poor law in which the destitute would be efficiently and more cheaply corralled into workhouses and deliberately treated harshly to discourage them from ever being a burden again.

Meanwhile the clergy and bishops of the Church of England

---

* The most recent such scheme had been devised by Berkshire magistrates at the village of Speenhamland in 1795, but by supplementing agricultural wages when food prices were high, its effect had been to keep workers' pay lower than it might otherwise have been. It was effectively a subsidy to farmers, not to their labourers.

were still preaching the old nostrums, not questioning the literal truth of the Bible and remorseless in their opposition to other faiths, especially Catholicism and Methodism. But often they spoke to near-empty churches and cathedrals, in parishes notionally held by an absentee incumbent who might darken a church's doors only once a year if the parishioners were lucky. There were evangelicals, of course, and nonconformists leaching congregations away, much to the established church's complacent exasperation, and energizing the British campaign against slavery. In the face of the torpor of the established church, it was no wonder that old superstitions and country practices survived as they had for generations, even alongside religious beliefs. With death so frequent, sudden, unexpected and inexplicable, and disease so frightening and generally incurable, it was scarcely surprising that belief in witches and cunning men continued to flourish.

Most people, especially in rural areas, had little stake in the country, no vote and no say in how their lives were run. Their politicians were remote figures whose names and appearances most would not recognize and for whom they could not vote. Even those property owners who were enfranchised generally found themselves living in constituencies where the member of parliament was selected by the local magnate whose patronage controlled it. This was part of an unreformed system which allowed pocket boroughs with scarcely any voters to persist at the expense of the new industrial towns whose populations were expanding exponentially. It was hard to distinguish between the two political parties, Tories and Whigs, whose differences were personal, tribal and attitudinal rather than principled or profound: the Tories were more ostentatiously defenders of church, state and status quo, the Whigs marginally more mercantile and minimally more reform-minded. Both drew their politicians from the same strata of society: aristocratic and landed scions (the Whigs particularly so), rather than the business or professional classes. Throughout the Regency period, a Tory administration was in office, from 1812 to 1827, led by one man, Lord Liverpool, the third-longest-serving prime minister after his eighteenth-century predecessors Sir Robert Walpole and the politician he most idolized, William Pitt the Younger. Liverpool and his colleagues ran the country with a minuscule civil service and relied on local magistrates and landed magnates to administer the counties and employ parish constables and nightwatchmen – and the militia if need be – to maintain law and order. In fact the country was lucky, in that its national ministers were diligent and responsible, mindful of their obligations and rarely personally corrupt, even though the electoral system that returned them to parliament was.

The men of Lord Liverpool's administration may have had titles and certainly had wealth and patronage, but they were not drawn from the very topmost echelons of society. Liverpool himself, whose name was Robert Jenkinson, was a resolutely uncharismatic prime minister. He was the son of a royal adviser, but came from a long line of country squires and almost certainly had Indian blood through his mother, who was the teenaged daughter of an East India Company civil servant. George Canning, one of Liverpool's associates, a future foreign secretary and briefly prime minister, was the son of a failed wine merchant and an actress. Robert Stewart, Viscount Castlereagh, Canning's bitter rival, was a member of the Irish aristocracy. The fourth leading member of the administration, the home secretary Viscount Sidmouth, the former Henry Addington, himself an ex-prime minister, was the son of a doctor and a schoolmaster's daughter. Liverpool and Canning would exhaust themselves in office, the former eventually incapacitated by a stroke in 1827, the latter dying just 119 days after succeeding to the highest office; and Castlereagh committed suicide by slitting his throat, worn down and unbalanced by constant criticism and public hostility. He was just one of nineteen parliamentarians who committed suicide during the thirty years after 1790; others succumbed to madness and ruin, duelling and stress. It was an unprecedentedly gruelling and demanding period. There was 'a distinctively *sturm-und-drang* quality about British patrician life' in the period, as the historian Linda Colley has described it, 'a special kind of emotionalism and violence'. These men of government had to cope with the massive challenges of war on two fronts and two continents, of establishing a peaceful post-war settlement of Europe, and of securing recovery at home; and with the challenges of insurrections, a growing demand for parliamentary and political reform and, not least, the question of Catholic emancipation. These were not negligible issues, but vital and immediate ones. The government's response was often unimaginative and occasionally maladroit, but considering the resources at its disposal, it is a wonder that the country was not even more unstable than it actually was. The calm, miniaturist world of Jane Austen's novels belies a seething and turbulent society underneath.

Above all this sat a tottering monarchy. By 1815 George III, on the throne for more than half a century, had retreated from any role in the government of the country. Old, mad and blind, he was confined to a small apartment within Windsor Castle – unseen in public, his days spent with his keepers, his beard long and unkempt. Sometimes he was restrained in a straitjacket, more often he would just talk incessantly, inconsequentially. At Christmas 1819 he spoke non-stop for fifty-eight hours. At other times he would spend hours playing the harpsichord, by then a largely obsolete instrument even in musically conservative Britain, though much to the old-fashioned taste of the Handel-loving monarch. By now he was oblivious to the world around him. It used to be thought that he may have suffered from the genetic blood dysfunction porphyria, but more recent diagnoses of his symptoms suggest that he probably had a bipolar disorder, a form of manic depression which affected him periodically for much of his reign. It had last been triggered by the death of his daughter, Princess Amelia, in 1811, and by 1815 it was evident that he would never get better. 'We do not expect the king's recovery,' his doctors had reported in April 1814. 'But it is not impossible.' Later that year they would add, consolingly: 'He never wants amusement and it is always satisfactory.' His long-suffering wife Queen Charlotte regularly visited but he no longer recognized her: 'The king, thank God, in a very calm state,' she wrote in January 1816. The government was aggravated by the scale of the fees and travelling expenses charged by the so-called mad doctors who visited him daily to assess his condition – they amounted to £35,000 a year – and tried to get them reduced but ultimately did not do so.

The king would live on for another five years, never knowing of the battles that had been fought notionally in his name. His subjects, in ignorance of the details of his final decline, could appreciate his dignity and diligence when he was in full command of his faculties: most of the qualities which he possessed, as *The Times* said when he finally died in January 1820, 'were imitable and attainable by all mankind' – a remarkable thought for the period. In the old man's place was his eldest son, the Prince Regent: self-centred, increasingly fat and steadily indolent, addicted to pleasure and careless of duty or obligation, reactionary and vainglorious, widely mocked in public and much despised. *The Times* would be much less forgiving when he died ten years after his father. 'What eye has wept for him?' it expostulated scornfully in July 1830:

15

What heart has heaved a throb of unmercenary sorrow?...If George IV ever had a friend, a devoted friend, in any rank of life we protest that the name of him or her has not yet reached us. An inveterate voluptuary, especially if he be an artificial person, is of all known beings the most selfish... the true repellent of human sympathy.

In the circumstances it was a wonder that the monarchy was not more challenged, as ministers certainly thought it would be, by violent revolution at any moment.

Much of our image of the Hanoverian dynasty in this period is drawn from the vivid cartoons of Gillray, Rowlandson and the Cruikshanks: George III and Charlotte eating their boiled eggs and spinach for breakfast, their son, leaning back complacently after a huge meal, waistcoat askew, stomach bulging, overflowing chamber pot close by. Yet, despite the example of revolutionary France, there was no serious attempt to topple the monarchy. When one of its more popular members, Princess Charlotte Augusta, the daughter of the Prince Regent, died in childbirth in November 1817 – had she and her baby survived, she rather than William IV, or Victoria, would have become monarch – there was an outpouring of sympathetic public grief. 'No public event in my time ever produced such a universal union of spontaneous sympathy,' wrote William Darter of Reading, many years afterwards. 'All business was suspended and shops closed; blinds were drawn down to the windows of private houses and even the poorest of the poor wore some humble token of sympathy.' The law courts and the Royal Exchange shut for a fortnight and the makers of ribbons eventually petitioned the government to shorten the period of official mourning in order to allow their businesses to resume, lest they go bankrupt.

This, then, was not quite the genteel Regency world of an old Quality Street chocolate box, nor even the comforting, largely affluent England we sometimes imagine from Jane Austen's novels. But then, as she remarked disingenuously in a letter written in December 1815 to the Prince Regent's librarian, the Rev. James Stanier Clarke: 'I think I may boast myself to be, with all possible vanity, the most unlearned and uninformed female who ever dared to be an authoress.' Yet her England was there too: a world where peaceful seasonal routines, country balls and harvest suppers, summer picnics and parties, marriages and elopements, persisted as they had for generations. What Austen sensed, but did not herself live to see, was how much the country would change in the years to follow.

1

'A burlesque upon war'

—JOHN QUINCY ADAMS TO HIS WIFE ABIGAIL, 1813

Unfortunately for the British, the early morning mist rising from the bayous of the marshy plain to the east of the city of New Orleans on Sunday 8 January 1815 was clearing fast as the tightly packed columns of redcoats crossed no man's land to attack the American lines. The start of their advance in the dawn light had been shrouded, but by the time they came within range of the American cannon at 650 yards the sun was coming out and they were in plain view, weighed down by their back-packs and struggling across the muddy ground. Not that the mist had particularly helped the British columns: the attack had started in confusion when the rocket launched overhead to signal the advance took the troops on the ground by surprise. Some stared up at it, baffled because they had not been told to expect it. By contrast it alerted the enemy to the imminence of the battle. So confused was the officer in charge of the 44th Regiment of foot that he neglected to order his men to collect the four-foot-long fascine bundles of ripe sugar-cane and ladders that were meant to fill the trench in front of the American redoubt and so enable them to scale the muddy breastwork wall. While the rest of the attackers ploughed onwards, they went back 500 yards to retrieve what they had forgotten, slithering about trying to carry the heavy, sticky cane bundles and catch up with the columns. From then on things only got worse.

The American cannon could scarcely miss and they poured forth grapeshot and canister shells, spraying red-hot iron balls into the struggling attackers and mowing down rank upon rank. Then, as those at the front got within musket range, the gunners stopped firing so that the cannon smoke would not obscure the view of the defenders' riflemen. The American militias, many of them experienced woodsmen from Tennessee and Kentucky who were used to hunting game, stood up behind their parapet and unleashed volley after volley into the faltering British ranks. As they did so, the drummers behind the parapet beat out 'Yankee Doodle'. It was 'the most awful and the grandest mixture of sounds to be conceived, as if the earth were cracking or the heavens had been rent asunder', wrote Captain John Cooke of the Monmouthshire Light Infantry. 'Give it to them, my boys,' shouted General Andrew Jackson, the American commander. 'Let us finish the business today.' In the cypress trees along the side of the battlefield there lurked militiamen and Choctaw Indians who had thrown in their lot with the Americans, firing into the sides of the columns as the soldiers staggered past as if into a high wind.

Sergeant John Cooper, of the 7th Fusiliers, wrote later:

At the word 'Forward!' the… lines approached the ditch under a murderous discharge of musketry; but crossing the ditch and scaling the parapet were found impossible without ladders. These had been prepared but the regiment that should have carried them left them behind and thereby caused in a few minutes a dreadful loss of men and officers while the enemy suffered little, being ensconced behind the parapet.

In front of the ditch, the attacking columns, many of them veterans who had faced the French in the battles of the Peninsular War, faltered, milled about, attempted to regroup, pressed forward, and finally began to melt away as they saw their officers and comrades dying before their eyes. Major General Sir Edward Pakenham, the British commander and brother-in-law of the Duke of Wellington, who minutes earlier had ordered the troops to attack without troubling to ensure they were all ready to do so, now spurred his horse forward to steady the line, crying: 'For shame! Lost from want of courage.' He was immediately shot through the knee, and then his horse was also hit and killed. As Pakenham tried to mount his aide's horse instead, another bullet tore through his spine and killed him outright. Almost immediately Major General Samuel Gibbs, leading one of the columns, was also mortally wounded under the raking fire in front of the parapet. The British had lost their two most senior generals within minutes of the start of the battle.

Those who reached the American line found themselves sliding about against the wall while being picked off by the militiamen, their white cross-belts making them perfect targets. Other units stopped in front of the wall, uncertain what to do. A few scattered groups did manage to scale the rampart, but they were quickly shot or forced to surrender. A Lieutenant Leavock of the 21st Fusiliers was so confused when he got to the top that he approached two American officers and demanded their swords, but they just laughed at him and told him he would have to surrender himself: 'You are alone and therefore ought to consider yourself our prisoner.' Another wounded officer who found himself staring down the barrel of a grubby Tennessee militiaman's musket sighed: 'What a disgrace for a British officer to have to surrender to a chimney sweep.'

Now a Highland regiment, the 93rd, raised from the clans in Sutherland, was thrown forward, dressed in their red tunics, tartan trews and hummel bonnets,* with bagpipers playing the regimental charge 'Monymusk'. They veered across the front of the American lines, trying to avoid the piles of dead and wounded men and those who were fleeing back. But their colonel was killed and they too halted before the rampart, standing stoically under fire at close range and awaiting orders before finally being told to retreat. They left 600 – two-thirds – of the regiment lying in the mud. A black West Indian regiment was diverted into the woods that flanked the field, but they too were beaten back by the militias and the Choctaws. 'Our grape and canister mowed down whole columns,' wrote the American General John Coffee, 'but that was nothing to the carnage of our rifles and muskets.' Out on the field, Sergeant Cooper remembered a man beside him being smashed to pieces by a cannon-ball:

> I felt something strike my cap; I took it off and found sticking to it a portion of his brain, about the size of a marble. A young man on my left got a wound on the top of his head… close to him another man had his arm so badly fractured near the shoulder that it was taken out of the cup. A few yards behind sat a black man with all the lower part of his face shot away; his eyes were gone and the bones of his brow all jagged and dripping blood. Near him in a ditch lay one of the 43rd trying to hold in his bowels.

'I could', said Surgeon William Lawrence of the Tennessee militia, 'have walked on the dead bodies of the British for one quarter of a mile without stepping on the ground.'

Most of the British troops had never wanted to be on the expedition

---

* Hummel bonnets were flat-topped, woollen knitted hats usually with a chequered band and sometimes with a feather or red pom-pom on top. They were favoured by several Scottish regiments in the period.

in the first place. Many were Irish or Scots (like some of the Americans behind the parapet) and had been coming to the end of their seven years' enlistment when they were shipped, unprepared and unexpectedly from Europe, thousands of miles over the Atlantic to fight a battle they did not want, across unfamiliar swamps and bayous, against troops who might almost have been their brothers. The West Indian troops with them shivered in their thin uniforms, designed for a Caribbean summer, not a raw Louisiana winter. The invasion force had suffered for more than a month since landing further down the delta. It had been a Herculean effort to drag themselves and their equipment, pushing and rowing barges with drafts too deep for the purpose for seventy miles up the shallow and sinuous bayous to the sugar-cane plantation where the battle finally took place. One group of soldiers, ordered to carry a cannon-ball each in their knapsacks, all drowned when their barge capsized. They went down, it was said, without a sound. The soldiers and sailors who accompanied them had been soaked by the freezing rain, half-starved and regularly harried by the enemy.

Probably, too, they would have been even more demoralized had they fully realized that the British commanders had targeted New Orleans not only for its strategic position at the mouth of the Mississippi river but also because of its rich potential for plunder. The Royal Navy had several empty barges ready offshore to carry off the loot. That is certainly what Lieutenant Colonel Thomas Mullins, commander of the 44th, the officer responsible for leaving behind the fascines and ladders, had thought. He believed his regiment was being sacrificed so that others could gain the honour of an easy victory. Perhaps that is why he forgot his role in the battle plan until it was too late. Mullins, who did not accompany his troops forward under fire, was later tried and cashiered for misbehaviour, though some historians since have thought he was a scapegoat and that it was his superiors who were really to blame for the debacle. In his magisterial *History of the British Army* J. W. Fortescue contended a century later that it was the naval commander Admiral Sir Alexander Cochrane who should have been held responsible and shot: 'the callous manner in which he deliberately placed the troops in a most dangerous situation and then worked his faithful blue-jackets to death to keep them there – all with the principal object of filling his own pockets – cannot be too strongly condemned.' It was, said Fortescue, the most striking warning upon record to British ministers against conducting operations onshore upon the sole advice of naval officers, a project wholly based on the prospect of prize money.

On the left bank of the Mississippi river a diversionary British attacking force managed to send the American defenders in the Kentucky militia flying in retreat, but they were alone and had to draw back themselves. The battle was all over by breakfast time. In less than half an hour, two generals, seven colonels, seventy-five officers and nearly 2,000 other ranks – almost half of those who took part in the attack – had been killed, wounded or captured. At least 300 were dead. The Americans lost thirteen killed and thirty-nine wounded. General Jackson said sanctimoniously: 'It appears that the unerring hand of providence shielded my men from the powers of balls, bombs and rockets when every ball and bomb from our guns carried with them the mission of death… I never had so grand and awful an idea of the resurrection as on that day.'

But it was not so much divine providence as lamentable planning, incompetent leadership and poor targeting by the British artillery, persistently shooting too high and missing the American lines, which lost the day. Jackson, the stern, self-righteous Presbyterian of Ulster ancestry, had prepared his defences well – and the British had given him every opportunity to do so – but on the day his troops had scarcely had to move to kill their attackers wholesale. In some ways the invasion had been a considerable feat of arms and endurance. Had the attack been launched before Christmas when the British first arrived – and pressed more resolutely then – it might well have succeeded. But the assault was too long delayed and then launched too haphazardly, and the outcome was, as the *Annual Register* recorded later, 'an enterprise which appears to have been undertaken with more courage than judgement'.

The battle of New Orleans was an utter disaster for the British and a complete humiliation. Major General John Lambert, in charge of the reserve, now found himself commander-in-chief and ordered the retreat. For the next ten days the two sides would sit glowering at each other, the British periodically venturing out under white flags to rescue their wounded, who had been crying out for days from the muddy plantation field, and to bury their dead. Finally the British withdrew, boarding the Royal Navy ships waiting offshore, down the delta, from which they had disembarked two months earlier. The navy had wanted to renew the attack, but the army had had enough: 'Kill plenty more, Admiral,' said one officer bitterly. 'Fewer rations will be required.'

───oපpo───

The battle marked the culmination of Britain's three-year war against the United States and was the last time the two countries faced each other in pitched warfare. Neither side knew – and the survivors would not find out for another two months – that the negotiators from the two nations had already reached an agreement to end hostilities a fortnight earlier, on Christmas Eve 1814 in the Belgian city of Ghent. Even after news of the settlement reached Washington in mid-February and was ratified by the Senate, word that the war was over took several more weeks to reach Louisiana. For Britain the campaign had been a distraction from the European conflict against Napoleon and the shipping of troops across the Atlantic had been an attempt to force a quick final victory following the French defeat in March 1814 and the emperor's abdication and exile to Elba. For many American politicians, too, there was a need to end the war quickly before it bankrupted the country: the national debt had increased from $45 million to $127 million in three years. New Orleans was in all senses a pointless battle in a futile war.

Hostilities had broken out in 1812 after several years of tension as the British attempted to impose a blockade on France to bring down Napoleon by strangling the French economy. To do this the Royal Navy was authorized to harry and stop ships even of neutral nations in case they were attempting to trade with the enemy. This meant primarily the United States, which was fast becoming an economic rival to Britain – the embargo was thus also a useful weapon in limiting American exports. The navy was additionally allowed to board American ships to detain any fugitive British sailors and even to impress American ones into naval service. This was naturally a source of considerable grievance to the young nation which had achieved independence by throwing off British rule only thirty years earlier. There was annoyance and spikiness in the relations between the two countries that had not diminished in the intervening years: exasperation on the British side that their American cousins were undermining the war effort against Napoleonic tyranny – even though only to a very small degree – and resentment among some American politicians that the British were still trying to impose themselves on their country. It is a measure of how unnecessary the war was that the orders in council by which the British government had imposed the sanctions were repealed as counterproductive before the conflict even got under way. British merchants themselves had opposed the embargo as interfering with their own freedom to trade.

But for the American warhawks – those clamouring for war with Britain – there was also a sense of unfinished business. Canada remained part of the British empire and needed to be annexed; but American loyalists had fled north after the War of Independence, and they and the rest of the Canadian population were determined to retain their own independence from the United States. When war finally broke out in 1812, it was regarded as an annoyance and a sideshow by the British government – 'the millstone of an American war,' said Viscount Castlereagh, the foreign secretary – and as an opportunity by those Americans who thought it would be a chance to seize the vast, underpopulated territory stretching along the St Lawrence Seaway to the Great Lakes. The British underestimated the Americans' military capabilities, just as they had during the War of Independence, and the Americans underestimated the British and Canadians' resolve to defend their land. Not all Americans wanted the war – most of New England was opposed because of its effect on their growing export trade – and on their side the British failed to appreciate that they could not consistently enlist the support of the Indian tribes of the Midwest, nor the support of Spanish and French residents in the South, to undermine the American war effort. Many Native American tribes supported the British – more than were on the American side – most prominently the Shawnees of Ohio, led by their charismatic leader Tecumseh, who was killed during a battle in 1813. They generally did so because of their opposition to white settler encroachment and the annexation of their traditional territory, but they could not be persuaded to support the redcoats in prolonged campaigns far from home.

27

The war meandered desultorily through two-and-a-half years of conflict – a 'burlesque upon war', as the future American president John Quincy Adams wrote home to his wife in Massachusetts. Repeated American attempts to invade Canada were beaten off, though US ships won small-scale engagements on the Great Lakes, and British incursions on the east coast of the United States were short-lived. American troops set fire to York, modern-day Toronto, and a British force briefly captured Washington in the summer of 1814, burned down most of the newly built government buildings, and set fire to the presidential mansion, but not before they had tucked into the meal that had been laid out for the hurriedly departed president James Madison. When the same troops moved on to attack Baltimore a few days later, however, they and the Royal Navy ships carrying them could not get past Fort McHenry and gave up the attempt. This was a minor engagement, though one that gave rise to the verses which now form the words of the American national anthem. They are from a poem written by a young Maryland lawyer, Francis Scott Key, who was watching the bombardment from on board one of the British warships, where he had gone to negotiate the release of prisoners.*

The truth was, however, that neither side could impose itself decisively on the other: the British lacked the will and the manpower (and tended to lose their generals in the heat of battle) and the Americans were short of professional soldiers and experienced or capable commanders. Apart from defending Canada, Britain scarcely had any

---

* Indeed, the War of 1812 is arguably now most remembered for the phrases that arose from it rather than the conflict, or its outcome. As well as Keys' 'O say can you see by the dawn's early light?', we have 'Don't give up the ship!', which is still a cherished motto of the US Navy, derived from the call of a dying American officer, Captain James Lawrence, as his vessel the *Chesapeake* went down following a duel with a British ship off Cape Cod; and 'Those are Regulars, by God!' – the anguished shout of the surprised British general Sir Phineas Riall as he succumbed to unexpected defeat at the battle of Street's Creek.

war aims: they could hardly have expected to reoccupy the United States. In the late summer of 1814, just as the British were burning what would become the White House (once the Americans had painted it to remove the scorch marks), teams from both sides settled down in Ghent to arrange a ceasefire and a peace treaty. Believing that the war with Napoleon was over, the British were confident of imposing terms on the Americans and the government sounded out the Duke of Wellington, fresh from his triumph in Spain, about taking command of the army in America to finish off the job. What was needed, wrote prime minister Liverpool, was to terminate the war with 'a brilliant success'. But Wellington was too acute for that. He urged the diplomatic ending of a war which could not be won, especially without naval control of the Great Lakes:

> That which appears to me to be wanting in America is not a general, or general officers and troops but a naval superiority on the lakes... in regard to your negotiation, I confess that I think you have no right from the state of the war to demand any concession of territory... You can get no territory; indeed the state of your military operations however creditable does not entitle you to any.

He suggested that his wife's brother Pakenham, who had been an impetuous commander under him at the battle of Salamanca during the Peninsular War, might be sent instead: 'he might not be the brightest genius but my partiality does not lead me astray when I tell you he is one of the best we have.' It was precisely that impetuosity which would cause Pakenham's downfall and death on the plain outside New Orleans. The Iron Duke's absence did not, however, prevent Jackson claiming to have beaten 'the boasted army of Lord

Wellington', and even some modern American historians seem to share that view. Had Wellington been there, the tactics would have been different and the outcome could well have been too.

New Orleans, like a great swathe of the rest of the central part of the country right up to the Canadian border, had only been part of the United States since 1803, when the government had acquired from France – in the Louisiana Purchase – an expanse of territory that encompassed all or part of fifteen modern US states. The local Cajun pirates made a calculated decision to side with General Jackson because they determined, correctly, that their nefarious offshore marauding would be tolerated more indulgently by the Americans than the British. The city of New Orleans had doubled in size in the previous ten years because of an influx of French refugees from Haiti, as well as Spanish and free blacks, and so was regarded by both sides as being of dubious loyalty. The British had hopes that the inhabitants would side with them against the American general, but in the end they remained loyal to the army in occupation – although Jackson imposed martial law on the city before the battle just to make sure of compliance and would be heckled by the city's residents for not lifting it afterwards. Any hopes that the Choctaws had of preserving their ancestral lands by supporting the Americans or that volunteering black slaves had of securing their freedom by enlisting would also be dashed by Jackson. It is estimated that 10 per cent of the American troops were black – though the general chose not to mention it in his account of the battle, nor did he make good his promise that they would be freed afterwards. 'Such monstrous deception and villainy could not, of course, be allowed to disgrace the pages of history and blacken the character of a man who wanted the applause and approbation of his country,' wrote one of them, James Roberts, who served with the Tennessee militia. Jackson, a

Tennessee plantation owner and slave holder himself, eventually became president in 1829 largely because of his status as the hero of New Orleans. Old Hickory's anti-British phobia, originally said to have derived from being humiliated as a child by British officers during the War of Independence and fuelled by the War of 1812, would remain with him throughout his long life.*

The Treaty of Ghent resolved none of the issues over which the war had supposedly been fought. Both sides settled for the status quo ante and left outstanding contentious issues to be resolved by discussion as they might have been all along. The British dropped their initial demands for a Native American Midwestern buffer state to limit white expansion westwards (thus abandoning tribes that had sided with them) and withdrew from the state of Maine, which they had partially occupied, so leaving the eastern Canadian border as it had been before the war and as it has remained ever since. For their part, the Americans recognized that the orders in council that had been the prime excuse for war had, in fact, been rescinded nearly three years earlier, that Canada was beyond their grasp, and that British impressments, unnecessary now that the sea war with Napoleon was over, could be settled by negotiation.

As soon as the details of the treaty – 'the Peace of Christmas Eve' – were received in Washington in February 1815, it was ratified immediately with relief. Nevertheless, news of the victory at New Orleans enabled President Madison to claim triumph in the war: it was, he said, a result 'highly honourable to the United States and terminates with particular felicity a campaign signalised by the most brilliant successes'. This was a considerable stretch. He himself had been

---

* Jackson acquired the nickname 'Old Hickory' during the War of 1812, hickory wood being particularly tough, unbending and strong.

one of the most belligerent warhawks, but he had been forced to flee into Virginia when the British occupied Washington. His ministers in charge of the war effort were largely incompetent, and the generals and admirals appointed to fight the campaigns were often inadequate, with a few exceptions such as Jackson and Winfield Scott (who would still be in charge of the Union army at the outbreak of the Civil War nearly fifty years later). Almost the only immediate political dividend for the president was that his opponents from the country's New England-based Federalist party, who had opposed the prosecution of what they called 'Mr Madison's war', were humiliated and electorally wiped out in the national euphoria that followed the battle of New Orleans.

What remained was to repatriate the prisoners of war. Many of the British captives opted to stay in America and melted into the hinterland, but there were also nearly 6,000 American prisoners in England who were desperate to get home. Most of them had been corralled in a new prison in the desolate faraway wastes of Dartmoor in Devon, where some had died of cholera and typhus. There were lengthy delays in sending the survivors back. With the resumption of hostilities in Europe that spring and the prospect of a return of the profitable trade with the United States following the end of the war, ships to carry the prisoners were in short supply and the owners of those that were available demanded exorbitant transport rates. The American prisoners were left kicking their heels, increasingly frustrated. When, on 6 April 1815, a Dartmoor guard churlishly refused to throw back a ball which had been hit over the wall by an American (were they playing cricket? – it is a possibility), the inmates rioted. Seven Americans were shot dead and thirty-two wounded in the ensuing mêlée before order was restored by the panicked Somerset militia guarding the prison. 'The Dartmoor massacre' briefly became almost as much a *cause célèbre* as the Boston massacre had been before the War of Independence, but it prodded Reuben G. Beasley, the American consul in London, into more energetic action to find ships to carry the men home – the British finally agreed to pay half the transport cost – and the Prince Regent offered compensation to relatives of the dead to help smooth over the crisis.

The Americans had got through the war by the skin of their teeth, but in a way survival intact against a mighty foreign empire was a triumph. They had asserted their independence and had a considerable military victory to boast about. The war's chief effect was on the American psyche: it is no coincidence that the decade following 1815 is known in the United States as the Era of Good Feelings. There was a gain in national self-confidence, as one of the Ghent negotiators, the Swiss-born banker Albert Gallatin, wrote: 'I must acknowledge that the war has been useful. The character of America stands now as high as ever on the European continent and higher than ever it did in Great Britain.' Self-confidence promoted trade (particularly with Britain) and eventually expansionism, westward now rather than northward into Canada: the 'manifest destiny' of mid-century America which took settlers across the Great Plains and the Rockies, the spread across the continent to the Pacific coast fostered by a sense of independence and God-given right. If Britain with its mighty and arrogant army could not occupy the United States, who could? The British would never try to fight the Americans again, but a lingering sense of Anglophobia lasted across the Atlantic for more than a century. Those who did not benefit from the War of 1812 were the Native American tribes, harried and forced from their ancestral territories largely by Jackson, and the enslaved black population, although more than 4,000 slaves escaped to the British lines during the war and moved on to Canada and England – where British courts refused

American demands that their 'property' should be handed back.

The British were glad to be quit of the war and to go home. As Sir Harry Smith, the veteran soldier who fought in a string of conflicts through the first half of the nineteenth century, wrote after news of the peace treaty finally reached the navy, while it anchored in Mobile Bay: 'We are all happy enough for we Peninsula soldiers saw that neither fame nor any military distinction could be acquired in this species of milito-nautico-guerilla plundering warfare.' In Canada, the British welcomed American troops into their lines: 'We received them very well, gave them a dinner and made our band play "Yankee Doodle" on drinking the President's health which gave them great pleasure,' wrote Lieutenant John Le Couteur. In his opinion, the end of a 'hot and unnatural war between kindred people' was worth celebrating, 'thank God!'

The end of the war came just in time for the troops to be shipped back to Europe to fight the French. In London, news that the US Senate had ratified the peace treaty arrived on 13 March 1815: four days after Napoleon escaped from Elba to embark on the Hundred Days campaign that culminated in the battle of Waterloo. That much larger battle took place 161 days – exactly twenty-three weeks – after the quagmire outside New Orleans. 'The morning of the 8th January', Andrew Jackson wrote in a letter a month later, 'will be ever remembered by the British nation and always hailed by every true American.' Actually, that is true only of Canadians who remember the war along their border as securing their independence. Somehow, at least as far as the British are concerned, the battle of New Orleans has been long forgotten.*

---

* Except possibly by the older generation as a pop song, once sung by the king of skiffle, Lonnie Donegan, which reached number two in the charts in 1959.

2

The peace of Europe

On 1 January 1815 an exhausted messenger rode up to the Minoritenplatz, a handsome cobbled square in central Vienna, close to the Hofburg Palace of the Hapsburg emperors, to deliver a very welcome message to Viscount Castlereagh, Britain's foreign secretary. The messenger had ridden hard for more than a week through the cold, wet and snowy European winter with an extremely important despatch for the British delegation staying at one of the grand mansions there. It told Castlereagh that the British and American delegations in Ghent had signed the peace treaty to end the war in the United States eight days earlier. In doing so they had lifted not just a financial burden from the Exchequer but a weight from the minister's mind.

Castlereagh, the astute, able and subtle man leading the British delegation at the Congress of Vienna, the great meeting of the leaders of Europe which was settling the future shape of the continent in the wake of Napoleon Bonaparte's defeat and exile to Elba the previous year, had been placed under increasing pressure to come home. The prime minister, Lord Liverpool, had been urging him for the previous two months to make progress towards negotiating a continental settlement at the congress or return to England, and MPs in the Commons were growing restive about what was going on. The man who led Liverpool's government in the House of

Commons* had been out of the country since the previous August and the negotiations at the congress were becoming both bogged down and threatening. Ministers did not generally go abroad – Castlereagh was the first foreign secretary to do so to negotiate a treaty – and to be so far away for such a length of time was unconscionable. When he had sailed across the Channel, he had expected to be abroad for a couple of months at most. The expense of the prolonged stay in the Austrian capital – the British delegation's entertainment bill to date included 10,000 bottles of wine – was causing murmuring in London. Castlereagh and Britain were regarded with suspicion and Britain's naval domination of the seas was feared by some of the other national delegations, which were mainly led by monarchs and heads of state rather than a mere minister. With so many countries with different interests attending the congress, the negotiations were fractious and difficult. The two most pressing remaining concerns were the future shapes and governments of Poland and Saxony. Neither were vital national interests for Britain but their future was thought essential to the stability of northern Europe. Castlereagh's attempt to establish a continental balance of power to prevent future conflicts was lost in the internecine quarrels and shifting alliances of the other negotiators.

However, the arrival of a peace settlement with America freed up the British position: it could now have a larger army back in Europe and would be a significant player in the balance of continental power, deploying both money and troops to assist its allies and ensure their allegiance. 'We have become more European and by the Spring we

---

*   As an Irish peer, from Ulster in Castlereagh's case, he was entitled to sit as an MP in the Commons; during his career he swapped between the constituencies of Down in Northern Ireland and Orford in Suffolk, both of which were controlled by family connections.

can have a very nice army on the Continent,' the foreign secretary remarked. The young Lord Apsley, with the delegation, wrote home to his relatives: 'The news of the American peace came like a shot here. Nobody expected it.'

Four days later, Castlereagh, generally regarded as a rather solemn figure, attended a reception organized by the British delegation where, to the astonishment of the guests, he was suddenly observed flinging himself into the dancing, his long legs kicking out vigorously, his thin face furrowed in concentration. Jean-Gabriel Eynard, the Swiss banker who was representing the Republic of Geneva at the congress, was astonished to watch him that evening:

> Lord Castlereagh was persuaded to move to a salon which had been prepared for dancing. He immediately began to waltz and did so for half an hour. At the moment when we thought he would take a rest, a Scottish reel was played and he immediately began to dance it, without a woman, with three other Englishmen. Nothing could be more curious than to see that fine face, cold and impassive, atop a body agitated by all the movements that the reel demands; at last, when the three Englishmen grew pale with fatigue, Lord Castlereagh was obliged to stop and announced: 'Oh! I am quite finished too.' As it was one o'clock, we retired, but I am certain that the minister resumed his dancing.

Such a sight would also have astonished Castlereagh's colleagues and rivals back in London. He was a serious-minded, intense man who had devoted himself to government service as a minister in difficult and demanding roles for most of the previous decade: first as minister for war and then, since 1812, as foreign secretary, in which capacity he had begun to improve the quality of the diplomatic service. He had a talent for making enemies, the most notable of whom was his colleague and rival George Canning, with whom he had famously fought a duel in 1809 when he believed Canning was going behind his back to the prime minister and undermining him (see page 55). Castlereagh was a poor public speaker, which scarcely helped him to present the government's case in the Commons, and he seemed indifferent to popularity or support. He was generally regarded as a cold fish. These shortcomings would undermine his achievements and prove increasingly burdensome to him in the years to come. For now, though, Castlereagh could enjoy the ball, as he had not enjoyed much of the previous four months. In his mid-forties, the British foreign secretary cut a sombre figure besides the flamboyance of the other delegates. Usually dressed in black, he was constantly negotiating, working and writing despatches home. This contrasted dramatically with the hereditary leaders of the other nations. They bickered about precedence, gleefully took part in all the activities organized by the Austrian court for their amusement, and, as often as not, hopped into bed with their mistresses or the courtesans who flitted about Vienna. Castlereagh's austere conduct differed also from that of his younger half-brother, Charles Stewart, the British ambassador to Prussia, who was enjoying himself to the full at the congress and getting into regular scrapes. In the words of a fellow officer, Stewart was 'a most gallant fellow, but perfectly mad'. He paraded about in his hussar officer's uniform, picking quarrels. At one point he tossed a coachman with whom he had fallen out into the Danube. He also touched up women and got drunk.* Stewart was widely known as 'Lord Pumpernickel' after an uncouth comic

---

* So drunk that one evening he forgot to close the French windows of his apartment and woke the next morning to find that his entire uniform with all its gold braid and diamond-encrusted insignia had been stolen in the night.

character in a popular contemporary play. Fortunately, most of the British delegation were not like him: they were aristocrats, but also civil servants and diplomats.

The day before the ball, in the wake of the news from Ghent, the foreign secretary had concluded an informal, secret agreement with the wily French royalist and Austrian negotiators, Talleyrand and Metternich, to form a mutually supportive alliance, such that if one of them was threatened with attack, the others would immediately come to their assistance with 150,000 men each. That would form useful security against both Russia and Prussia, whose ambitions in eastern Europe they all regarded with suspicion. Tsar Alexander I, who was leading the Russian delegation, was championing an independent Polish state, but this was seen as no more than a ruse to disguise his country's true intentions. Poland would not be a buffer against westward Russian expansion as the French and Austrians had hoped, but a puppet state to enable Russian influence to creep into northern Europe. Prussia, meanwhile, was demanding to take over the independent kingdom of Saxony – a smaller German state that had made the mistake of siding with Napoleon at the battle of Leipzig in 1813. Annexation of Saxony would allow Prussia to increase its domination of Germany and the Baltic region, and even to make incursions into Scandinavia. The Prussian king Frederick William III was even threatening war if his country did not get its way. This would all upset the balance of power on the continent that Castlereagh was striving to create and which would be the cornerstone of British foreign policy throughout the coming century.

Such were the febrile manoeuvrings in Vienna between countries that had fought each other and swapped allegiances during the previous years of fighting – Prussia had been on Napoleon's side until recently – and had only come together in a grand alliance in

1813 once the Napoleonic regime was seen to be vulnerable. France, whose negotiator Talleyrand was now angling for his country's restoration among the great powers, had only become a monarchy again following Napoleon's abdication the previous April. In Charles-Maurice de Talleyrand-Périgord – recently made a prince by the returning king Louis XVIII – the French had a formidable negotiator, a man who had survived the upheavals of the previous thirty years of his country's history through charm, shrewdness and cunning and made himself indispensable to a succession of regimes: first to Louis XVI, then to Napoleon, whose peace treaties he had negotiated, and now as foreign minister to the restored monarchy. He might be, in Napoleon's phrase, 'a shit in silk stockings' and he was now in his sixties, but if anyone was capable of regaining influence for his country, it was him.

The Congress of Vienna had been the idea, the previous summer, of Prince Klemens von Metternich, the handsome, charming, supple – and philandering – Austrian foreign minister, after the allied powers had finally united against Napoleon and pushed him into retreat following the battle of Leipzig – also known as the Battle of the Nations – in the autumn of 1813. The allied armies had occupied Paris and forced the emperor's abdication. Bonaparte had convulsed Europe for nearly a quarter of a century, fought enormous battles across much of it, laid waste to swathes across its countries, occupied its cities, confiscated their wealth, and forced their young men to fight and die for him, but he was dealt with in a gentlemanly fashion. He was promised a generous pension, allowed to keep a guard of 600 troops, and inaugurated as the ruler and owner of the agreeable Mediterranean island of Elba, midway between the western coast of Italy and his home island of Corsica. The allies thought he would want to stay there. Now it was time to unpick the mess his depredations had wrought and restore stability and order. In doing so, they had been extraordinarily generous to France, confiscating scarcely any of its territory and not seeking punitive reparations. Louis XVIII was committed to paying Napoleon's pension, though he had not got round to doing so, which by the end of 1814 was a source of grievance to the former emperor. Probably more damaging to the future prospects of peace was the fact that the settlement was so mild that both Napoleon and many of his former troops came to believe that they had not really been defeated at all and so were reluctant to accept the end of hostilities.

Metternich saw the congress as a way of settling the future disposition of Europe, in his capital city, at his orchestration and under his control, so that he could manipulate it and achieve a settlement in which the Hapsburg empire, its influence and its territories were safely preserved. Perhaps even he had not realized quite how many would turn up: emperors and kings, princes and dukes, foreign ministers and ambassadors. It was not only the first international gathering of its sort but perhaps the most glittering ever. 'All Europe assembled in my ante-chamber,' Metternich wrote to his wife as the parties gathered. Someone counted 200 separate delegations. In that respect it was much like a modern summit, with not only governments but lobbyists and interest groups circling round the delegations: some demanding the abolition of slavery or of piracy, others calling for civil rights for Jews in central Europe. Individual landowners turned up demanding restitution of their property and cities sent representatives demanding compensation for their losses. There were also those whose works of art and sculptures had been looted and deposited in the Louvre: they wanted them back, but they were going to be disappointed – that too had been part of the agreement with France to end the war.

Vienna was at this time the third-largest city in Europe with a population of about 250,000 people, but the influx of foreign retinues, troops and hangers-on swelled its size by tens of thousands more. The Austrian foreign minister quietly arranged a network of spies, recruited as waiters and servants, to keep an eye on the guests and to report back on whom they were seeing, what they were saying – and who they were sleeping with.

The visitors all had to be accommodated in quarters appropriate to their status. They had to be fed and watered, and they had to be entertained and kept happy. The effort very nearly bankrupted the Austrian state. Even the Russian tsar, Alexander I, resplendent in a green uniform and conscious of his importance as the deity-ordained sovereign head of a great power, was busily occupied with a succession of mistresses. He was by turns capricious and suspicious, devout and distracted, an absolute, mystical monarch in thrall to the ideas of the eighteenth-century enlightenment, so long as they did not impinge on his own divine right. Alexander would, it was said, willingly have consented to make everyone free as long as everyone willingly did what he wanted. On his visit to Britain in the summer of 1814, crowds had flocked to catch a glimpse of the tsar, but his autocratic and insensitive manner had not gone down well. Like many another Russian leader before and since, he was suspicious of the intentions of the western Europeans even as he sought to emulate them and was convinced that they would combine to do Russia down, or fail to appreciate or respect its role in the world. Diplomacy was not his strongest suit.

The Baroness du Montet, an observer, wrote:

In the mornings the kings, if they are not engaged in playing soldiers, go for strolls on foot; when there are no grand parades

or hunts they pay calls; in a word they live the lives of young
bachelors. In the evenings they put on full dress uniform, they
shine at the truly fairytale parties given for them by the Emperor
of Austria… history is taking a rest, the sovereigns are amusing
themselves, they are on holiday and they are enjoying it.

As the Prince de Ligne famously said: '*Le congrès ne marche pas,
mais il danse*' – the congress does not walk, but it dances.* Or, in the
words of a deeply frustrated Castlereagh: 'We are impeded by the
succession of fetes and private Balls – they waste a great deal of
valuable time.'

The congress was a nest of competing egos and duplicitous diplomats, intriguing and plotting their demands under their capricious
rulers. Back in London, Lord Liverpool, prime minister of a country
which no longer had an absolute monarch at its head, summed up
the British attitude in a letter to the Duke of Wellington in December
1814. Only one leader – who was not in Vienna – seemed grateful
and reliable at all:

> The more I hear and see of the different courts of Europe, the
> more convinced I am that the King of France is… the only sover-
> eign in whom we can have any real confidence. The Emperor of
> Russia is profligate from vanity and self-sufficiency, if not from
> principle. The King of Prussia may be a well-meaning man, but
> he is the dupe of the Emperor of Russia. The Emperor of Austria
> I believe to be an honest man but he has a minister in whom no
> one can trust.

---

* The Prince's words pun on the French verb *marcher*, which can mean both 'walk'
and 'work' (in the sense of 'function successfully').

Louis XVIII, the younger brother of the executed king, was perhaps tolerated only because he was better known to the British than the others, having spent the previous twenty years in exile in England.

The Austrians arranged regular balls, masques and dances most nights of the week, and there were also outings, dinner parties and picnics.* National delegations too held levees and banquets. The now totally deaf Beethoven made his last concert appearances and conducted his Seventh Symphony one evening, and Antonio Salieri was also on hand to conduct *Fidelio*. One day in November there was even a boar hunt. The boars were helpfully herded into a park for the purpose of being shot and set running at intervals in front of the guns. 'From time to time five or six beasts were released and forced to pass the row of sovereigns, who were placed according to rank, so that if the emperors missed the unfortunate wild boars, the kings would have the honour of taking aim at them and if they missed then it was the turn of the princes, then of the dukes, then of the field marshals and then of the more lowly,' recorded the banker Eynard. 'This hunt, which is nothing more than an assassination of wild boar, lasted all morning and the monarchs had the glory of killing 500 of them. The fat king of Wurtemberg, who rather resembles a wild boar himself, killed 35…'

One night the Spanish Riding School was taken over for the grandest ball of the entire congress, at which a fake medieval tournament was staged with knights jousting for the honour of representing the twenty-four *belles d'amour*, one of whom was Metternich's seventeen-year-old daughter. The hall was furnished with two long

---

* When the author was the *Guardian*'s European Affairs Editor in the late 1990s, during the first Austrian presidency of the European Union, Austria laid on similar celebrations for visitors. There were no boar hunts but Beethoven's 'Ode to Joy' was frequently played.

galleries, filled with gilded armchairs, and chandeliers glittered over the scene. The wives and mistresses vied to outdo each other with the splendour of their gowns. Talleyrand's niece by marriage Dorothée, thirty-nine years his junior, who acted as his mistress as well as his hostess, remarked: 'I do indeed believe we shall wear every pearl and diamond to be found in Hungary, Bohemia and Austria.' Princess Esterhazy's costume alone was estimated to have cost six million francs, and even Lady Castlereagh, regarded by the continentals as a dowdy, plump figure, wore her husband's Order of the Garter in her hair. 'She is very fat and dresses so young, so tight and so naked,' wrote the extremely ungallant Austrian general Schwarzenberg. The English had not been able to visit the continent, except as soldiers, for many years, and so their provincial fashion sense tended to be looked down upon by Europe's aristocratic sophisticates. Now they had the chance to tour abroad again, they were flooding back, especially to Paris. 'It is raining Englishmen,' Metternich had complained to his wife earlier that summer.

As the representative of the one power that had fought Napoleon throughout and had promised to pay its allies, Castlereagh himself was one of the key players at the congress, together with Metternich, Talleyrand and Tsar Alexander I. Unlike many of the other participants, Britain did not have territorial ambitions, but the country's government was concerned to promote a settlement of European boundaries that would preserve peace and prevent another prolonged war, and it was prepared to pay its allies for their military and diplomatic support. It had assumed that the congress could be wrapped up in a few weeks, but that took no account of the competing claims of Russia and Prussia, not to mention the rulers of smaller statelets scattered across the continent, some of which had suffered badly in the Napoleonic wars and whose delegates now demanded compensation, or at least the restitution of lost territory – or anyway suzerainty over other people in other lands. Laboriously and at its leisure, the congress carved up the continent. As Talleyrand's protégé Count Auguste de La Garde-Chambonas noted: 'A kingdom was cut to bits or enlarged at a ball; an indemnity was granted in the course of a dinner; a constitution was planned during a hunt [while] everyone was engrossed with pleasure.'

In agreeing the secret great powers' treaty with Talleyrand and Metternich, Castlereagh had considerably exceeded his authority, but as the news inevitably seeped out, it had a chastening effect on the other delegations and gave space for compromises. Prussia in particular reduced its demands for Saxony and backed away from its threat of going to war unless it got it, and the Russians were offered the Duchy of Warsaw rather than authority over the whole of Poland. This was promising: Castlereagh saw the agreement only as a financial obligation but it additionally gave Britain assurances that the pact would apply to the defence of the Low Countries, particularly the Scheldt estuary in Holland, safeguarding Britain from invasion from that quarter. This was a strategic cause close to the foreign secretary's heart, since he had been one of those implicated in organizing the disastrous Walcheren expedition six years earlier, when British troops had been sent to occupy an island at the mouth of the river and had been forced to retreat in disarray.* For Metternich the agreement gave Austria powerful potential allies against Russia, and for Talleyrand it meant that France was back, its influence restored without

---

* The Walcheren campaign was intended to open a second front against the French and blockade Antwerp and Flushing, the busiest ports in Europe, but the British invasion force was decimated by fever – 4,000 of the 40,000 troops died, only 106 of them in combat. It was soon estimated that 40 per cent of the entire force was incapacitated and the plan was aborted after six weeks.

Napoleon. 'France is no longer isolated in Europe,' he told Louis XVIII back in Paris. In London, the cautious Lord Liverpool was also gratified, though slightly taken aback by his foreign secretary's decisiveness: 'I am sure it gives us the only chance of coming out of the Congress with credit,' he wrote.

Now Castlereagh could return home. The Duke of Wellington, newly installed as Britain's ambassador in Paris, journeyed across Europe to take his place at the congress. The only substantive issue that remained unresolved for the British was securing agreement for the abolition of the slave trade. Under some moral pressure from the abolition movement back in England, Castlereagh had devoted considerable time to trying to square the other maritime powers to abolish the human transports, but it was not a simple matter. Countries such as Spain and Portugal were suspicious of British motives. They argued that British colonies in the Caribbean were already well stocked with slaves, so preventing future trade would benefit British-owned plantations there at the expense of European ones. They were demanding delays, opt-outs and finally compensation for such an agreement. Talleyrand even rejected Castlereagh's offer of the island of Trinidad because France wanted the restoration of Bourbon rule over the kingdom of Naples in return for agreeing to abolish its part in the trade five years hence. In the end the low politics of bribery – Portugal secured £200,000 and Spain £400,000 from Britain – achieved promises to end the trade eventually, at some time in the future, maybe. The delegations finally signed up to a declaration that the slave trade was 'repugnant to the principles of humanity and morality'. It was a small, venal step – but it was the first time at least that an issue of human rights had ever been considered at an international conference. In fact, Napoleon himself pre-empted the French decision by issuing a proclamation, as part of his diplomatic

manoeuvring on his return to France, banning the trade with immediate effect.

Wellington was given a hero's welcome on his arrival in Vienna in
early February 1815. His agreement to attend the congress was greeted
with some relief by ministers in London who feared that he would be
assassinated if he stayed in Paris. He was not a natural diplomat, but
he was shrewd, he spoke French, the language of protocol, and he
came garlanded with military success and prestige as 'the Conqueror
of the Conqueror of the world'. His first words at the first session he
attended were jocular: 'What have you done, gentlemen?' To which
Metternich replied suavely: 'Nothing, absolutely nothing.'

Castlereagh, who had told Metternich that the agreement with
Austria and France was the start of a golden age of mutual coopera-
tion in creating a Concert of Europe, headed for the Channel in the
middle of February after helping Wellington to settle in. His account
of his negotiations would not be universally praised in London,
but there was grudging respect for what he had achieved. His old
enemy Canning conceded in a private letter to the Tory politician
William Huskisson that the agreements were not 'indiscreditable…
He returns surely with great advantages', and even the veteran anti-
slavery campaigner William Wilberforce agreed that the declaration
had been all that could be done.

But by that time the congress had been overtaken by a shocking
and momentous event. On 26 February, a week before Castlereagh
arrived back at Dover, Napoleon escaped from Elba. No one knew
what the former emperor's intentions were or, for a while, even where
he was. He had slipped off the island while Sir Neil Campbell, the
British officer notionally keeping an eye on him, was away seeing his
mistress in Italy, and it was not until Campbell turned up in Genoa
four days later asking whether anyone had seen Napoleon that word

of his escape began to spread. The news took ten days to reach Vienna. Metternich initially left the sealed dispatch marked 'urgent' on his dressing table while he tried to get some sleep. Talleyrand reacted imperturbably a few hours later when he received Metternich's belated note, which he gave to Dorothée, his mistress, to read out to him. At the same time, Wellington, preparing for a morning's hunting, was told the news and relayed it to his companions from the British delegation, who all burst out laughing. There was no laughing in Paris, however. When he read the telegram, fat, elderly Louis XVIII exclaimed dolefully: 'It is revolution once more!'

As the leaders gathered to discuss the revelation, opinion was divided as to where Napoleon might have gone. Talleyrand thought he would have headed for Italy on the basis that he might be lynched if he landed in France, and Wellington agreed. But Metternich knew better: he thought he would head for Paris. That indeed was Napoleon's plan. He did not think he would be harmed: 'I shall reach there without firing a shot,' he said; and he was right. He landed with about a thousand followers at Golfe-Juan between Cannes and Antibes on 1 March and was neither arrested nor molested as he made his way through the fringes of the French Alps north to Grenoble. The king and the French army blustered that they were ready to arrest him – his old comrade Marshal Ney proclaimed that he would bring him back to Paris in an iron cage ('He's not the sort of bird I'd want in any cage of mine,' muttered the king). But although Napoleon's welcome was not effusive, the opposition melted away and his old soldiers and generals, including Ney, began rallying to him once more.

Outside Grenoble, on 7 March, there was a famous confrontation when Napoleon stood before the 5th Infantry Regiment, who had been sent to arrest him, opened his greatcoat and dared them to fire. The troops went over to him en masse with shouts of '*Vive l'empereur!'* As recruitment to his cause accelerated the further north he marched, it quickly became clear that he would not be stopped by what one newspaper, *Le Moniteur*, had described scornfully as a few rural policemen. A satirical broadsheet rhyme of the time in Paris caught the flavour:

> What news? Good God!
> The Tiger has broken out of his den,
> The Monster was three days at sea,
> The Wretch has landed at Fréjus,
> The Brigand has arrived at Antibes,
> The Invader has reached Grenoble,
> The General has entered Lyons,
> Napoleon slept last night at Fontainebleau,
> The Emperor proceeds to the Tuileries today,
> His Imperial Majesty will address his loyal subjects tomorrow.

With his troops melting away, Louis XVIII decided to flee, and by midnight on the 19th his carriage had rumbled north out of the capital, leaving Paris to the forces now clustering around Napoleon. Such was the power of his name that all Europe seemed once more at his mercy. The emperor entered the capital the following day.

Things had, however, changed in the year he had been away. The French stock market plunged on news of his return and many were disinclined to resume an endless war on his behalf. If it was hard for French royalists to persuade people to fight and die for the long-exiled fat old king, most except for Napoleon's most diehard supporters were not that keen on resuming the war either. It has been calculated that Napoleon's armies had lost at least a million men in the campaigns of the previous twenty years. There was a demand for

constitutional government to curb the emperor's powers in line with
those constraints Louis XVIII had had to accept – 'that blackguard
has ruined France for me,' Napoleon exclaimed – and he could no
longer trust his ministers, some of whom were negotiating privately
with Talleyrand and Metternich. Rebels rose against the emperor in
the Vendée and Brittany, and although they were eventually defeated
by the Napoleonic forces, it required an army of 30,000 men to do
so – troops he could have done with in the coming campaign.

Worst of all, the European leaders were still together in Vienna, so
could not be seduced or picked off one by one by Napoleon. Under
the looming threat of his return, the bickering and frivolity stopped.
However much Napoleon declared that he wanted to negotiate a
peaceful return to power, they were uniting against him and pledging
troops to form a massive international army of more than half a
million men: 'If we are to undertake the job, we must leave nothing
to chance,' said Castlereagh, back in Britain. It must be done on the
largest scale, inundating France from all directions. To bolster their
resolve, the eight largest powers had already agreed a declaration on
13 March, making Napoleon an outlaw with whom there could be no
negotiation. Talleyrand, who drafted the initial document, had wanted
to go further, calling the emperor a wild beast and a bandit, but his
statement was watered down by Metternich. The smaller countries
such as Denmark and Bavaria were not consulted or included. What
the eight signed was clear enough. It stated: 'The Powers declare that
Napoleon Buonaparte has placed himself outside all human relations
and that, as the enemy and disturber of the peace of the world, he
has delivered himself up to public justice.' There could be no turning
back. Europe had effectively declared war on one man, not a nation:
the allies were at war with Napoleon Bonaparte, not with France. But
the powers had also effectively initiated the principle of intervening

in the internal affairs of another country. That did not concern Talley-rand. He wrote to Louis, who was now in Ghent: 'It is very strong: there has never been a document of so much power and importance, signed by all the sovereigns of Europe.'

In Vienna Tsar Alexander touched Wellington on the shoulder: 'It is for you to save the world again,' he said. This was flattering, though perhaps not what it seemed: the tsar was keen to lead the allied armies against Napoleon himself and was not pleased when the Russian army of 200,000 men was placed in reserve, left in Poland in case the French broke through, rather than in the forefront of the allied ranks. As it was, the duke was placed in charge of the gathering allied army in Flanders. Lord Liverpool's government promised £5 million to its European allies in support of the military offensive, and the Rothschild banking family raised an immediate £250,000 for the armies gathering along the French border, largely by manipulating the exchange rate with the franc.* Astonishingly, Napoleon quickly managed to assemble an army of more than 100,000 men, but within weeks there would be armies all around the French border ready to repel him. All Europe now held its breath.

* The Rothschilds, a German Jewish banking family, whose wealth was already immense, were established across Europe by the early nineteenth century with brothers based in Paris, Vienna and Naples as well as London, where Nathan Roths-child essentially underwrote the British war effort in its latter stages.

3

'A fearful interval'

—WILLIAM WILBERFORCE, DIARY, APRIL 1815

Viscount Castlereagh was perhaps not the best man to present the government's case to MPs as Leader of the House of Commons: in the words of Winston Churchill, 'seldom has that office been filled by a man with fewer natural qualifications for it.' He was a poor speaker, but, worse, he seemed to have an arrogant disdain for explaining himself, or the government's policy. It made him easily misunderstood – some would grow to regard him as a tyrant because he was the voice of a government that would resort to repressive policies after the war was over – but with his senior colleagues, including the prime minister, in the House of Lords, he was the person who had to do the job.

'Our friends *en première ligne* in the House of Commons have proved themselves not equal to the burden,' Liverpool had written disparagingly of their ministerial colleagues to Castlereagh in January, urging him to come home from Vienna. In a letter to Wellington, he added: 'The restoration of general peace, though it may relieve the country from great difficulties, does not make the government more easy to be conducted in the House of Commons.' So it was that Castlereagh appeared in the Commons for the first time in nearly a year in March 1815, both to explain the negotiations in Vienna and, by then, following the escape from Elba, to present the government's case for confronting Napoleon anew.

The outcome of the debate on the congress and the decision to go to war against Napoleon which arose from it was not necessarily a foregone conclusion. Although the government was united and could command a majority in the Commons against a fractious and frustrated opposition, party discipline was not what it later became and there were those questioning why Britain should go to war again in defence of the Bourbon monarchy which had now fled from its own country. Among these critics was the Duke of Wellington's older brother, Lord Wellesley, though his stance was probably dictated by frustrated political ambition and pique. Wellington himself canvassed privately whether it might be better if the throne was passed instead to a new Bourbon generation, Louis's younger cousin, Louis Philippe, the Duke of Orléans, but was told by Castlereagh that the current king must be supported 'for the present'.* Privately it seems that the foreign secretary had some sympathy with the idea of replacing King Louis – despite his reactionary later reputation, he was not particularly keen on absolutist monarchy – but publicly in the Commons that spring he insisted that it was a war for national security, that Britain could not back away from its European allies and should not be fettered by internal opposition at home.

In all this, Castlereagh received unequivocal backing from Lord Liverpool. Even at 200 years' distance the man who was prime minister continuously for nearly fifteen years, from 1812 to 1827, is hard to get into focus. He remains a dim, somehow unmemorable figure, alone among Britain's most significant prime ministers. The words used to describe him are usually equable, mild, prudent and good-natured; even his three portraits by Sir Thomas Lawrence – from 1796, 1820 and 1826 – show a bland, benign, undistinguished

---

* Louis Philippe eventually became king in 1830 and was deposed in 1848.

face. He was, said Charles Long, a ministerial colleague, one of the best-tempered men living and was described by the Whig George Tierney as a man who was ready to turn out in all weathers to defend the government. The worst that people said of him was that he could be irritable and fidgety – 'Grand Figitalis' some called him – but considering the length of time he served and the stress he was under for much of it, that was not surprising.

Both he and Castlereagh operated for years under considerable strain, with a small though dedicated civil service, inadequate colleagues and unreliable allies both at home in parliament and abroad, and under more public scrutiny and ridicule than their predecessors had generally experienced. These were not men born to be bureaucrats, indeed they were not necessarily born to have an administrative career at all. The historian Roger Knight says of them: 'Aristocratic ministers, unused to the long hours of administration and opposition in the House, were particularly vulnerable to stress and fatigue.' In a series of governments they had to cope with the unprecedented challenges of a prolonged continental war, which lasted more than three times longer than the Second World War 130 years later; a prolonged threat of invasion; the disastrous 1809 Walcheren campaign; the assassination of the prime minister, Spencer Perceval, in 1812; and the madness of the king and establishment of a regency. Such challenges were unique in their time and have not been equalled since. The ministers would also continue serving amid considerable domestic upheavals for years to come after the war. In such circumstances – communicating laboriously by letter with lengthy time delays in conveying instructions and reacting to distant events, operating at long range, almost by feel – it is remarkable that their administration was as effective as it was.

Robert Jenkinson – known patronizingly by his more aristocratic opponents as 'Jenky' and by others, equally scornfully, as the 'Arch Mediocrity' – was the son of Charles Jenkinson, the organizer of patronage during Pitt the Younger's administration, so politics was in his blood and he was never destined for anything else. He did not even have much of a family fortune behind him, though he eventually inherited the aristocratic titles bestowed on his father for services rendered. In 1815 both he and Castlereagh were only in their mid-forties, though they had both already served in government almost continuously for nearly a decade. Both men had been shaped in their conservatism by the French Revolution. As a teenaged Oxford undergraduate in France, Liverpool had been in the crowd watching the storming of the Bastille in 1789, and Castlereagh, a Cambridge undergraduate, had visited the country two years later when the revolution was at its height. Any youthful sympathy they might have shown for the ideals of the revolution – Castlereagh had allegedly once drunk a toast to the rope that should hang the last king – was knocked out of them in the process. Their subsequent political careers – both entered the Commons in their twenties – were focused on preventing anything similar happening to overturn the established order in Britain.

Liverpool trusted Castlereagh. They had scarcely discussed Britain's position before the Congress of Vienna, and although Liverpool thought the triple alliance agreement was bold, he did not disown it. While it was hard to second-guess what was going on in Vienna from London, the two men had kept up a constant correspondence and they generally agreed with each other on principles. As Liverpool's biographer Norman Gash says: 'Few British foreign secretaries have enjoyed so much latitude as Castlereagh at Vienna; few have been supported so steadfastly by their prime minister.'

The vivid and immediate threat of Napoleon's return meant that parliamentary criticism of government policy following the congress was more muted in the spring of 1815 than it might otherwise have been. Actually, Vienna and what was happening there were so remote from people's lives that most Britons had little interest in the outcome. Liverpool wrote to Castlereagh in January 1815: 'very few people give themselves any anxiety about what is passing at Vienna, except in so far as it is connected with expense.' Castlereagh's late return to London meant that he was unable to appear in the Commons before 20 March, by which time the emperor was arriving back in Paris.

There were other issues which threatened to be much more difficult for the government that spring. Chief among them was the imposition of a protective tariff against corn imports – the Corn Laws – and there was also the fractious and uncertain position of the monarchy, which took up more parliamentary time than the progress of the war in America had. The Corn Importation Bill was introduced just as Napoleon was escaping from Elba. Designed to protect landowner incomes once the war was over, with grain prices expected to fall, the regulations prevented wheat imports into the country until the domestic price reached eighty shillings a quarter,* a figure not obtained except in wartime. That inevitably meant that the price of bread remained high. The domestic price of wheat had halved in two years: from 118 shillings and nine pence a quarter in January 1813 to sixty shillings and eight pence in January 1815, largely owing to good harvests and also partly to a long-term trend in improved farming methods. This precipitous price fall was terribly worrying to farmers, especially if cheaper foreign grain imports flooded the market now that there were no longer blockades on European or American supplies. They demanded protection from such compe-

---

* A quarter was eight bushels, equivalent to 480 lb or 217 kg.

tition and so did landowners who saw their rental income falling. Landowners were the dominant and most influential interest group in the country and, although ministers would have preferred a sliding scale of charges on grain imports to moderate bread prices, they bowed to the agricultural interest's demand for a tariff barrier that would effectively keep out all imports, whatever the cost to the poor in high bread prices. This ran counter to the general economic principle of free trade and it would also lead to wage inflation – workers earning a pound a week and having to pay more than a shilling a loaf needed higher pay to survive – and to public disorder, but for the moment the farmers' interests were paramount. The government could not be blamed for the bad weather which would cause harvest failures in 1816, scarcity driving up the price of bread. But, in protecting farmers' livelihoods and landowners' rents, ministers stored up political problems for the future. There were food riots in London and provincial towns across the country from Merthyr Tydfil to Glasgow in 1816, and these soon fed into previously quiescent demands for political reforms, to secure fairer representation of other interests. Ministers' windows were smashed and troops were called out (see Chapter 13). Soon harsher, more repressive measures against dissent would be imposed. The Corn Laws dominated the cost of food and remained a focus of discontent for thirty years until the law was finally abandoned at the cost of internecine fighting and the temporary destruction of the old Tory party of the landed interest in 1846.

The Corn Laws were a protectionist measure rather than a revnue-raising one, but other sources were needed following the government's political decision – applauded at the time – to abolish income tax in 1816. In its place came other unwelcome taxes: duties on wine and spirits, carriages, horses and dogs, servants, newspapers and even windows in warehouses, all to raise about £5 million.

Although the injustices and inequities of the unreformed House of Commons were well known and had been campaigned against since the last decades of the eighteenth century, pressure for political reform was largely in abeyance during the war. The members of the House of Commons in 1815 were almost all from the landed aristocracy and gentry: men of property, and they needed to be, for fighting contested elections – to boroughs or corporations as well as to parliament – was ruinously expensive. The Yorkshire election of 1807 was said to have cost its candidates £250,000 by the time electors had been bribed, supporters and thugs hired, drinks bought, and returning officers' dues and printing costs paid. Constituencies were contested on an arcane number of bases with varying electorates: in some any men who paid the poor rates could vote, in others any men resident for the last six months – the 'potwallopers' who had a family and boiled a pot there – were eligible. Boroughs had their own different voting regulations and qualifications. There were corporation boroughs where only members of the corporation could vote and burgage boroughs in which voters had to have ancient property qualifications.* Oxford and Cambridge Universities had two seats each. Many constituencies were in the gift or under the influence of an aristocratic family – who determined who could vote – or could be bought for a steep price just like a piece of property. Gatton in Surrey was a parish which was said to have only 135 inhabitants and

---

* Burgage derived from the medieval term for borough, and in such towns ownership of particular properties gave an entitlement to vote – a right that could be bought and sold so that it was possible for a candidate, or his sponsor, to buy up all the burgage votes and hence get elected. Among such boroughs were towns like Appleby, Chippenham, Horsham, Droitwich and East Grinstead. They were indeed rotten boroughs, though it was the more egregiously depopulated and voterless constituencies such as Old Sarum which would increasingly cause popular outrage before the 1832 Reform Act swept them away.

six houses, but it was bought and sold on a regular basis: the last
time would be in 1830 for £180,000. Notoriously, places such as the
bleak hill-top of Old Sarum or the Suffolk coastal village of Dunwich,
which had largely fallen into the sea, returned MPs, whereas the
fast-expanding cities of Manchester, Birmingham and Leeds had no
separate representation at all. The eleven southern seaboard counties
between the Wash and the Severn, with Wiltshire added, contained
more than half the borough seats in England. Less well noticed
by history, the House of Lords was being subtly changed through
this period: the peerage had expanded rapidly, by more than 200
members, in the fifty years between the American War of Independence and the Great Reform Act of 1832. Many of those who were
ennobled had done the state some service, as politicians, judges,
diplomats and military heroes.

But men such as Liverpool and Castlereagh were in no particular
hurry to reform the House of Commons, even though they recognized the system was corrupt, because they believed it protected men
of property and conservative instincts. It certainly protected a Tory
majority in the Commons between 1807 and 1830. Whig patronage
was there too, but was much less extensive than the number of
Tory-controlled seats. While the war was going on, the opposition
was not going to challenge the system. As Earl Grey, the man whose
government eventually carried the Reform Bill in 1832, told the Lords
in 1810:

I doubt much whether there exists a very general disposition in
favour of [reform]. Until this country shall have expressed its
opinion upon this subject, the examples of the other nations of
Europe should deter us from any precipitate attempt to hurry on

to premature or violent operation a measure on which the best interests of the nation so essentially depend.

William Lamb, who became the Whig prime minister as Lord Melbourne in the 1830s, was given the Peterborough constituency in 1816 by its patron Lord Fitzwilliam on condition that he would oppose reform. He was happy to do so, saying he thought it was unnecessary and that the people did not wish it, though he added: 'if the people should ever become seriously and perseveringly desirous of it, I should think it my duty to support it.' It was not essentially in the interests of electors to challenge the status quo either: the vote was part of their property too, like their homes, and was a valuable commodity – though many did not use it in constituencies where that property made them liable to be assessed for tax. Only in some of the borough seats with wider franchises and looser patronage – Westminster was an example – was it possible to elect a radical MP.

This then was the nature of the House of Commons that listened to Castlereagh in the spring of 1815. The most heated debate was on 28 April as Napoleon was recruiting his forces in France. A succession of MPs supported a motion to prevent the country being involved in a war 'on the ground of the executive power in France being vested in any particular person'. More to the point, as the radical Whig Samuel Whitbread asked: was Britain at war, or peace? By the time he proposed the anti-war motion in the Commons on 28 April 1815, Whitbread was approaching the end of his tether. He had been a radical throughout his twenty-five-year parliamentary career – a source of disappointment to his Tory father, who had hoped he would follow him into the family brewing business, especially when Samuel supplanted him as MP for Bedford in 1790. Despite his family's immense wealth – his personal income was about £30,000 a year, drawn from 12,000 acres of Bedfordshire and the brewery's profits – and his education at Eton and both Oxford and Cambridge, Whitbread was snubbed for 'coarseness' by the aristocratic Whigs. Presumably this was on account of his origins in trade. But his radicalism and obstreperousness did not make him popular beyond the small Radical group in the Commons. Whitbread was 'vulgar, overbearing and becoming past endurance', said Richard Brinsley Sheridan, the former MP and playwright, who had fallen out with him over the management of the Drury Lane Theatre and had lost his seat on the board. As his career in the Commons progressed, Whitbread did indeed pick fights and could be perverse in the causes he espoused. The government's response to Napoleon's return that spring made him almost hysterical: Castlereagh was worse than Bonaparte, he declared; this was a war for the extermination of one man and an incursion into the rights of another nation to pick its own leader.

Whitbread and others argued that it was not for Britain and its allies to decide the government of France and that Napoleon should be negotiated with, as had happened to a limited extent at the time of his abdication the previous year. Perhaps the government should wait to see whether his intentions were aggressive or not: would he cross the borders of France and launch an attack? If he stayed in Paris, there was no cause for war. Instead, the allied declaration at Vienna outlawing him was, said John Smyth, one of the members for Cambridge University, an act of aggression against France. Thomas Coke, the great Norfolk landowner and agriculturalist, argued that the abettors of war were the enemies, not the friends, of the country, and William Wilberforce hawked his conscience into the debate – all wars were terrible and unpredictable, but Napoleon was a liar. He really did not want to have to vote on the matter. Privately, in his diary, the great anti-slavery campaigner conceded his mixed feelings:

'I spoke ill because indecisively, as indeed I felt in one sense; for my own judgement would be for treating with Bonaparte if we were free; but we are so committed with the Allies that we could not honestly separate from them.' It was, as he said, 'a fearful interval'.

The *Hansard* report of the debate shows Castlereagh's oratorical shortcomings, even allowing for the rhetorical style of the period. He did not think that the safety of the world was 'to be sought by an alienation from those Powers of the Continent by whose assistance we brought the former contest to a happy issue'. If they had not acted then,

> Napoleon would not only have been left in possession of the most fertile parts of Europe of which possession was so pregnant with danger to us, but [also] to the independent powers now in a state of the most vigorous exertion against him [which] would have remained completely subservient to his will... The only rational question was whether we should place any reliance on this man and by that reliance afford that time which he required in order to recover and organise his means.

He was, however, hopeful of a 'glorious result and that the exertions of the confederacy, actuated as all its members were, by a strong sense of the necessity of the case, would succeed in producing the complete establishment of a solid peace and the security of general freedom and independence'. With such words ringing in their ears, the 273 MPs voted down the motion to prevent war, though seventy-two – mainly radicals – supported it. They have been generally unnoticed by history and indeed their concerns seem to have been little noticed at the time. The government's view that Napoleon was not to be trusted and needed to be defeated seems to have been generally accepted. As Wilberforce wrote in his diary: 'It is amazing how little people seem moved, generally I think for war.'

———∞———

The question of whether Britain was actually at war occupied the thoughts of more than some radical MPs, however. It played on the mind of the Duke of Wellington too, once he arrived in Brussels in early April. The need to prepare for a battle was urgent, but organizing the allied forces was difficult in the absence of any real knowledge of what Napoleon intended, or where he would lead his army if he crossed the country's borders. Even in mid-May, the duke was writing:

> In the situation in which we are placed at present neither at war, or at peace, unable on that account to patrol up to the enemy and ascertain his position by view or to act offensively upon any part of his line, it is difficult if not impossible to combine our operations because there are no data upon which to found a combination.

It was a considerable feat for the British to get their troops onto the field in Belgium anyway. In 1814, 47,000 British troops had been paid off following the ending of hostilities. After more than twenty years of war recruitment was increasingly hard – one reason why the American war had had to be brought to an end was the difficulty of finding more troops to fight it – and the local militias which had previously been a source of men were also short of recruits. The army had come home from Europe, and getting troops and equipment back across the Channel to counter the imminent arrival of Napoleon was a considerable logistical challenge. The government's promise of 150,000 was far from being obtained, for many units which had fought in the Spanish peninsular campaign had been disbanded and other troops were still making their way back from the United States. To attempt to make the promised number, the government had to disburse subsidies to the Dutch and Prussians. During the whole course of the war, from 1793, Britain paid its allies nearly £68 million in subsidies to fight – almost half of that in the last three years of the conflict.

Wellington fretted about the British manpower and equipment shortages, particularly the lack of artillery – he wanted 150 cannon but had received only forty-two by May. In early June, however, he had a force of 25,000 British, 6,000 members of the King's German Legion and 11,000 Hanoverian troops, though many of them were new recruits. This was supplemented by 17,000 Dutch and Belgian troops, 6,000 Brunswickers and nearly 3,000 from Nassau. Many of the Dutch, Belgians and Germans had fought for Napoleon at periods during the preceding wars and their loyalty was uncertain, as well as their willingness to fight. The Belgians in particular had just found themselves unwillingly annexed to Holland at Vienna, so were scarcely happy to be led into battle by the young Dutch Prince of Orange. If anything, they would have preferred Napoleon. The duke did not think much of the calibre of his young, inexperienced British staff officers either and constantly badgered ministers back home for others, preferably those who knew him and whom he trusted. Wellington wrote to the Prince Regent on 15 April 1815:

> I might have expected that the generals and staff formed by me in the last war would have been allowed to come to me again, but instead of that I am overloaded with people I have never seen before; and it appears to be purposely intended to keep those out of my way whom I wished to have.

This was understandable grumbling, but in fact Wellington eventually got most of the staff officers he wanted.

In all, by the time Napoleon crossed the border into Belgium, the duke had an army of about 68,000 – approximately a third of them British – to confront Napoleon's 72,000, but there were also separately 48,000 Prussians under the command of Marshal Blücher. Initially, although Wellington had been named commander-in-chief of the army in Flanders by the allied powers in Vienna, there was some doubt whether he would actually be in charge of the entire army. The newly crowned Dutch king William I – known to the British as the Old Frog because of his overhanging upper lip and wide-set eyes – wanted his son, the young and inexperienced Prince of Orange – the Young Frog, also called Slender Billy and Silly Billy – at least to command the Dutch-Belgian contingent separately from the British. The prince himself was all for invading France directly, wherever Napoleon and his army were. Fortescue says sardonically in his *History of the British Army* that the Dutch king 'may well have thought that a crown adds an augmentation to the brain as well as an adornment to the brow'. In early May, Wellington threatened his Dutch ally that he would break off all relations with him unless he fell into line. Fortunately wiser counsel prevailed, and in the end, with studied diplomacy, the duke got his way and prevailed over the prince and his father: he would indeed command the entire Anglo-Dutch army at the battle of Waterloo.

4

'The damnedest millstone'

—DUKE OF WELLINGTON, JULY 1818

Of all the domestic problems an early nineteenth-century government had to bear, perhaps the trickiest and most sensitive was that of the royal family. The king and his relatives took up more parliamentary time and were more politically divisive – in the case of the Prince Regent, partisanly so – than almost any other domestic issue. They were also a significant drain on the national exchequer in an era when the scope for government expenditure, apart from on war and defence, was limited. There were just so many relatives requiring pensions. In 1812, at a time when the government was raising about £15 million a year from income tax and borrowing on a large scale to finance two wars, the prime minister Spencer Perceval proposed a bill – which passed without division in the Commons – that the royal household should receive a grant of £180,000 a year, with an additional grant of £100,000 to the Prince Regent for the cost of taking up royal duties from his father. The government did not dare, however, to take over the cost of the prince's debts, which at that stage amounted to £552,000. Ministers knew they would not get that through parliament.

After Perceval's assassination in May that year,* Lord Liverpool

---

* Spencer Perceval was shot in the lobby of the House of Commons on 11 May 1812 by a deranged businessman named John Bellingham who was aggrieved that the

and his government spent considerable time wrestling with the lavish financial demands of the prince and his brothers and trying to head them off. In an era when the sovereign expected to play a central role in the making and unmaking of governments and in the promotion and demotion of ministers and could be crossed, overruled or ignored only at the prime minister's peril, the state of the monarchy was crucially important. When the Prince Regent assumed his father's constitutional role, he also wanted to get his own way in areas such as the choosing of ambassadors and candidates for bishoprics as of right. He could be obstinate if he felt thwarted.

For ministers in 1815, the least of their troubles was with the old, mad king, deaf and blind, locked up in a few of the royal apartments at Windsor Castle. Much more problematic was the Prince Regent's ongoing and highly public attempts to divest himself of his tiresome and long-estranged wife, Caroline of Brunswick. Beyond that, there was the question of who was to marry their young and wilful daughter, the teenaged Princess Charlotte, who, after her father, was next in line to the throne as heir apparent. The Prince of Wales had been appointed regent in 1811 under the terms of the – rather wonderfully named – Care of King During his Illness, etc. Act, once it became clear that his father was never going to recover from his latest bout of insanity and could no longer carry on the business of state. The king's heir was the only possible candidate. Tory politicians were ambivalent and had put off making such a decision for as long as possible – just as they had headed off the prince's ambitions nearly a quarter of a century earlier during George III's first temporary collapse in 1788. Their caution now came about because the prince

government had refused to compensate him after he was falsely imprisoned for debt for five years in Russia. He was tried and executed within a week.

had ostentatiously sided then with the Whig radicals, such as Charles James Fox, who were his cronies.* If he was given his head, ministers feared that he would unilaterally turf them out and replace them with the opposition. This was still the sense they had in 1811, but they had been slow to appreciate that the prince had changed with age and was now increasingly conservative, even reactionary, in outlook. He was out of sympathy with the Whigs' growing support for Catholic emancipation and their reluctance to give full, unquestioning support to the war with France. But ministers had to get a regency bill through parliament in order for the prince to succeed to his father's duties, and they delayed until the matter could be put off no longer. They were accordingly relieved when the prince signalled that he had no plans to change the political make-up of the administration (the Whigs were relieved too as it removed any responsibility on them to endorse Tory policies).

But the regency still left the prince's position anomalous. He had most of the powers of the king, but he would have to wait until his father's death before he could ascend the throne. And his long years of waiting so far had scarcely made him a more decorous or consensual figure. Probably no prince before him had been so recognizable from the public prints and cartoons, nor more lampooned and more publicly ridiculed, for his licentiousness, debauchery, gluttony and drunkenness. George III in his younger, lucid days could chat amiably to passing peasants without being recognized. On one such jaunt when he was staying at Cheltenham to take the waters, he was engaged by a country farmer who asked in the course of their chat whether he had ever seen the king. After being told yes, the man

---

* Fox was dead by 1811, as were many of his contemporaries, and the highly partisan politics of the 1780s had abated under the pressure of the war.

said: 'Our neighbours say he's a good sort of man but dresses very plain.' To which the king answered: 'Aye, as plain as you see me now.' No one could have said that of his son, the grossly fat, gout-ridden and gumboil-eyed prince with rouged cheeks, sensuous lips and grotesque dark, curly wig.

Anyone passing the windows of a print shop would see all too recognizable caricatures of the prince, drawn by venomously talented artists such as Gillray, Rowlandson, Lewis Marks, William Heath and latterly the young George Cruikshank, commenting relentlessly on the latest excesses. Even if some passers-by did not understand the satirical depictions of the prince shown as a plump and greedy potentate with an enormous backside, clad in absurdly tight military uniforms, or as an oriental Buddha, or as a giant whale (as Prince of Wales), or even as a velocipede bicycle for one of his mistresses to ride on, the wordy captions left little ambiguity for those who could read. The cartoonists' image of the prince as a voluptuous wastrel had a devastating effect on his public reputation in places such as London and Bath where politicians and opinionated society gathered. He did not hide away: they could see him riding in Rotten Row, or driving a phaeton carriage; they could glimpse him at the opera or the theatre and hear the boos that greeted him – and so could the cartoonists. When he went to Bath or Brighton, his reputation followed him. An ostentatiously theatrical figure, the prince's flamboyant lifestyle and flagrant liaisons were constantly on show. The surprise is how little was concealed.

Periodically, the prince would attempt to buy off the cartoonists – George Cruikshank was paid £100 in 1820 'for a pledge not to caricature His Majesty in any immoral situation' – and bribes were offered to newspaper editors to change their editorial stances or to modify their criticisms. If all else failed, the prince's private secretary Sir Benjamin Bloomfield might be sent out into Pall Mall to buy up the most vicious illustrations, or to pay for the copperplate so that they could not be reproduced.* Attempts to squash opposition legally were strikingly unsuccessful. In 1812 the *Morning Post*, which had previously been bribed, went so far over the top as to describe the prince as 'an Adonis of loveliness', which prompted the rival *Examiner* to retaliate with an attack written by the journalist Leigh Hunt:

> this Adonis of loveliness was a corpulent gentleman of fifty! This delightful, blissful, wise, pleasurable, honourable, virtuous, true and immortal prince [was] a violator of his word, a libertine over head and ears in debt and disgrace, a despiser of domestic ties, the companion of gamblers and demi-reps,† a man who has just closed off half a century without one single claim on the gratitude of his country or the respect of posterity.

For traducing and vilifying the prince, 'a foul, atrocious and malignant libel', Hunt and his brother, the paper's editor, were fined £500 each and sentenced to two years' imprisonment following a boisterous trial, but of course such harshness did nothing at all for the prince's reputation or popularity. Indeed, it secured the hatred of the Hunts' friends, including literary figures such as Shelley, Hazlitt and Charles Lamb. Hunt served his two years in the Surrey County Gaol in

---

* Even though he certainly did not laugh at them, remarkably the prince kept many of the cartoons about himself, including those he had paid to suppress, which is why so many are still known. The collection was eventually sold a century later to the Library of Congress to raise money in order to enhance George V's stamp collection. When originals of these prints surface at auction these days, they can fetch thousands of pounds.

† A demi-rep was slang for a woman of easy virtue.

relatively congenial conditions.* Yet the prince's ridiculous appearance belied his sharp, though indolent, intelligence – buried from years of underuse – and his cultivated aesthetic taste. He was, wrote Lord Byron, 'a finished gentleman from top to toe', or, as the Duke of Wellington more astutely had it, 'the most extraordinary compound of talent, wit, buffoonery, obstinacy and good feeling – in short, a medley of the most opposite qualities, with a great preponderance of good'. The prince had had a harshly disciplined upbringing at the hands of his parents and had made up for it ever since. His roguish charm did not work on everybody. When she met him in London in the summer of 1814, the terrifically snobbish Grand Duchess of Oldenburg, sister of Tsar Alexander I, told her brother: 'He is a man visibly used up by dissipation and rather disgusting. His much boasted affability is the most licentious, I may even say obscene strain I have ever listened to… [he has] a brazen way of looking where eyes should not go.' Presumably the king had tried one of his favourite dirty jokes out on her.

This behaviour was all a far cry from the fusty, Germanic, rule- and precedence-bound provincial propriety of George III's court. No other British prince would have had the extravagance and wit to have built the Royal Pavilion at Brighton in the shape of a small oriental

---

* James Henry Leigh Hunt was a meteoric figure in Regency journalism. The government had unsuccessfully tried to prosecute the radical *Examiner* several times in the previous few years because of its support for Catholic emancipation and Irish independence, but its attack on the prince took it too far and its usual counsel, the radical Whig MP Henry Brougham, could not save the brothers. In jail, where he served the full two years until February 1815, Leigh Hunt was joined by his growing family and allowed to decorate his room, install a piano and a bookcase, tend the garden outside – and to continue writing and publishing the newspaper. He also had regular celebrity visitors, including Lord Byron, Jeremy Bentham, William Hazlitt, and Charles and Mary Lamb. Hunt's eventual release from prison was celebrated in an early poem by the young John Keats, and in the following years he became a friend and versifying emulator and chronicler of the romantic poets. Unlike them he lived into old age.

palace, of a sort that neither he nor his architect had ever seen (see pages 132–3). And no one else either would have commissioned such a place, to replace his earlier rather more soberly designed villa there, in early 1815, when he was personally £339,000 in debt. Probably no other royal prince has been so enthralled by literature, great fan as he was of Jane Austen and Walter Scott. And no other royal prince has made such a ludicrous spectacle of himself as George did with his succession of highly visible mistresses and his relentless public vendetta against his ghastly wife. In 1815 this too was in full swing.

There is an interesting account of a visit to the prince's court from an unusual source: the diary kept by a Persian ambassador, Mirza Abul Hassan Khan, which was written during his nine months' stay in London in 1809–10 while a friendship treaty between the two countries was finalized. Abul Hassan encountered the prince several times at balls and dinners and was very impressed by his friendliness. The diary references are extremely fulsome, but the prince seems to have been genuinely interested in the exotic ambassador and sought him out, inviting him to visit the palace gardens whenever he felt melancholy or homesick and to ride one of the horses from the royal stables. On 3 February 1810 he attended a dinner the prince arranged in his honour:

> We proceeded through rows of handsome footmen, richly attired and saw a myriad beautifully coiffed ladies standing beneath the gold and silver and crystal chandeliers. Thousands of wax candles lighted the rooms and alcoves… The prince graciously placed me on his right hand and showed me great condescension. [He said:] 'Every place has its particular attractions. God the Creator has given us the flowers of spring and the fruits of summer – as well as pomegranate-breasted beauties! Since he has brought you to

this land, banish sorrow from your heart and enjoy it!' Then the conversation turned to affairs of the heart. The Prince asked: 'Thin women or fat – which do you prefer?'

For himself, the prince (like Hassan) preferred plump women, but he should never have married Caroline of Brunswick in April 1795. This was not least because he had already semi-secretly married his mistress, the twice-widowed Maria Fitzherbert, whose shortcomings were not only that she was a distinctly non-virginal commoner but, much worse, a Roman Catholic. Their liaison was common knowledge in the prince's circle and was the subject of gossip and cartoons by Gillray and others. That marriage in 1785 could not be acknowledged, so the union with the stout and smelly German princess ten years later was an arranged dynastic match for reasons of state and the begetting of a legitimate heir. The prince may have already had as many as six illegitimate offspring with a succession of mistresses. He and Caroline seem to have loathed each other at first sight. The prince famously reeled away from her embrace on their initial meeting, saying to his companion, Lord Malmesbury, 'Harris, I am not well; pray get me a glass of brandy', and walked out, while Caroline muttered: 'My God! Is he always like that? He's very fat and nowhere near as handsome as his portrait…' The reason for his distaste was probably that the princess, short, buxom and lascivious, was not over-hygienic in either her infrequently changed underclothes or her person. He needed her dowry, though, and the settlement the government would give them as a married couple, as he was at that time £600,000 in debt. In such circumstances, the wedding night was a fiasco: the prince was drunk and appalled to discover that his bride was also not a virgin ('I have every reason to believe… for not only on the first night there was no appearance of blood, but her manners were not those of a novice,' he wrote to Malmesbury). Caroline claimed he spent the night asleep in the grate, but they managed to make love, on his reckoning, three times on the first two days after the wedding.

The couple soon separated but not before Caroline had given birth to their only child, Charlotte, who was to be shuttled between governesses and maids of honour, was given limited access to her improvident mother on her father's orders, and saw little of him either for much of her childhood. In the meantime, the prince took a succession of mistresses and Caroline flirted more or less publicly with lovers and gentleman callers. The gossip was so strong at one stage that the government held 'a delicate investigation' into the rumours about her infidelity, which cautiously reached no definite conclusion. All the while, the stories about her and her ill treatment by the prince served only to improve her public popularity and damage his, much to his annoyance. As Jane Austen wrote: 'Poor woman. I shall support her as long as I can because she is a Woman and because I hate her Husband… [If] I must give up the Princess, I am resolved at least always to think that she would have been respectable, if the Prince had behaved tolerably by her at first.' Both partners were stuck, unable to divorce because of the scandal that would inevitably emerge from a court case. Caroline whiled away the hours of social isolation by making wax dolls of the prince and sticking pins in them. She also increased the embarrassment for both prince and government by openly associating with the Whig opposition and soliciting the advice of politicians such as Samuel Whitbread and Henry Brougham in support of her cause.

By 1814 Caroline had had enough of being excluded from court events, and after Napoleon's abdication had opened the continent once more to visitors, having secured a pension of £35,000 a year from the government – only too keen to see her go – she left for a prolonged jaunt around Europe and the Mediterranean, accompanied by a louche retinue of followers and hangers-on. The Prince Regent cheerfully toasted her departure the same night: 'To the Princess of Wales's damnation and may she never return to England.' Caroline soon took up with a swarthy aristocratic Italian companion named Bartolomeo Pergami, or Bergami,* with whom she canoodled across Italy, Tunis, Malta, Athens, Constantinople and Jerusalem (which, in imitation of Christ, she entered riding on a donkey) before coming to rest at the Villa d'Este overlooking Lake Como. It was a progress followed with ribaldry by the cartoonists back home and with exasperation by the government. Ministers paid Baron Ompteda, Hanover's ambassador to the Vatican, to spy on her activities and bribe her servants while she was in Italy with the purpose of discovering evidence of her adultery. The reports back were encouraging – there were plenty of colourful stories – but it seemed legally inconclusive from the point of view of proving misconduct, and so she remained a source of Europe-wide fun and scandal until her vengeful return, to claim her rights as queen of England, in the wake of George III's death in 1820. This, and the new king's determination to have nothing to do with her ever again, led the government eventually into the quagmire of a prolonged public hearing in Westminster Hall into Caroline's alleged adultery, a political crisis and a decision ultimately to drop the case against her, which in turn led to rioting in the streets by her London supporters and the stoning of ministers' houses by the mob. The final, humiliating act saw her being turned noisily away from her husband's coronation at Westminster Abbey the following year and officials' steadfast refusal to offer her an invitation to the banquet

---

* His name was spelled both ways by English contemporaries.

that followed it. When she died three weeks later, at last the king was free. Six years earlier, however, in 1815, the prince had another difficult woman on his hands: his sole legitimate child Charlotte, headstrong, voluptuous like her mother and capricious – as many teenaged girls are, even those who are second in line to the throne and perhaps especially those who have had a neglectful upbringing. Lady Charlotte Campbell, one of Caroline's ladies-in-waiting, wrote an incisive description of Charlotte in 1811, when she was fifteen:

> above middle height, extremely spread for her age, her bosom full but finely shaped; her shoulders large… a nature to become soon spoiled and without much care and exercise she will shortly lose all beauty in fat and clumsiness… Her features very fine. Their expression is… noble… She has a hesitation in her speech, amounting almost to a stammer; an additional proof if any were wanting of her being her father's own child but in everything she is his very image. I fear that she is capricious, self-willed and obstinate. I think she is kind-hearted, clever and enthusiastic. Her faults have evidently never been checked, nor her virtues fostered.

In 1812 Charlotte fell for a handsome young captain of the Light Dragoons called Charles Hesse. He had taken to calling on her at her mother's apartment in Kensington Gardens, where Caroline would allegedly close the door, leaving the young couple alone together, with the cheering words: '*Amusez-vous.*' When he heard this, the Prince Regent was furious and sought the advice of Lord Eldon, the Lord Chancellor, who said if she had been his daughter he'd have locked her up. Eldon's family money came from coal mining, which drew the haughty response from the princess: 'What would the king say if he could know that his granddaughter had been compared to the granddaughter of a collier?'

An attempt to betroth her to the Prince of Orange – 'Silly Billy', the young man who would command the Dutch division at Waterloo – foundered in 1814 when she discovered she would be expected to live in Holland for part of the year. Then, when in retaliation her father tried to insist that she should stay in seclusion at Windsor, seeing only her grandmother, the queen, she fled to her mother's house and had to be coaxed back. Such high jinks were naturally the gossip of the town, even in the days before tabloid newspapers. The public naturally sided not with the outraged father but with the spirited teenager and her mother – who promptly left on her continental jaunt without even saying goodbye, or troubling to meet her daughter again. By now Charlotte had fixed her attention on an alternative European prince, Leopold of Saxe-Coburg-Saalfeld, an impecunious young German officer in the tsar's army. The year 1815 would be spent persuading her father to meet him and give his approval to the match instead of that with the Prince of Orange: 'no arguments, no threats shall ever bend me to marry this detested Dutchman,' she wrote.

Finally, in 1816, Charlotte got her way, and she and Leopold were married to general rejoicing. It was to be a huge shock, therefore, when she died suddenly in November 1817, probably of post-partum bleeding, following the birth of a still-born son after an arduous two-day labour. She was only twenty-one years old. Naturally, the prince and Caroline were blamed for the disaster, for not being present, for allowing their daughter to be attended by an incompetent doctor, Sir Richard Croft.* Charlotte died at Claremont House,

---

* Actually Croft was an accoucheur, a sort of celebrity midwife: he had kept qualified physicians away from the bedside and had not performed an emergency caesarean

near Esher, some way outside London, which the couple had been given as a wedding present. That too became a source of criticism, because she had been left so far from proper London doctors. John Wilson Croker, a Tory MP and indefatigable letter-writer, wrote to Robert Peel, who at that stage was the government's chief secretary in Ireland, a few days later: 'the public is in a sulky humour, waiting for any fair or unfair excuse to fly into a passion… If there should arise any division in the Royal Family, it will be the match to fire the gunpowder.' In another letter to Peel at about the same time, he wrote:

> I am satisfied that nothing could have saved her, nor even the child, but in an affair of such vital importance to herself, to her offspring, to her family, to the nation and to Europe, surely precautions should have been taken which you or I in our private families would have thought necessary if our wives were to lie in at a great distance from immediate assistance or additional advice.

Had she lived, Charlotte would have succeeded her father when he died in 1830. As it was, with the death of the heir to the succession and with the Prince Regent clearly unable to have another legitimate child with his estranged but not divorced wife, attention turned to his younger, though middle-aged, brothers to do the decent thing for England, get married and produce an heir to the throne. They were not an inspiring lot: 'By God!' said the Duke of Wellington, 'They are the damnedest millstone about the necks of any government that can be imagined.' Only two were legally married and they had

---

which might have saved both mother and baby. Croft was so unnerved that he would shoot himself a few months later while attending another, similar, labour.

not succeeded in producing a child. That left the dukes of Clarence, Kent and Cambridge, and they public-spiritedly expected to be offered financial incentives by parliament if they were going to marry and father offspring. In this they were largely disappointed. The oldest, Clarence, who would become William IV, had produced ten illegitimate children with his long-term mistress, the Irish actress Mrs Jordan, but he was already into his mid-fifties and his hurried marriage to the twenty-five-year-old German princess Adelaide did not produce the desired result. Fortunately, the Duke of Kent, who had hoped for a pension from the government to clear his debts,* married Leopold's sister, the dowager princess of Leiningen, and they eventually managed to provide the child who would be queen for most of the century: Victoria. Charlotte's widower Leopold was himself consoled by being made the first king of the Belgians, with the support of the British, after the creation of Belgium in 1831.

———— ✺ ————

It was not just boos that the Prince Regent had to face when attending the opera or being driven through the street. There was a real undercurrent of violence in national life. His father had been attacked by a deranged woman armed with a penknife in the 1780s, and he himself may have been shot at while returning from the State Opening of Parliament in 1817. Two round holes appeared in the window of his

---

* 'As for the payment of my debts,' the duke told a friend, 'I don't call them great. The nation, on the contrary, is greatly my debtor.' He had hoped for an annual pension of £25,000, plus £12,000 to cover his wedding expenses, but had to make do with £6,000 a year instead. The baby was born – 'pretty, as plump as a partridge' and, more importantly, healthy – on 24 May 1819 and was christened Alexandrina Victoria. Her first name was chosen in honour of the tsar, because the duke knew it would annoy the Prince Regent. There was inevitably a scene at the christening as the duke and regent squabbled over what names the baby should receive. The Duke of Kent died before his daughter was a year old, so did not benefit much from the pension.

carriage, though no bullets were found. Captain Rees Gronow of the Foot Guards, who was close to the scene, was convinced it had been an assassination attempt as the prince was driven past a 'mob of blackguards ripe for mischief… I can speak from personal knowledge that a shot was fired and it was aimed at the royal carriage.'

Nor was that the only attempt on a royal personage: the prince's brother, the Duke of Cumberland, was attacked by his valet in his apartment at St James's Palace one night in May 1810 in what appears to have been an attempt at murder. The duke was only saved from being chopped to pieces with a sabre because of his nightcap and the thickness of the bed curtains, though he received several severe cuts around the head and throat and nearly had his thumb severed. The valet, a Corsican named Joseph Sellis, then rushed to his room and cut his own throat. At the time it was supposed that the man had a grievance against the duke, but many years later a darker story circulated. The duke's former private secretary, a Captain Charles Jones, wrote that on Christmas Eve 1815 he had been told by Cumberland that he had been forced to kill Sellis in self-defence because the man had been 'threatening to propagate a report' about him, though he did not elaborate further. Was this a veiled hint that the valet was planning to accuse him of homosexuality? If so, it would have been a devastating charge. Homosexuality was still punishable by death – forty-six people were executed in England for sodomy between 1810 and the last execution in 1835 – and even lesser sentences were savage: time in the stocks and prolonged imprisonment were common. While it is highly unlikely that a member of the royal family would have been publicly accused of such a crime, still less charged with it, gossip would inevitably have got around.

5

'An idea of the Regions of Pluto'

—ROBERT PARKER OF BATH,
ON VISITING IRON WORKINGS, 1805

By the start of the Napoleonic wars in the 1790s, the Industrial Revolution in Britain was already well under way. Coal mines and ironworks were disfiguring the landscapes of Wales and the Midlands; there were cotton mills spinning out reams of yarn and steam-engine sheds were powering nascent factories; iron rails were propelling wagons jerkily along tracks and canals were snaking laboriously across the country to transport goods more smoothly and efficiently and in greater bulk than had ever been possible before. During the following twenty years, British manufacturing industry geared up for the war effort and enterprising men could become rich in supplying the government, or investing in its bonds, issued to fund the war debt. If Napoleon really did say in his bitter final exile that Britain was a nation of shopkeepers, it should have been a compliment: it was British wealth and trade, reaching out worldwide, which financed the prolonged military campaigns to defeat him, paid for allies and made victory possible. British workers were not conscripted, as French and other European young men were, to fight their governments' wars: they stayed at home to work in the factories and on the farms which fuelled prosperity as well as the war effort. As the historian Roger Knight has noted:

The historical headlines have been usurped by Napoleon and Wellington, the drama of Waterloo and the Congress of Vienna. The foundations of military victory, though, lay in the industrial capacity of cannon founders, the expertise of gunsmiths in their machine shops, the diligence of shipbuilders and the makers of ropes, uniforms, gun-carriages and gunpowder, the hard work of those who toiled in the increasingly efficient agricultural sector, the merchant seamen whose ships transported vital stores and food and the crews of packet ships who provided the means of communication throughout the year. In turn, none of this could have been achieved without the men who signed and passed contracts across tables in government departments, the civil servants who drafted documents… and the international merchants and dealers who traded in the City.

But heavy industry was developing and expanding in volume and profitability anyway during the last years of the eighteenth century and the first years of the nineteenth. Production of pig iron was less than 100,000 tons a year in 1790; fifteen years later it was 250,000 tons. In 1788 there were only eight blast furnaces in South Wales; in 1806 there were forty-seven, and by 1812 the figure had reached ninety. Similarly in the Black Country: six blast furnaces in Staffordshire in 1788 had become ninety by 1820. From the north-east 704,000 chaldrons of coal were exported along the coast and overseas in 1790; by 1815 the figure was 1,048,000 chaldrons.* In addition, the amount of coal sent to London in the same twenty-five-year span rose from 753,000 chaldrons to 1,148,000. The availability of cheap coal was

---

* A chaldron (derived from cauldron) is an ancient measure of volume, used mainly for coal. It amounted to approximately 28 cwt (hundredweight) or 3,136 lb (1,422 kg) and was roughly regarded as the amount a coal wagon could safely carry.

the making of an industrial centre such as Birmingham, where, as a visiting Frenchman wrote in the 1780s: 'It cannot be too often said … that it is the abundance of coal which… performed this miracle and has created in the midst of a human desert a town of 40,000 inhabitants who live in comfort and enjoy all the conveniences of life.'

There were probably about 7,000 colliers working the coal barges down the coast from Newcastle in the 1790s, paid about a pound a week, or six to eleven guineas for a sea trip to London during wartime: a round journey that might take several weeks. This was considerably more than an agricultural labourer could expect to earn.

Visitors who ventured into coal-mining areas were astonished and appalled at the vistas, which many described as a vision of hell. This was an industrial version of the idea of the sublime in nature that the romantic poets were popularizing: the great power of the natural world harnessed and bent to man's will and ingenuity. Blast furnaces glowed permanently by day and night and belched red-grey smoke to darken the sky. Men were staggered by the scale and ambition of the undertakings: John Wesley described the famous iron bridge which crossed a gorge of the River Severn in Shropshire as being like the Colossus of Rhodes (to a modern eye it appears quite small, though beautifully elegant in design and no mean feat of engineering). An Italian traveller in 1787 described the area as:

> a veritable descent into the infernal regions. A dense column of smoke arose from the earth, volumes of steam were ejected from the fire engines; a blacker cloud issued from a tower in which was a forge and smoke arose from a mountain of burning coals which burst out in turbid flames… night already falling added to the impressiveness of the scene which could only be compared to the regions so powerfully described by Virgil.

Passing the same area nearly twenty years later, Robert Parker from Bath was similarly impressed:

> You are at once surrounded with coal pits and iron stone pits, steam engines, furnaces and forges, innumerable, immense beds of coal blazing around, burning into coke for the furnaces and chimneys pouring out thick volumes of smoke in all directions as far as the eye can reach; this appearance, with the black faces of all the men I saw, gave me an idea of the Regions of Pluto.

If such places were terrifying to visitors, they were appalling to work in: hot and dusty with choking fumes and the stench of sulphur, dangerous and unprotected, for men, women and children. In coal mines there was an ever-present threat of devastating explosions caused by fire-damp. The worst of them at the time was the Felling disaster at a colliery near Gateshead, in what is now Tyne and Wear but was then part of County Durham, when ninety-two miners were killed in May 1812. The following year another explosion in the same pit on Christmas Eve 1813 killed a further twenty-two men and boys.

These tragedies were the impulses behind Sir Humphry Davy's development of the safety lamp that bears his name, which was first exhibited in December 1815. Miners needed illumination underground, but naked flames frequently ignited gases and the safety lamp attempted to prevent this by encasing the lit candle within a wire gauze frame. In the autumn of 1815 local clergy in Newcastle appealed to Davy, who was the leading and most famous scientist of the day, to find a solution to prevent explosions. He and his assistant Michael Faraday discovered that the so-called fire-damp which caused explosions was methane gas, but that this needed considerable heat to ignite. Their experimentation showed that when carbon dioxide was present, after the oxygen in the air had been burned off by a candle flame encased in the gauze tube, the surrounding temperature was cooled and the methane would not catch fire. It seems probable that it was actually Faraday, whose achievements in the fields of electricity and magnetism would eventually surpass Davy's, who was responsible for developing the gauze cover – not that he got great credit from Davy, nor a place of honour at the Newcastle reception, nor the set of plate presented to his boss by the grateful coal owners of the north-east. The lamp was, Faraday later observed in lecture notes, 'the result of pure experimental deduction… no accident… but the consequence of a regular scientific investigation'. It was only a limited success: the gauze tended to rust and it also prevented much illumination, but it was one of the first preventative measures to be adopted during the Industrial Revolution. It did not stop pit disasters though.

Steam powered many of these new enterprises. It enabled coal to be hauled to the surface, looms to be driven in mills, water to be pumped out of Cornish tin mines, forges to be powered, glass to be blown and pottery to be baked, corn to be ground, paper to be manufactured and, increasingly, engines to be driven along tracks, carrying cargoes to canals. These machines were great sights which people would travel miles to see; by 1800 there were perhaps 2,000 steam engines working in Britain. They supplemented the water wheels at factories, such as the wheel, fifty foot in diameter, that powered the blowing cylinders for a blast furnace at Merthyr Tydfil.

The canal system was spreading too. Starting in the late eighteenth century, canals had already created a transport network linking the towns of the Midlands and the north and had had a marked effect on the prosperity and industrial growth of the regions. The barges from the Lancashire and Staffordshire coalfields halved the cost of coal to the factories of Birmingham and the mills of Manchester. The boom in canal-building was prompted not just by the economic benefits they brought, however: the companies that built them were funded by share issues and speculators saw a good return on their investment – many of the canal companies paid dividends of 20 per cent a year. Every stage of a canal that was opened was greeted by civic authorities along the way with ceremonial rejoicing and brass bands and flags, for they knew it brought prosperity. The Leeds and Liverpool Canal ran for 127 miles by the time it was finished in 1816 and connected a network that stretched from Hull on the east coast to the Mersey on the west. It was the making of Bradford, which saluted the canal as 'one of the noblest works of the kind that perhaps are to be found in the Universe', and its completion reduced transport costs across the region by four-fifths. These were wonders of the age: the network of canals surrounding and winding through Birmingham was the making of its prosperity, with coal delivered on barges fuelling its workshops, gunmakers and metal-bashers.

The benefits spread south. The Kennet and Avon Canal, linking the Thames at Reading to the Avon at Bath ninety miles away, was opened in 1810. The Grand Junction Canal was being cut across the east Midlands to link Nottinghamshire and Leicestershire with the Warwick and Birmingham Canal and then down to the capital. In 1814 the Grand Union Canal completed the links between the Midlands, the Trent and the Humber with London and the Thames, and so also down the Kennet and Avon to the West Country. The following year, the Worcester and Birmingham Canal opened up the River Severn to the Midlands towns, and the Stratford-upon-Avon Canal joined them to the River Avon and Warwick, and on to the Grand Junction. Crossing the Pennines, the Rochdale Canal was completed in 1804 and the Huddersfield in 1811. In London itself the

Regent's Canal was begun in 1812, an eight-and-a-half-mile channel across the length of the north side of the capital, joining the Grand Union Canal and linking Paddington with Limehouse and the docks. This canal, planned with gracious permission from the prince to use his name, was part of a wider scheme to create Regent's Park and grand housing running down into central London along Regent Street. The canals were built by the brute strength of thousands of navvies, using picks and shovels. With locks to surmount hills and even iron-trough aqueducts to bridge valleys and rivers – at Longdon over the River Tern in Shropshire, at Pontcysyllte near Llangollen, and at Wolverton in Buckinghamshire – the canals were major engineering feats, a freight transport network in its time to rival the modern motorway system.

Where the canals reached the sea or open water, modern ports were being built to take the trade. Liverpool had fifty acres of docks by 1824, and in London the navvies were soon cutting through the East End, beyond the Tower of London, to create docks for shipping. The West India Dock on the Isle of Dogs was first in 1799, followed by docks at Wapping and Blackwall and the Grand Surrey Basin in 1807. These were huge endeavours with warehouses and thirty-foot brick walls surrounding them: great acts of confidence in the future of Britain as the pre-eminent maritime trading nation, built even as Napoleon was trying to starve the country out of the European war with a continental blockade against its imports. The blockade was certainly permeable: the fishermen and smugglers of Channel ports such as Deal on the Kent coast made a profitable living importing luxury goods from France and exporting British goods including weapons and even boots to the French ports; they also periodically carried escaping French prisoners of war for a price. This trade was busily carried on, seemingly oblivious to the fact that both William

Pitt the Younger and then Lord Liverpool spent long periods a couple of miles down the coast at Walmer Castle, overlooking the Channel, as lord wardens of the Cinque Ports. It was almost a toss-up for the government whether the military secrets the coastal fishermen sold to the French authorities were worth less than the secrets they brought back. On one occasion an exasperated Pitt ordered all the boats of the port to be burned by the coastguard.*

———✦———

Roads were also being improved, both in design and construction, and turnpike companies flourished, charging travellers to use their roads. With the exception of the motorways we know today, the pattern of most routes was being finally settled, not along the upland, hill-top tracks that had been used since time immemorial, but surveyed and laid out by engineers – men such as Thomas Telford, John McAdam and John Rennie – along valley bottoms and using straighter and wider lines than the previous tracks and lanes. Each turnpike was built and operated by a private company, usually financed initially by share offers, and each had to be authorized by a separate Act of Parliament. Their roads were hard to avoid on major routes (the companies also tended to block off side roads so travellers had to use them), and they were marked by toll-booths and gates to ensure that everyone paid. They did, however, allow quicker travel times. In the case of a route such as London to Holyhead on Anglesey, from which ships sailed to Ireland, the government stepped in and underwrote the cost of the road because the sparse population in north Wales made a turnpike uneconomic. The state of the previous road also left

* The picturesque smugglers' cottages remain in Deal's narrow side streets, some still with their hidden tunnels built to conceal contraband; they are now tastefully decorated as weekend retreats and holiday lets.

it little choice: in the first three months of 1810 it was found that the mail coach was between one and five hours late on seventy-one days out of eighty-five – and delays meant it missed the tide. As Telford, who designed the road, wrote: 'This road, so essential for maintaining the communication between six or seven million of His Majesty's subjects on one side of the Irish Channel and twelve million on the other, could never be put into a proper state of repair and safety if it is to be left to local interests to support and maintain it.'

Telford's roads were carefully constructed on a base of solid stone, forty feet wide with drainage channels, retaining walls and depots every quarter mile for storing gravel; there were no gradients steeper than one in thirty, and the surface was gravelled, not constructed haphazardly of large stones and rocks. In the 1780s a four-horse post-chaise took four days for the 260-mile journey from London to Holyhead; by 1808 the journey had been reduced to thirty-eight hours, and by the 1820s to twenty-eight. Even a French traveller was impressed in the 1830s: 'The superiority of the English roads over those of the greater part of Europe and more especially of France cannot be contested.' The writer and agriculturalist Arthur Young wrote in 1813: 'I remember the roads of Oxfordshire forty years ago when they were in a condition formidable to the bones of all who travelled on wheels. A noble change has taken place…'

Scottish-born John McAdam favoured a different, cheaper system of road construction to Telford's: layers of compacted small stones and chippings which gave a firmer surface, together with a slight camber from the middle of the road to allow surface water to run off. By 1815, as roads surveyor in Bristol, McAdam was building roads in the area similar in design to those used today.

Stagecoaches, bowling along at seven or eight miles an hour, were the quickest form of transport over long distances, but the journey would be arduous and uncomfortable. Travelling inside was marginally warmer, though more stuffy and cramped, while sitting outside, up with the driver and guard, was a cheaper but colder experience. Passengers could break their journeys overnight at coaching inns. This in itself could be gruelling if the beds were damp, the bedding dirty and the bed bugs active, and passengers were well advised to take their own sheets. Alternatively, they could travel through the night, though this was more dangerous as roads were not lit. Towns on the mail-coach routes, with several inns, probably provided a more competitive service and the passing trade boosted their prosperity. Newbury, half-way between London and Bath on the thirty-six-hour journey, was so convenient for a night's stopover that at the turn of the nineteenth century it boasted at least eight inns along just one stretch of the town's London Road.

The George and Pelican was probably the best and certainly the most illustrious: George III and his family (hence 'George' added to the inn's name) and Lord Nelson all stayed there, and it is where the Berkshire magistrates gathered in 1795 to agree a system of outdoor relief for the destitute workers of the county (see page 11). It was perhaps an incongruously affluent place to choose, rather like devising unemployment benefit at the Ritz. At some stage an anonymous rascal scratched this verse on one of the inn's windows:

> The famous inn at Speenhamland
> That stands below the hill,
> May well be called The Pelican
> From its enormous bill.

If they were short of entertainment, those staying there overnight could stroll next door to a theatre grand enough to be showing Mr

Sheridan's latest play, or later Joey Grimaldi's newest touring show. The Pelican and the theatre are long gone, though many other coaching inns of the period survive across the country as modern hotels and pubs. Few towns on the main routes lacked stopover inns where horses could be changed and refreshments and a bed for the night obtained: the Bear at Oxford, the Cock and the Bull at Stony Stratford, the Spread Eagle at Midhurst, the Angel at Bury St Edmunds (which features in *The Pickwick Papers*), the George at Stamford, and hundreds more.

Members of the working class who could not afford the fares could only walk. A man like the radical weaver Samuel Bamford grew used to tramping from Middleton in Lancashire down to London and back, striding along for twenty to thirty miles a day, begging milk and bread at farmhouse kitchens and sleeping in barns and haystacks. This was nothing unusual: the writer Thomas Holcroft claimed that his father, a shoemaker turned peddler, had frequently walked sixty miles a day on his rounds in the mid-eighteenth century. Even in cities, men walked to their jobs. If they did not need to find work beyond their locality, however, many folk never strayed more than a few miles from home.

The canals were soon to be superseded by the railways, whose tracks were laid by the sons of the men who dug the canals. By the 1820s investors in canals were looking elsewhere for better returns on their money – to gas and public utilities companies (200 provincial gas supply companies were founded between 1816 and 1830) and to the insurance market. It would be the 1840s before investors would turn to the railways.

The country was not yet fully industrialized and it was still possible to come across a mill or factory by a river in the middle of fields, as a French engineer noted in 1816 when he visited the Vale of Llangollen:

After a long and exhausting walk, I came into the valley on a fine autumn evening just as the sun was setting. Never had I seen such an imposing sight. In the midst of the luxuriant woodlands, still flourishing with all their natural freshness, arose whirlwinds of flame and smoke, continual eruptions from the craters of industry. There were blast furnaces, forges, limekilns, piles of coal being coked, workshops, fine mansions, villages built in an amphitheatre around the flanks of the valley. At the bottom was a foaming torrent, while above it the canal, enclosed in its iron envelope, hung like something enchanted on its high slender pillars, a supreme work of architecture, elegant and unadorned and this magnificent achievement was the outcome of the bold-ness and daring of one of my friends!

The owners of the new, mechanized factories were keen to show what wonders their machinery could perform. One of the most remarkable efforts – what would now be called a publicity stunt – took place on 11 June 1811 in the Berkshire town of Newbury, only a few miles from where the Speenhamland magistrates' meeting had attempted to improve the wages of local agricultural labourers a few years earlier. Now a local mill owner called John Coxeter, who had recently intro-duced new looms in his factory, boasted to Sir John Throckmorton, a wealthy landowner with a fine Palladian mansion at Buckland in the north of the county, that he could take a coat from his back, reduce it to wool and remake it again within twenty-four hours, much as a Hong Kong tailor might today. Sir John had a better idea: how about making him a coat that he could wear to dinner less than a day after it had been a fleece on the back of a sheep? The two gentlemen settled on a wager of 1,000 guineas and accordingly Throckmorton sent his shepherd Francis Druett at five o'clock in the morning with two

Southdown sheep to Coxeter's mill for them to be shorn. The wool was washed, stubbed, roved, spun and woven, then the cloth was scoured, fulled, tented, raised, sheared, dyed and dressed. By four o'clock in the afternoon it was ready for a local tailor, James White, to cut the cloth and nine employees sat ready with their needles already threaded to make up the coat. They finished at twenty past six, an hour and a half early, and Throckmorton appeared, wearing the coat, before a cheering crowd of 5,000 people outside the mill. Sir John went off to dine with his friends at a local inn, and the two unfortunate sheep were slaughtered and roasted whole and distributed to the crowd, who washed their meals down with 120 gallons of ale that Coxeter, having won his bet, had thoughtfully provided. But it did not ultimately save the Berkshire woollen industry, which could not compete with the expanding mills of Yorkshire, nor match the cheapness of the cotton being spun in industrial Lancashire.*

For skilled workers in industries such as weaving, the new mills and the machinery they contained were an economic threat: producing more cloth, more quickly and with fewer hands than had previously been possible. They could no longer work from home at their own pace with holidays when the work was done and orders complete. Instead, they were absorbed into the factories, working longer hours for less money and getting used to the new disciplines that came with the new organization of labour: clocks and whistles to ensure good time-keeping, and knockers-up, armed with long poles, paid to rap on workers' windows in the early mornings to make sure they were out of their beds in time for shifts. Their days were no longer their own.

---

* The coat still exists: a cutaway hunting jacket with a high collar and double rows of buttons in a rather drab damson colour – a shade that was then fashionable and known as Wellington, named as so much else in the period was. It may be seen on display at the Throckmorton ancestral family home at Coughton Court in Warwickshire.

The new mills took advantage of the streams and rivers running down off the Pennines and the Derbyshire Peak District to harness energy and increase productive efficiency. The villages and small towns around them – places such as Bury, Bolton and Blackburn – grew larger as the owners increased their workforces. In the first thirty years of the nineteenth century the number of cotton-spinning factories increased by a third, but the amount of raw cotton their machines processed increased tenfold. Not all businesses succeeded, but the ones that did tended to be concentrated within urban settlements, with ready access to a workforce and to transport links. The new mills were soon being built, by the turn of the century, with brick walls and iron joists to increase the strength of the floors for machinery and to reduce the risk of the frequent fires that were suffered by older, wooden mills. Their construction meant too that they could be built higher and bigger: a boost to trade all round. By the start of the nineteenth century the towns where factories were situated were growing at an ever faster rate. Leeds was expanding by about 150 new houses a year in the 1770s and 1780s – houses for mill workers, back-to-backs and terraces – then by 200 a year in the 1790s, and by 900 a year in the first years of the new century. The towns of Manchester and nearby Salford formed the largest conurbation outside London, though they were still small by later standards – they could still be walked across from end to end in less than an hour, having a circumference of only four or five miles. Even so they were expanding rapidly.

The mills and factories now worked all day and through the night. 'I saw the workers issue forth at 7 o'clock, a wonderful crowd of young people… a new set then goes in for the night, for the mills never leave off working… These cotton mills, seven stories high and filled with inhabitants, remind me of a first rate man of war and when they are lighted up on a dark night look most luminously beautiful,' wrote

John Byng after visiting Richard Arkwright's mill at Cromford in Derbyshire in 1790. But he did not have to work there. Many others were appalled and made queasy both by the spectacle of child labour and by the loss of individual freedom. The radical satirical novelist Thomas Love Peacock burst out with real anger in his novel *Headlong Hall*, written in 1815:

> Where is the spinning wheel now and every simple and insulated occupation of the industrious cottager? Wherever this boasted machinery is established, the children of the poor are death-doomed from their cradles. Look for one moment at midnight into a cotton mill, amidst the smell of oil, the smoke of lamps, the rattling of wheels, the dizzy and complicated motions of diabolical mechanism: contemplate the little human machines that keep play with the revolutions of the iron work, robbed at that hour of their natural rest, as of air and exercise by day; observe their pale and ghastly features, more ghastly in that baleful and malignant light and tell me if you do not fancy yourself on the threshold of Virgil's hell… Nor is the lot of the parents more enviable. Sedentary victims of unhealthy toil, they have neither the corporeal energy of the savage, nor the mental acquisitions of the civilised man. Mind indeed they have scarcely animal life. They are mere automata, component parts of the enormous machines which administer to the pampered appetites of the few, who consider themselves the most valuable portion of a state because they consume in indolence the fruits of the earth and contribute nothing to the benefit of the community.

Workers and especially craftsmen were becoming restive as the system became more firmly established. They had lost their old freedoms, their old skills had been devalued and their incomes reduced. In 1812 and then in 1816 the harvest was bad and wheat prices shot up, making men more desperate. The discontent with the factory system would diversify into complaints about food shortages and destitution and then into demands for political reform to allow the complaints of working men to be heard and taken into account: a series of protest movements the authorities would first repress and then seek to subvert.

It was not just entrepreneurs, businessmen and factory owners who were doing well in the early years of the nineteenth century: speculators were too. Buying stocks and shares in the canal companies was highly profitable, but so was investing in insurance and buying government bonds as the national debt rose to pay for the war. About 60,000 people held government bonds in 1760, 100,000 by 1780, and 250,000 by 1815. Investing in private companies was risky in a downturn, but the bonds gave a good return and boosted the rise of the middle class. With their surplus cash they bought consumer goods and luxuries, in turn helping the rise of manufacturers such as Wedgwood and Chippendale, Sheraton and Hepplewhite. They could buy tea, as Jane Austen did, not online but by post, ordering from catalogues and having their goods delivered by peddlers and hawkers. They might read the latest novels and attend plays and could imitate the latest fashions from London.

In 1803 the evangelical moralist and magistrate Patrick Colquhoun *

---

* Colquhoun, a former Lord Provost of Glasgow, moved to London in 1789 where, like an eighteenth-century Mary Whitehouse, he railed against the moral decline of the nation as demonstrated by the sexual profligacy and improvidence of the working classes. He thought that they needed to be taught habits of frugality and thrift and should not be paid more than subsistence wages, so that they would not be tempted to indulge their appetites. How this squared with the vast crime wave he perceived was harder to say, but his statistical analysis was part of his attempt to delineate the structure of society and his figures have generally been accepted by historians as broadly

calculated the incomes of the various groups in the population as part of his estimate of the social structure of England and Wales, from the king (average annual income £200,000) to the 30,500 Chelsea, Chatham and Greenwich pensioners (average annual income £10). In between there were 2,000 eminent merchants and bankers (£2,600 per annum), 40,500 higher civil servants, lesser merchants and manufacturers (£800), 1,000 eminent clergymen (£500), 500 persons employed in theatrical pursuits (£200), 160,000 farmers (£120), 445,726 artisans, mechanics and skilled labourers (£55), 340,000 agricultural labourers (£31), 50,000 common soldiers (£29), and 260,179 paupers in miscellaneous employment (£10). The calculation was that about one in four of the population belonged in families with an income of at least £120 a year, but to approximate to gentility, one needed at least £300 a year – although an income of £250 meant you probably had spare money for investment. It was possible, though not common, to rise from relatively humble beginnings to wealth and status, through luck or application. Lord Chancellor Eldon's grandfather, as we have seen from Princess Charlotte's remarks, was a clerk to a Newcastle coal merchant, and his father started as an apprentice in the coal business; Viscount Sidmouth, the home secretary who had been prime minister as Henry Addington, was the grandson of a teacher. But these were exceptional: most power in the land, especially in the unreformed House of Commons, still resided with the landed aristocracy.

---

reliable. Funnily enough, he and the Society for the Suppression of Vice, which he supported, were much keener on cracking down on the poor than on the wealthier members of society – Colquhoun thought he deserved a government pension for his work and privately wrote asking for one, though he did not get it. As William Cobbett wrote, he and his fellow campaigners were 'anti-everything that is calculated to draw the people together and to afford them a chance of communicating their ideas; anti-everything which does not tend to abject subjection'.

If the middle classes were doing quite well for themselves, the plight of the poor was beginning to give rise to alarm among reformers and those worried about public disorder. The Rev. Johnson Grant stopped in Bakewell, Derbyshire in 1809 and watched the workers:

> I passed a cotton manufactory; the people all coming out to dinner, for it was already one o'clock. From the glance I had of their appearance, the observations I made were these: They were pale and their hats were covered with shreds of cotton. Exclusive of want of exercise, the general bane of all manufactures, the light particles of cotton must be inhaled with the breath and occasion pulmonary affections. Owners of factories should consider this... Let every person then order his work people to bathe every morning and let him have a piece of playground for them, wherein some athletic and innocent exercise might be enjoyed for an hour or two each day... let them drink much water.

Many were more alarmed by the workers' moral state. The topographer Richard Ayton was concerned by workers in the Swansea Valley in 1814:

> Women in all parts of Wales are employed in offices of the hardest and dirtiest drudgery, like the men. On the banks of the canal I saw little companies of them chipping the large coals into small pieces for the furnaces without shoes or stockings, their clothes hanging about them, released for the sake of ease from pins and strings and their faces as black as the coals except when channelled by the streams of perspiration that trickled down them... I am particularly struck with the wretched, filthy, ragged appearance of the lower orders of people. The women are beyond all

sufferance, dirty and slovenly and, as they unfortunately all dress alike, there is no competition among them and they are equally unmoved by the love of cleanliness and the shame of dirt. Few of them ever wear shoes or socks, though some do wear stocking legs, reaching down to the ankles and attached by a loop to the great toe; their outer garments are always woollen, as coarse as a horse cloth and of a dark colour that does not require washing; on their heads they wear a man's hat, sometimes without a brim, sometimes without a crown and sometimes without a brim or a crown; and thus generally disguised, they present a form of more roughness and rudeness in the shape of women than I ever saw in any other part of the kingdom... But there is a far more serious subject for reproof... in the corruption of morals and manners which the increase of manufactories has occasioned among the people within the last half-century... the streets of Swansea are almost as notorious for scenes of loud and shameless profligacy as the Point at Portsmouth. That this degeneracy results from the increase of manufactories and the consequent attraction of a larger population to one point there can be no doubt.

Some factory owners and employers were trying to circumvent such desolation and dislocation. They were building model houses for their best employees: homes built in clusters, with gardens. Those at Belper and Darley Abbey near Derby, or near the Marshall, Benyon and Bage flax mill at Shrewsbury, were early examples. But the best known and best proselytized were Robert Owen's factories at New Lanark, near Glasgow. Owen, a Welshman who had risen in the drapery business in London and Manchester, had fallen in love with and married the daughter of the company's proprietor David Dale. Becoming manager and then part-owner of the business in 1810 and raising £60,000 from Manchester investors, he was able to put into practice some of the ideas garnered when he was a member of the Manchester Literary and Philosophical Society in the 1790s. Dale's Chorton Twist Company was no small backwoods outfit: it was already one of the largest businesses in Britain, its four mills having 6,000 spindles. It housed its workers in tenements and had 2,000 employees, a quarter of them orphan children from poorhouse charities mainly in Edinburgh. Dale was actually a good employer and may not have been given sufficient credit for his relatively humane attitudes by his son-in-law, who was at pains to emphasize the improvements he himself subsequently made. Owen wrote that the workforce lived in poor conditions, without sanitation, families crowded together in a single room; there was little education for the children, and drunkenness and theft were rife. As with many factory populations, they were reliant on the 'truck system', which forced employees to spend their wages buying inferior goods at inflated prices in company stores.

Owen's big idea was that treating employees more humanely would improve not only their lives but those of the community and would accordingly increase productivity. Education would naturally produce better, more rational people. To improve their character, their environment had to be made better. One of his first moves was to introduce schooling for the children and to ban those under the age of ten from working in the textile mills altogether. This had the additional benefit of freeing their mothers to work longer themselves. There was to be no physical punishment and overall working hours were reduced from thirteen hours a day to ten. He also modified the truck system so that employees were offered good-quality produce at near cost price, with savings from bulk buying ploughed back into the business – a sort of prototype cooperative movement. When his partners in the mills grew restive at the effect on profits, he bought them out, raising money from the utilitarian philosopher Jeremy Bentham and the Quaker William Allen among others who were interested in his social experiment.

So Owen was able to push ahead with his scheme, and to make his ideas better known, he spread the word in books, articles and speeches. Visitors to see his philosophy in action at New Lanark included other reformers, politicians and even the tsar of Russia. His book *The Formation of Character* was published in 1813, updated as *A New View of Society* in 1814. It would be a new utopian moral world and not one governed by religion, though it would be respectful of others' beliefs. A large degree of order and regimentation was involved. 'Train any population rationally and they will be rational,' Owen asserted in his 1814 book. 'Furnish honest and useful employment to those so trained and such employments they will greatly prefer to dishonest or injurious occupations. It is beyond all calculation the interest of every government to provide that training and that employment and to provide both is easily practicable.' Workers would not, as Bentham assumed, make choices that were automatically or inherently rational for the greater good, nor would they share identical aspirations and uniform motivations for themselves. They must be *educated* to make right decisions.

To incentivize the workers, there was no corporal punishment and no fines, as in other factories, but a system of coloured cubes, placed by each loom, a different colour according to the quality and quantity of work produced, so that each could see how others were doing – and of course be spurred to greater effort. In time Owen's vision would encompass not just education but training, care for the young and the elderly, improved health for all and better treatment for women: 'equal in education, rights, privileges and personal liberty'. As he told his employees when he opened what he called New Lanark's Institute for the Formation of Character on New Year's Day 1816: 'I know that society may be formed so as to exist without crime, without poverty, with health greatly improved, with little if any misery and with intelligence and happiness increased a hundredfold: and no obstacle whatsoever intervenes at this moment except ignorance to prevent such a state of society from becoming universal.'

Such a major magnate could demand a hearing, and in April 1816 Owen was called before a committee of the House of Commons, chaired by Robert Peel, father of the future prime minister and an industrialist himself, to expound his views to incredulous MPs:

QUESTION: At what age do you take children into your mills?
OWEN: At ten and upwards.
Q: Why do you not employ children at an earlier age?
OWEN: Because I consider it to be injurious to the children and not beneficial to the proprietors.
Q: What reasons have you to suppose it is injurious to the children to be employed at an earlier age?
OWEN: Seventeen years ago a number of individuals with myself purchased the New Lanark establishment from Mr Dale. I found that there were 500 children who had been taken from the poor-houses, chiefly in Edinburgh, and those children were generally from the age of five or six to seven to eight. The hours at that time were thirteen. Although these children were well fed, their limbs were very generally deformed, their growth was stunted and, although one of the best schoolmasters was engaged to instruct these children regularly every night, in general they made very slow progress, even in learning the common alphabet. I came to the

conclusion that the children were injured by being taken into the mills at this early age and employed for so many hours, therefore as soon as I had it in my power, I adopted regulations to put an end to a system which appeared to me to be so injurious.

Q: Do you give instruction to any part of your population?

OWEN: Yes, to the children from three years old upwards and to every other part of the population that choose to receive it.

Q: If you do not employ children under ten, what would you do with them?

OWEN: Instruct them and give them exercise.

Q: Would not there be a danger of their acquiring, by that time, vicious habits, for want of regular occupation?

OWEN: My own experience leads me to say that I found quite the reverse, that their habits have been good in proportion to the extent of their instruction.

Clearly this man's ideas were quite impractical and would never work. Thirty years later, Peel's son as prime minister would still be opposing the reduction of factory shifts to ten hours or the ending of child labour. Then and since, Owen has also been criticized from the Left for patronizing the poor and assuming he knew what was best for them. As the brief-lived radical newspaper *Black Dwarf* said in 1817:

It is very amusing to hear Mr Owen talk of re-moralising the poor. Does he not think that the rich are a little more in want of remoralising? Reduce the herd of locusts that prey upon the honey of the hive and think they do the bees a most essential service by robbing them… the poor will not want your splendid erections for the cultivation of misery and the subjugation of the mind.

Owen would eventually be disillusioned at New Lanark. He sold up and attempted to start new communities on similar principles at New Harmony in Indiana and at Tytherley in Hampshire, but these projects would fail. Later still Owen would attempt to set up a trade union. In some ways his proposals were prototypes for socialism. He would doubtless be gratified to know how widely his ideas, considered so eccentric at the time, have been taken up since.

⸺ ☙ ⸺

For many agricultural workers life was harder and more precarious than in the towns and factories, and starvation was a real possibility after bad harvests or in the spring months when food stocks were running low. Most lived in little better than hovels and were in thrall to their masters, local farmers or landowners. Harsh laws contained them and their freedom to raise food on their own account was increasingly circumscribed. Common land and open pastures held in common were being fenced off and essentially seized by local landowners, who could employ lawyers to defend their actions and point to the so-called 'Inclosure' Acts that successive parliaments had passed from the mid-eighteenth century. It was a process of annexation that had been going on for a long time – many of the peasants' revolts of the medieval period had been provoked by the loss of common land – but it gained strength and frequency in the seventy years following 1760, and by the early years of the nineteenth century most of the available and cultivable land across England had been closed off to villagers whose ancestors had farmed on it for centuries. The motivations behind this were financial: enclosed land was more profitable – more crops could be grown, or more animals reared, more cheaply and efficiently, and higher rents could be charged to tenants. On the estates of Wales, Scotland and parts of Ireland, similar processes were happening. The lairds and landowners were clearing their estates for sheep and cattle-grazing, depopulating the Scottish Highlands of the clans who had loyally followed them into battle during the revolt of 1745, in pursuit of profit and the sensibilities of the sublime, deserted landscapes of untamed nature.

The effects of clearing the land across the British Isles were harsh, reducing agricultural workers to the status of serfs, reliant on seasonal employment and low wages, and eventually depopulating the countryside. Perhaps the most potent protest against what was happening was Oliver Goldsmith's poem *The Deserted Village*, published in 1770 with its famous refrain: 'Ill fares the land, to hast'ning ills a prey,/ Where wealth accumulates and men decay'; and its equally subversive couplet: 'The law locks up the man who steals a goose from off the common,/ But lets the greater felon loose/ Who steals the common from off the goose.' Not that the wealthy took much notice: if they did not want the land for commercial purposes, they could always use it to create the great open landscaped vistas designed for them by Capability Brown or Humphry Repton. Demolishing whole villages to improve the view or replacing them with more picturesque ruins was far from unknown. The gracious living we associate with the Palladian mansions of the Georgian aristocracy was not achieved without a human cost locally, and in some cases it was financed by the profits of the slave trade.

There was another practice which had a devastating effect: clearing the ground for game shooting. The improvement in gun technology – shorter barrels, breech-loading from the 1780s – made the common pheasant, a challenging bird to shoot with its sudden, swooping, low-level flight, into a feasible target for sport. The bird required careful rearing, but large flocks could be built up each year and they needed ground cover to lurk in – rhododendrons, newly introduced from the Indian Himalayas, were both picturesque and ideal for the purpose. Expenditure on pheasants by the great house-holds spiralled. At Longleat, £264 was spent on buying birds in 1790 and that figure had become £400 by 1810; at Belvoir, expenditure quintupled in the same period. Then, gamekeepers were needed, both to rear the birds, until essentially they became half-tame, ready for blasting, and to protect the property, especially from poachers. The fact that, like most game birds, the pheasant was a grain-eater and so had the potential to lay waste to farmers' crops was neither here nor there to shooting enthusiasts.

Gradually the game laws were strengthened to protect the bird for the aristocracy and from farmers, peasants and poachers. While at the start of the eighteenth century poaching had been punishable with fines or brief imprisonment, under the harsh Black Act in 1723 it became one of fifty new capital offences. Between 1760 and 1820 fifty additional game acts were passed, and gamekeepers became not only zealous enforcers of the law on their masters' behalf, but also for that reason much hated and despised and accordingly targets them-selves. Somehow, countrymen could not see how the birds could be other people's property: weren't they free as the air? They were not marked as belonging to anyone. In the words of the rhymester in *The Claughton Wood Poachers*: 'I'm sure there is no mark on them as any man can claim their own,/ So if a man can finger one, why can't he bring it home?' If he did, he faced six months' imprisonment for a first offence and a year and a whipping for the second. No wonder there were regular battles between poachers and gamekeepers, sometimes deaths and occasionally hangings – and the rural poor were definitely on the poachers' side.

This was clearly shown in a celebrated affray between rival platoons of gamekeepers and poachers in Gloucestershire in January

1816. The fight followed the death of a young labourer on an estate owned by Lord Ducie near Berkeley the previous November. Tom Till had been caught by shot from a remotely operated spring gun in a wood while out poaching and was killed. Vowing revenge, a group of local poachers led by a respected young farmer named John Allen congregated the following January in a field on the neighbouring Berkeley Castle estate and confronted a combined force of keepers from several local estates. The fight was supposed to be unarmed, but in the mêlée a gun went off and shooting began. One keeper was killed and six wounded.

As the poachers fled, Colonel Berkeley gathered his forces in pursuit, scouring every house in the area and finally surrounding Allen's farmhouse at Moreton. The farmer surrendered, whereupon Berkeley beat him to the ground with a cudgel. Eleven of the gang, 'all young men of decent appearance, respectably connected', were subsequently tried at Gloucester. Nine were transported, but Allen and the man alleged to have fired the shot were hanged. Thereafter the local doctor Edward Jenner – the man who had devised vaccination as a cure for smallpox – who had given evidence of the dead gamekeeper's injuries at the trial, found himself ostracized and forced to move from the area. Meanwhile Colonel Berkeley, completely indifferent to local anger, not only commissioned a painting of what became known as the Berkeley Castle Poaching Affray (the picture still hangs in the castle) but also exhibited in a glass case a branch of a tree that had been peppered with shot during the fight.

<hr>

Farm labourers' wages were much lower than those of factory workers and tradesmen: on the farm workers might get eight shillings a week, while a miner could earn twenty-five shillings and a spinner in Manchester thirty shillings. The proximity of alternative work in the north probably boosted agricultural wages there, though a farm labourer would not have a spinner's skills, but in the rural south absolute poverty was endemic. Many subsisted, particularly in bad times, on potatoes and salt, washed down with 'tea' made from water poured on burned crusts. A wet-weather coat for a labourer cost three times his weekly wage. 'It is but little in the present state of things that the belly can spare for the back,' it was said. For many the only hope of freedom from want was, as the Northamptonshire peasant poet John Clare wrote, the grave. Clare certainly knew rural poverty: he tried his hand as a pot-boy, gardener, militiaman and lime-burner before having to fall back on parish relief in 1817. Such hardship was hard to escape: those slipping away from the farm to walk to town in search of better work might find themselves arrested and sent home, carted back under arrest by parish officers, if they tried begging for food along the way in parishes and towns where they did not belong.

Once in a city like London, they might find work hard to come by and end up grubbing in the streets, scraping between the cobbles for dropped coins or even the nails from horses' hooves. In the biggest, most bustling metropolis in the world, a city bursting with small workshops and companies, work could still be cyclical and employment precarious even for the skilled. For the poor crowding its streets, life here could be very hard indeed. This was the state of the city a few years before *Oliver Twist* (or indeed before the young Charles Dickens headed for Warren's Blacking Factory near Charing Cross in 1824): dirty, smelly, disease-ridden and overcrowded. It had an extraordinarily diverse working population: newly arrived country boys, as well as Londoners born and bred, Irish immigrants huddled four families to a room in the slums of Marylebone, and beggars on the streets. There was Charles McGee, an immaculately dressed one-eyed Jamaican who begged daily at Ludgate Circus; or Joseph Johnson, a former sailor, who had fashioned a wooden model of a Royal Navy ship which he wore on his head and who earned his money singing sea shanties in the street. William Dorrell was an inspector of pavements in St Giles's parish, one of the most notorious slum districts of the city around the area of Seven Dials, north of Covent Garden. Investigating the problem of begging in 1815, he told MPs: 'I have said, "Why do you not go out to work?" And they have said to me, "We get more by begging than we do by work."'

These were the sort of people who terrified men like Colquhoun and the poet Robert Southey: wastrels and brutes, as they saw them, masterless men given over to drunkenness and debauchery, seen in a way that would be familiar to tabloid readers two centuries hence. The great and immediate fear was that they would run out of control, like the *sans-culottes* of Paris during the French Revolution only thirty years before, or indeed the hooligans who had wrought havoc across London during the anti-Catholic Gordon Riots of 1780. At that time the army had had to be called out to restore order and nearly 300 people had been killed as well as much property destroyed. There were indeed occasional twitches of disorder to discomfort and alarm respectable folk. There was a time, wrote Southey, 'when I believed in the persuadability of man and had the mania of man-mending. Experience has taught me better.'

It was the moral corruption of the poor that such men hated, and the cure for it, evangelical campaigners believed, was enforced discipline and ruthless hard-heartedness: 'to harden the heart and do efficient good', according to the Philanthropic Society. The poor needed to be taught to work harder and not indulge themselves with idle pleasures such as drink. Their children needed to be brought up to work too, from the age of four perhaps, so that they should not follow their parents into bad habits. It was this philosophy that brought about the New Poor Law and the workhouse system a few years later, in the 1830s: no more 'outdoor' relief in the home; the destitute should be corralled in workhouses where they could be made to work and kept an eye on. As Jeremy Bentham said, it was an indisputable truth that 'the more strictly we are watched, the better we behave'. That would teach the feckless poor the error of their ways. It would be a cheerless existence, deprived of idle pleasures.

But not everyone agreed that harshness would have the desired effect, as the economist and writer Arthur Young wrote:

> For whom are they to be sober? For whom are they to save? If I am diligent, shall I have leave to build a cottage? If I am sober, shall I have land for a cow? If I am frugal, will I have half an acre of potatoes? You offer me no motives; you have nothing but a parish officer and a workhouse! Bring me another pot...

Black people were by no means unusual sights in London and across Britain in the early nineteenth century. Many were servants, but there were also tradesmen and craftsmen among them, and writers and actors – and campaigners for the abolition of the slave trade. Many of their names have been lost, though some even of the poorest were idiosyncratic or notable enough for their memory to survive. It has been estimated by the historian Gretchen Gerzina, based on burial registers, that between 1 and 3 per cent of Londoners of the period were black.* There were also long-standing black commun-

---

* This may be roughly comparable in scale with the size of the community of Pakistani origin (2.7 per cent) in Greater London in the 2011 census (black Londoners now represent approximately 15 per cent of the capital's population).

ities in the slave-trading ports of Liverpool and Bristol, although slavery itself was no longer legal in Britain. In a landmark court ruling in the Somerset case in 1772, Lord Mansfield had laid down that a former slave could not be taken from the country by force or sold against their will.* On a visit to England in 1805 an American visitor, Benjamin Silliman, was highly impressed – or perhaps just shocked – that the English did not have slaves:

> A black footman is considered as a great acquisition and consequently negro servants are sought for and caressed. An ill-dressed or starving negro is never seen in England and in some instances even alliances are formed between them and white girls of the lower orders of society... As there are no slaves in England, perhaps the English have not learned to regard negroes as a degraded class of men, as we do in the United States, where we have never seen them in any other condition.

The slave traders of Bristol and Liverpool had made too much money out of their dreadful business to have any scruples and fought long and hard to preserve it. But the trade in the British empire was abolished by Act of Parliament in 1807, thanks largely to evangelical campaigners such as William Wilberforce, and thereafter most

---

* Lord Mansfield, the Lord Chief Justice, himself had a mixed-race relative living with his family at Kenwood House in Hampstead. Dido Elizabeth Belle – the child of a liaison between his nephew, the career naval officer Sir John Lindsay, and an African slave – spent much of her life at Kenwood, helped Mansfield with his correspondence, and was painted, reputedly by Zoffany, with her cousin Lady Elizabeth Murray. The Somerset v. Stewart judgment of 1772 was Mansfield's most famous and enduring. He ruled that a slave, James Somerset, who had been brought to England by his master Charles Stewart and who had escaped and been recaptured, could not be forcibly returned to slavery elsewhere. Although the judgment applied in a particular case, it effectively created the general principle that slavery was not permissible within Britain; in the words of Somerset's counsel: 'This air is too pure for a slave to breathe in.'

Britons began to regard the trafficking of slaves as barbaric, to look down on the United States, and to take a high-minded attitude to other European countries which were slower to follow the British lead – as Castlereagh did at the Congress of Vienna.

In late eighteenth-century London there had been a number of celebrated black inhabitants. Among them was Olaudah Equiano, who had been a slave in America after being born in Nigeria, but who came to London as a free man in his twenties. He wrote his autobiography, *The Interesting Narrative of the Life of Olaudah Equiano*, later married a white woman in deepest rural Cambridgeshire, and died in his early fifties in 1797. Equally celebrated in his day was Ignatius Sancho, an actor, composer and writer who had a grocery shop in Mayfair, had his portrait painted by Gainsborough, and is thought to have been the first black man ever to vote in an English election. He died in 1780.

A generation or two younger, there was Jamaican-born Robert Wedderburn, son of a slave mother and a Scottish plantation owner, who came to Britain as a young man and joined the campaign for abolition. He spoke at public meetings with such vehemence – 'tell slaves to murder their masters as soon as they please,' a police spy reported him as telling one meeting – that he ended up in prison several times. Then there was William Davidson, another Jamaican son of a mixed marriage (his white father had been the island's attorney general) who came to Britain, was secretary of the shoemakers' union and was eventually executed – 'Black Davidson' – for his part in the Cato Street conspiracy to murder the cabinet in 1819 (see pages 131 and 277).

Some of the black servant population had been brought to England by their masters, others had bought their freedom in the Caribbean or United States. Following the Napoleonic wars there was an influx of black former soldiers and sailors, though they did not receive pensions like their white comrades. Joseph Johnson, the beggar sailor with a ship on his head, had been wounded in the war, but as he had been serving on a merchant ship at the time, he was not eligible for any help at all from the Admiralty in his destitution. Later in the nineteenth century this influx would peter out.

There were also lascars, Indians from the subcontinent and south Asia, who had fought in the navy and ended up in England; Huguenots and French refugees from the revolution; and Jews, many from Germany, making their way in trade and banking. The Rothschilds helped finance the war effort, while at the other end of the social scale Ikey Solomon, born in Houndsditch in east London in 1787, went into business on his own account as a pawnbroker, pickpocket and fence of stolen property. He served four years in the hulks for stealing money in 1810 and was about to stand trial on other charges of theft and receiving in May 1827 when he made a dramatic escape while being escorted back to Newgate jail after a hearing. The guards had apparently not realized that the driver of the hackney cab in which he was being carried was actually his father-in-law and they also seem to have made something of an error of judgement in allowing the cab to take a lengthy diversion via Petticoat Lane (one version of the story says they were kindly giving Mrs Solomon a lift home after the hearing on their way back to the jail). In any event, Ikey's friends were waiting and sprang him from custody, whereupon he managed to get away to New York. Ikey is generally held to have been the model for Fagin in *Oliver Twist*, though he was a rather more respectable-looking figure than Dickens's character. Solomon's wife and children were transported to a penal colony in Tasmania following her conviction for receiving stolen goods. Ikey opted to join them and he and his wife spent much of the rest of their lives expiating for their crimes there.

6

'The Great Wen'*

—WILLIAM COBBETT

ate on the afternoon of Monday 17 October 1814, George Crick, a clerk at the Meux Horseshoe Brewery at the bottom of Tottenham Court Road,† noticed that an iron hoop weighing seven hundredweight had split and slipped off one of the giant vats, twenty-two feet high, in which 135,000 gallons of porter were slowly maturing. He did not think much of it at the time because such a slippage happened several times a year and had 'not been attended by any serious consequence' before. Nevertheless he dropped a note to one of the brewery's partners just to let him know. Then, about an hour later, the vat burst open and its collapse precipitated the explosion of several other huge barrels, producing a fifteen-foot-high tidal wave of beer which smashed down the side wall of the brewery and flooded down the street towards the rookeries of St Giles and Seven Dials. Something over 320,000 gallons of beer poured through the area, and Crick and his colleagues found themselves waist deep in the brew. Down New Street – now New Oxford Street – a four-year-old child called Hannah Banfield was having tea with her mother Mary in the first-floor apartment where they lived. The flood swept through the room, hurling the little girl through a partition

---

* A 'wen' is a tumour or cyst.

† The brewery was approximately on the site now occupied by the Dominion Theatre.

wall, killing her and washing her mother out of the window. At the Tavistock Arms in Great Russell Street, a fourteen-year-old barmaid called Eleanor Cooper was overcome and drowned as she scoured pots in the yard, and in a basement nearby a group of mourners, all Irish immigrants who had been holding a wake for the two-year-old son of a friend who had died the previous day, were submerged and five of them drowned. The body of the child's mother, Ann Saville, was found floating among the wreckage of the barrels an hour later. Eight people were killed in the accident, the worst brewery explosion in British history, though none of them were Meux employees. At the inquest it was found that the barrel had been rotten. Had the explosion happened an hour later, it was said, many more would have been killed because the men who lived in the area would have been home from work by then. As it was, the inquest verdict was that the deaths had been caused by misfortune and the brewery company was able to reclaim £7,000 from the government for the excise duty it had already paid on the maturing beer. It did not contribute to the fund set up to help those whose homes had been inundated by the flood – they were, after all, immigrant Irish slum-dwellers – nor did the incident result in the censure of Henry Meux, the brewery's owner, or its managers, still less in the collapse of the company. He sailed on and would eventually be awarded a baronetcy.

The Horseshoe Brewery was expanding, but it was only the sixth-largest such beer company in London at the time of the explosion, just one of thousands of family-run businesses in the bustling capital. London did not have the heavy manufacturing industries of growing towns such as Manchester, but it was the trading capital of the world, as well as its largest city. By 1811 it had more than a million inhabitants: about a twelfth of the total in England, Scotland and Wales. Its population had expanded by 100,000 people – nearly 10 per cent – in the previous ten years, and within the next thirty years it would double in size. London generated at this time about a quarter of the country's wealth.

That wealth came from banking and trading and from small manu-facturing companies serving London's growing consumer market: watchmakers, jewellers, sugar refiners, carriage-builders, paper manufacturers, printers, silk weavers, hatters and tailors. Visitors marvelled at the range of products in the shops, almost as much as they were left breathless by the energy and bustle of its inhabitants, who seemed constantly on the move, pushing, shoving and shouting. One German visitor in the 1780s wrote: 'The stranger in London will be struck with astonishment when he sees the innumerable kinds of merchandise displayed before his eyes in thousands of well-fitted-up shops, for I believe there is no city in the world which in this respect can be compared to London.' In London, wrote Casanova, who visited in the 1760s, 'everything is easy to him who has money and is not afraid of spending it'.

Charles Lamb wrote to William and Dorothy Wordsworth at home in the Lake District:

> I have formed as many and as intense local attachments as any of you mountaineers can have done with dead nature. The lighted shops of the Strand and Fleet Street, the innumerable trades, tradesmen and customers, coaches, wagons, playhouses, all the bustle and wickedness round about Covent Garden, the very women of the town, the watchmen, drunken scenes, rattles – life awake, if you awake, at all hours of the night, the impossibility of being dull in Fleet Street, the crowds, the very dirt and mud, the sun shining upon houses and pavements, the print shops, the old book stalls... coffee houses, steams of soups from kitchens,

the pantomimes – London itself a pantomime and a masquerade
– all these things work themselves into my mind and feed me...
and I often shed tears... from fullness of joy at so much in life.

Just as today, a visitor who paused to ponder or look around in wonder
was liable to be run over. 'You stop and bump! a porter runs against
you shouting "By your leave," after he has knocked you down,' wrote
Georg Christoph Lichtenberg, the German writer and scientist who
visited London twice in the 1770s. The poet Robert Southey, stopping
at a pastry cook's shop one day in 1812, asked her why she kept her
window open in all weathers. She told him that if she did not, she
would lose forty or fifty shillings a day, because many busy passing
customers picked up buns and biscuits as they passed the window
and threw their pennies in so they did not have to stop and go into
the shop to pay for them. Clearly an early form of takeaway: as the
historian Judith Flanders points out, if her estimate was reliable and
she was selling penny buns, that equated to about 500 customers a
day hurrying past and grabbing their breakfasts on the run. 'Was there
ever so indefatigable a people?' wrote Southey, impressed.

All was hurry and vibrancy. And noise: there was a constant buzz
of shouts and calls from pedestrians and street vendors (and, at night,
watchmen calling the time), but also the grind and clatter of horses'
hooves and iron-rimmed wheels on granite street surfaces, making it
difficult for many to make themselves heard above the torrent – what
the Victorian journalist Henry Mayhew would later call 'the uninter-
rupted and crashing roar'. The rush started in the middle of the night
as drovers herded livestock into Smithfield market, and carts brought
fish to Billingsgate and vegetables to Covent Garden. Then the long
trudge to work began: men rising early, walking as much as ten or
twelve miles to be at their posts by seven o'clock. Tens of thousands

of workers were crossing the city every day to get to and from their employment: clerks trudging from outlying Brixton and Lambeth, Islington and Pentonville to reach their counting houses in the City; dockers and labourers from Soho and Seven Dials heading for their employment in the East End's new docks and the noisome leather-works, soap-rendering plants and other noxious factories downriver; dressmakers and tailors on piecework; glass-blowers and brewery workers; tile-makers and sugar processors; shop-workers and appren-tices needing to get to their shops and workshops early to sweep the floors, dust the produce, wash the windows and pavements, and polish up the handles of the big front doors ready for the first customers of the morning.

London was absorbing nearby villages which were becoming suburbs, but even areas that were already fashionable and well-to-do in the centre of town had a varied social mix. Mayfair was the haunt of the dandies, but it still had a market and a range of tradesmen, including butchers herding cattle in the streets and slaughtering them in their backstreet yards: a woman living in Brook Street complained in 1801 that the stables behind her house were so crowded on market days that she could not get her carriage out without running the risk of being gored by bullocks. Particular areas had their own speciali-ties: cabinet-makers and furniture manufacturers around Tottenham Court Road; clock-makers and craftsmen in precision metalwork in Clerkenwell; coach-makers in Long Acre near Covent Garden's vegetable market. By the 1840s it was estimated that there were 40,000 tailors, dressmakers and milliners, many of them in Soho and Holborn, and by then 200,000 people would be tramping to the City each day. The hours were long: twelve-hour days, sometimes later in the shops and at busy periods, before the long trail back home again; six days a week and no holidays, work precarious, wages undercut, and the threat of unemployment at any time if orders dropped off or an employer went bankrupt.

Many were fuelled by ambition, sobriety, thrift and religiosity. They had before them the knowledge that many of London's most successful company owners had started like them: the original Samuel Whitbread, who had begun at the age of fourteen as a brewer's apprentice; William Fortnum, who had been a royal footman and gone into the grocery business with his landlord Hugh Mason; or James Lock, the apprentice hatter who had inherited his employer's business. And, if not secular ambition, there was always piety. The Church of England had its great City churches and was jealous of its long-standing privileges and wealthy communicants, but the denominations that were really growing were the nonconformist churches stretching out into the suburbs. Their sense of moral engagement and occasionally political involvement – as over the campaign against slavery – and their emphasis on personal conversion and commitment had much greater resonance than the complacent pieties and disengagement of the established church, many of whose clergy were absent from the parishes they were supposed to serve. The London Churches Act of 1711 had set aside money for the construction of fifty new Anglican churches across the capital, but a century later only ten of them had been built. By contrast, in 1812 there were 256 chapels and places of worship for dissenters, many more than the 186 churches of the established religion. These were the people whose growing wealth and philanthropy had founded a string of hospitals across London in the eighteenth century: lying-in hospitals for mothers in labour, foundling homes for orphans, even the Lock Hospital for venereal cases. If the care was basic, the capital was nonetheless perhaps the best-provided city for the sick in the western world.

Thousands had found their hearts 'strangely warmed' at John Wesley's outdoor rallies, or the more radical messages of George Whitefield's mass gatherings at Blackheath.* Baptists, Presbyterians and Quakers were now respectable, Methodists less so because they were perceived to be more politically radical, but Catholics were still beyond the pale. Catholicism was the religion of the slum-dwelling Irish, an alien creed whose adherents owed allegiance to a foreign potentate in Rome and whose last English king had been ejected in the Glorious Revolution in 1688 when he had supposedly become too absolutist for his own good. By 1815 there was pressure from some senior politicians, foremost among them George Canning, the rebel Tory former minister, to alleviate the restrictions on Catholics: to emancipate them from the seventeenth-century Test Acts that restricted their employment and their ability to stand for public office, become MPs, run corporations or even attend university if they would not take an oath denying their religious beliefs. The pressure was caused largely by recognition of the need to pacify Ireland, but also because the government urgently wanted to recruit Catholic Irish troops to fight its wars and struggled to do so if they had to forswear their religion first. Many politicians, however, were not yet convinced of the need for this reform, fearing that emancipation would undermine the very pillars of the state. The chief obstacle was the Prince Regent himself, who was adamantly opposed and determinedly holding to the monarchical oath to uphold the Church of England – in this if in little else – morally or spiritually. Catholic emancipation would take a prolonged parliamentary struggle and another dozen years following 1815 to pass into law and only came

---

* 'Strangely warmed' was how John Wesley described his own feelings at the time of his spiritual awakening.

about when senior Tories such as Robert Peel changed their minds and gave up resisting the inevitable.

—❧—

For those with money to spare, if not to burn, London offered copious pleasures: not only the pubs, gin shops and shebeens that could be found on every street (at one time in the mid-eighteenth century it was believed that one house in every eight in London sold drink), but also a wide range of entertainments. There were giants on the London stage, playing Shakespeare in varying styles as well as farces and pantomimes. John Philip Kemble had largely retired from acting and gone into theatre management by this stage, though he had nearly been bankrupted by the fire that destroyed the Theatre Royal, Covent Garden in 1808.* He had then been almost ruined by the 'old price' riots which accompanied the opening of the replacement new theatre, forcing its temporary closure the following year, when he tried to increase the seat prices to reduce his losses. The rival Drury Lane Theatre had burned down a few months after the Theatre Royal, entirely bankrupting its owner Richard Brinsley Sheridan. Now both theatres had been rebuilt, and coming up fast to great acclaim at Drury Lane was the fiery and unstable young actor Edmund Kean, who had made his debut in London in 1814, playing the great Shakespearean roles. His naturalistic acting was 'like reading Shakespeare by flashes of lightning', according to Coleridge, though he was also described in unfriendlier fashion by

---

* Kemble's older sister, Sarah Siddons, the greatest actress of her day, famous for her heart-stopping portrayal of Lady Macbeth, had retired in 1812, giving the audience at Covent Garden an impromptu eight-minute farewell speech in mid-performance following the sleep-walking scene, after which the ovation was so great that the play could not continue. Two other Kemble siblings, Charles and Stephen, were continuing to act.

Leigh Hunt as having 'a voice like a hackney coachman's at one in the morning'. Kean was pioneering a new, less formal and declamatory way of acting, in contrast to Kemble's more mannered, stately style, which included pausing for applause at the end of speeches. Kean enthralled audiences – and also returned Shakespeare's texts to their original state, dropping Nahum Tate's happy ending to *King Lear*, which had been played for more than 100 years. Shortly afterwards Kean's great rival Charles Macready would follow him to London, appearing at Covent Garden, initially in less classical roles because he feared comparison with Kean.

The biggest star in the London theatre, though, was the clown Joseph Grimaldi, who in 1815, aged thirty-six, was at the height of his powers and in huge demand – to the annoyance of the rival theatre owners, Charles Dibdin at Sadler's Wells and John Fawcett at Covent Garden, who both wanted him to appear exclusively for them. Trying to satisfy all parties and maintain his precarious earnings, that summer Joey would race by cab from performing at the Surrey Theatre in Southwark, south of the river, up to Sadler's Wells in Islington, and then down to perform the same evening at Covent Garden.

Joey was highly popular with audiences: a London lad who had started in the theatre with his Anglo-Italian father when he was a small child and had grown up to make the stock pantomime part of Harlequin his own. His exotic costumes and white face make-up have been common to clowns ever since, but it was his balletic athleticism which thrilled audiences and his cheeky, irreverent Cockney wit – 'Here we are again!' – that made them roar with laughter. In part, the manic energy was an attempt to earn enough money to keep himself solvent – actors were not well paid – but it did not do him any good. Fawcett withheld Grimaldi's money because he was appearing at other theatres without permission that summer, and Dibdin would soon sack him when he demanded twelve guineas a week (as opposed to twelve pounds: a twelve-shilling difference), two benefit performances allowing him to profit from all the night's takings, and a release to tour the provinces for six weeks every summer. Dibdin maintained he could not afford it and replaced Grimaldi with Signor Paulo, a rival clown, though one who copied his costume and make-up. Both Joey and Edmund Kean would end their lives crippled, alcoholic and near-destitute. Acting was not yet a respectable profession, and ramshackle touring companies, like the Crummles' in *Nicholas Nickleby*, would continue for many years to come, performing in provincial theatres and even barns.

On Thursday 22 June 1815, the day that news of the previous Sunday's battle of Waterloo appeared in *The Times*, the newspaper also carried an advertisement for that week's programme at Sadler's Wells:

> A new dance called *THE PLOUGHBOY*; a comic song by Mr Sloman; a favourite pantomime called *THE MERMAID*: clown Mr Grimaldi. The entertainments to conclude with a new Melo-drama called *THE RED HANDS; or Welsh Chieftains*. Box 4 shillings, Pit 2s, Gallery 1s, Doors opened at half past five, and begin at half past six; places kept till half past seven.

The Wells' chief novelty at this time was its on-stage tank on which miniature depictions of sea fights and battles, such as Trafalgar and the siege of Gibraltar, could be staged in water three feet deep, with model ships crewed by midgets and children. It was a remarkable spectacle, although the water was only irregularly changed, so it became malodorous and deeply unhygienic (not helped by the cast sometimes bathing in it following performances). On this June week, however, disappointed patrons were informed 'that in consequence of the extraordinary expensive preparation making for a Ship Launch on real Water, no Aquatic Scene can be exhibited this week'. If that did not appeal, theatre-goers could go to Drury Lane to see Mr Kean in *Rule a Wife and Have a Wife* with, second on the bill, *Charles the Bold*; or, the following evening, to Covent Garden to see *The Duenna* with Mr Sinclair as Carlos and Miss Stephens as Clara, during which, in the course of the evening, 'Black-Eyed Susan' would be sung and there would also be a farce and other entertainments. For land-based spectacle, they could go instead to Astley's Royal Amphitheatre across the river in Lambeth to watch 'at half-past six precisely… a new, splendid serio-comic equestrian pantomime with extraordinary preparations'; these included a real horse-race and a real fox chace (*sic*), as well as a comic musical piece called *KING HENRY VIII AND THE COBBLER* and concluding with *THE SAILOR'S LOVE, or Constancy Rewarded*, two shows nightly. Audiences certainly got their money's worth.

Theatre was not the only entertainment in London, of course. There were the pleasure gardens spread across the capital, most prominently at Vauxhall Gardens in Lambeth. Huge crowds of spectators could be swallowed up in the leafy walks there – 60,000 allegedly during one day's holiday in the 1780s – and, if they were not there to canoodle with their wives, mistresses and girlfriends in the so-called dark walks under the trees, they could be entertained with concerts and recitals in the 150-foot-wide rotunda, or astonished by spectacles such as the world's first parachute jump from a balloon, made by a Frenchman in 1802, and, above all, thrilled by the firework shows. One was scheduled for Friday 23 June 1815, presided over by Signor Bologna according to the previous day's *Times*. Entrance was not cheap at three shillings and sixpence (four shillings to see the fireworks) and the park was beginning to fade in attractiveness, though it would remain open for another forty years. That week, London also had concerts: Pio Cianchettini, having recovered from his indisposition, was promising a vocal and instrumental concert of his works at the Argyll Rooms the following Monday. There was a panorama portrait of Paris 'as now fortifying by Bonaparte' – an advertisement evidently inserted before news of Waterloo came through – as well as exhibitions, sermons and meetings. There was also, of course, a need to convert the Catholic Irish from their papist ways, with an ingenious proposal to speak to them in their own tongue:

ANNUAL MEETING of the BAPTIST SOCIETY for PRO-MOTING the GOSPEL in IRELAND: Breakfast at 7 o'clock, the Chair to be taken at 8 precisely. The principal objects are to establish schools in Ireland for teaching the native Irish language and to employ persons to read the Holy Scriptures in Irish to their neighbours.

No wonder visitors were dazzled.

———— ✺ ————

For those of a legalistic or ghoulish turn of mind, there were often public executions to attend. The gallows at Tyburn had fallen out of use after 1783 and now executions in the capital were conducted in the street by Newgate prison, next to the Old Bailey court, or outside the Horsemonger Lane Gaol across the river.* The latter offered a better view, but the former was where the most infamous criminals were throttled to death.

* Horsemonger Lane Gaol was the alternative name for the Surrey County Gaol, where the journalist Leigh Hunt was imprisoned for lampooning the Prince Regent.

In 1815 the most notorious case of the year was that of Eliza Fenning, a pretty twenty-two-year-old cook who had been accused of attempting to poison her new employers, the Turner family, who lived in Chancery Lane, none of whom had died. The incident had occurred on 21 March – the day after Napoleon had arrived back in Paris – when Fenning, the daughter of a Irish former soldier, had cooked the family dumplings with their lunchtime meal. Everyone, including Fenning herself, had apparently fallen sick, though they had recovered within a few hours by the time a doctor was called. Maybe it was adulterated flour, or contaminated water – neither unknown in London in those days – but no one seems to have checked that possibility. The following day Orlibar Turner, the young woman's suspicious employer, claimed to have found traces of arsenic in the dumpling residue – not that he was qualified to discover it – though he alleged he had discovered enough to kill the whole family several times over, not just make them mildly sick. Following this allega-tion, the frightened young cook was hauled off to prison, the first step in a terrifying vortex leading inexorably to the gallows. The trial a few weeks later was a travesty – prisoners at this stage were not allowed to speak in their own defence, or indeed officially to be legally represented. Much was made of Fenning's supposedly suspicious character – her being Irish (though she was actually a Methodist rather than a Catholic) and her liking for reading books. The evidence was almost entirely circumstantial and non-scientific; the judge was energetically biased against Fenning and the jury found her guilty after ten minutes' deliberation. She was sentenced to hang.

It was a terrifying indictment of the savagery and arbitrariness of the law. The whole case seems explicable only in terms of con-temporary middle-class fears of being poisoned by their employees and concern about the subversiveness and radical tendencies of the

Irish – though Fenning, born in Suffolk, had spent most of her life in London and her family lived just around the corner from the Turners in Red Lion Street. In the face of a well-honed newspaper panic that she must be guilty if the court had said so and despite a campaign led by Methodist ministers pleading her innocence, there was no clemency and no reprieve and the young woman went to the scaffold outside Newgate a week after the battle of Waterloo. Her anguished cry – 'Before the just and almighty God, and by the faith of the holy sacrament I have taken, I am innocent of the offence with which I am charged' – may have echoed poignantly across the crowd outside the Old Bailey.* Fenning was dressed all in white for the occasion to indicate her innocence (some said it would have been her wedding gown) and the execution was watched by a crowd of as many as 40,000, most of them clearly sympathetic to her plight. Any of those who attended would have seen an affecting spectacle and a triple bill, because two men were hanged at the same time.

Fenning's family was charged with a bill for fourteen shillings and sixpence to cover the executioner's fee and to reclaim her body (she could be buried privately because she had not been convicted of murder), but they had to borrow from sympathizers in order to do so. The funeral procession through Holborn and Bloomsbury a few days later was accompanied by 10,000 people, despite the authorities' attempts to harass the mourners. 'The ultimate fate of the criminal is the best proof that [her claims of innocence] have no foundation in truth,' the *Observer* reported smugly. Meanwhile, the Turners'

---

* Fenning's famous last words were reported by a journalist supporter of hers, William Hone, and they were probably embellished, especially as it is questionable how far they would have carried across such a huge crowd. Fenning was literate and wrote letters from Newgate petitioning for her innocence, though these may have been improved for publication by Hone.

solicitor told a journalist that his clients had done what was proper by ensuring that the girl was hanged: 'Nobody would be safe if these Irish wretches [are] suffered to get into respectable families.'

Such a case was notorious and sordid, but it was only one of a number of hangings in London that year. The number of executions increased dramatically following the end of the Napoleonic wars, with an expansion in what constituted hanging offences. In the four years between 1806 and 1810 there were fifty-three executions in London, 12 per cent of the 428 people sentenced to death in England and Wales, the rest being commuted to transportation. Between 1811 and 1815 there were eighty-five hangings, and between 1816 and 1820, 140 (13 per cent of the 1,058 capital-crime convictions). The figures rose similarly across England and Wales as a whole: 374 executions between 1811 and 1815, 518 between 1816 and 1820.

Capital crimes were expanding as the authorities panicked about subversion and would only be restricted to crimes of murder and treason in the 1830s when the government realized that juries simply would not convict prisoners to hang for minor offences such as theft. As if hanging were not enough in the meantime, for really serious crimes medieval-style mutilation might also be involved. The radicals involved in the Cato Street conspiracy in 1820 were sentenced to be publicly hanged, drawn and quartered, though in the event they were merely decapitated by the masked executioner with a surgical knife after they had been throttled by the noose.

Short of an execution, there were other punishment spectacles to be had. The pillory was still available, though decreasingly used, to humiliate those sentenced for crimes of subversion and sodomy (which was still also a capital offence). The condemned, paraded through the streets with their heads and hands fastened through a board, were defenceless against the ordure, stones, dead cats,

stinking fish and excrement flung in their faces by jeering crowds
for an hour or more. Worse could happen – they might be blinded
by the stones and in one case in 1815 a prisoner died after his ordeal.
Eventually MPs called for the punishment to be stopped, though not
because of the harm to those subjected to it. The trouble was that
sometimes crowds sympathized with the criminal, such as the printer
sentenced in 1797 for publishing Thomas Paine's banned pamphlet
The Age of Reason, and left him alone – and where was the punishment or retribution in that?

—∞∞∞—

In 1815 two architects, both in their early sixties and born within a
few months of each other, were changing the appearance and design
of British buildings. They were John Soane, the prickly and paranoid
designer of the Bank of England and Dulwich Picture Gallery, and
his rival John Nash, the ingenious and energetic architect of a wide
range of country homes for the gentry, who had been taken up by
the Prince Regent and whose workload was accordingly expanding
exponentially.

With the exception of Sir Christopher Wren, few men have had
such an influence on the face of London as Nash, and few have had
such a spendthrift or capricious employer as his patron, the prince.
In the year of Waterloo Nash was engaged in designing the regent's
stately pleasure dome in Brighton, transforming what had once been
a farmhouse that had been enlarged and enlarged again in the classical style only a decade earlier by Henry Holland, into an exotic
mock-Indian palace, sitting squatly near the seafront, with domes
and turrets, gothic touches, mock-Chinese interiors, a music room,
banqueting suite, gallery and apartments. Holland's walls survived,
submerged under the iron framework and stucco surface as the

pavilion was expanded piecemeal. The Indian features – they were called 'Hindoo' style at the time – were apparently first conceived by Humphry Repton, Nash's sometime partner, but they were carried into effect by Nash himself. Neither architects nor prince, of course, had ever been anywhere near India or seen anything other than pictures of Mughal designs from the sketchbooks of travellers such as Thomas and William Daniell, whose *Oriental Scenery* was published from 1795. Even Nash's biographer Sir John Summerson, writing in the 1930s, found the pavilion hard to love: 'The decoration, laid so thickly over these classical bones, has no consistent affinity with any known style. It is a coalition of ideas formed in Nash's imagination with the addition of specific decorative adjuncts supplied and largely designed by tradesmen,' he wrote:

> In its own day it was the target of every wag. Byron, Cobbett, Wilberforce, Hazlitt, Sydney Smith – all had their fun with it, mingling contempt with laughter. To radicals it was a red rag, to connoisseurs a monster of stylistic impurity. Today it is simply a minor historical monument and to the citizens of Brighton a familiar curio containing halls which may be hired for lectures and concerts.

The pavilion was a huge extravaganza, largely impractical to live in and the prince himself never stayed there after 1822. As Summerson says, once it was finished in 1823, the king lost interest, even though the conversion had cost the enormous sum of £160,000.

But the prince's patronage would transform the fortunes of the growing town around his pavilion forever, turning it into a fashionable resort for the dandies and members of the court circle who would follow him there. They started by renting local cottages – the prince's mistress Mrs Fitzherbert had been one of the first to do so in the 1780s – and gradually a series of spec-built terraces and squares were constructed, spreading westwards towards Hove. Indeed, wherever Regency society moved for pleasure the speculative building of stuccoed villas, terraces, squares and crescents followed: in Cheltenham, Hastings and St Leonards, Exeter and Reading. And the same was true of London – in Hampstead and Pimlico, but chiefly and most ostentatiously in Nash's reconfiguring of Regent's Park and Regent Street.

This was his other grand project of the period, starting with the redevelopment of what had previously been called Marylebone Park in the Repton style, with a lake and picturesquely sited clumps of trees to form the vista. But that was just the start of the scheme. The Regent's Park would have middle-class villas and terraces and crescents around it and be fringed by its canal, heavily promoted by Nash as he was the canal company's chief shareholder. Then, in place of the capital's dingy, narrow, mean and crowded streets, there would be a wide boulevard sweeping down to Oxford Street and the Strand and on to the prince's residence at Carlton House, overlooking St James's Park. The aim was to make London the most distinguished and imposing capital city in the world and, especially, to beat Paris and Vienna. Nothing now could stall Nash's celebrity – not even an unfortunate accident, witnessed by the crowned heads of Europe during their visit to London in August 1814, when a temporary wooden pagoda he had designed on a bridge over a stream in St James's Park burned down in a firework accident and two people died.

The planning stage for Regent Street was under way by 1813 when an Act of Parliament gave permission for the development to be built. The work would take a further decade and a half, though not all of Nash's plans or those of his fellow architects would get built. There were difficulties acquiring some of the land from owners such as Sir James Langham, who wanted too much money, and the post-war economic slump also delayed building, but enough was completed to create an elegant and affluent street in the heart of the capital of an expanding global empire. Regent Street, curving down from the park, was supposedly modelled on the broad vistas of Oxford's college-lined High Street, but was actually threaded between gardens too expensive to be bought by the developers. It was an urban realization of what contemporary romantics saw as the picturesque: long, varied views into the distance, interspersed with such eye-catching details as All Souls Church. Now, when much of Nash's plan and many of his buildings have been lost or replaced, including the world's first covered shopping arcade next to his Royal Opera House, it is some-times hard to see the original scheme. But enough remains – not least the grand terraces south of the park – to sense what Nash had in mind.

Nash's fall would be great once his patron George IV had died in 1830. A Commons committee accused him of 'inexcusable irregulari-ties and great negligence' as the cost of another project, rebuilding Buckingham House for the king, spiralled out of control.* This was largely because George IV had kept changing his mind, but Nash was ruined and would die insolvent. For a hundred years his work and that of his followers would be dismissed as meretricious and trashy – impractical, jerry-built houses disguising brickwork and cast-iron frames with a layer of stucco and surface elegance – but now of course they are highly prized and hugely valuable.

Nash was a charmer. The Tory diarist Mrs Arbuthnot described

---

* At this date it was still known as Buckingham House, after its original owner the Duke of Buckingham. It became a royal palace when Queen Victoria made it her official London residence after 1837.

him as 'a very clever, odd amusing man with a face like a monkey's but civil and good humoured to the greatest degree'. But he was not a details man. He had not needed to be in the extravagant days of the early Regency when he was hustling to gain favour with the prince and other rich clients. Sir John Soane, who was much more meticulous, once told him that he had met 'few persons so anxious of fame and who would make more sacrifices at the altar of public approbation than yourself'. The two men were rivals, mutually wary, and Soane in particular was suspicious of Nash's flashiness, though they would occasionally collaborate. Both were self-made men, rising by talent albeit with the help of wealthy patrons: Soane was the son of an Oxfordshire bricklayer (and reputedly had started as a hod-carrier himself) and Nash was a Welsh millwright's son – proof that men of special skill could make their way to affluence and success and even social acceptability.*

If for Nash 1815 was a year of commercial achievement, for Soane it turned into an *annus horribilis*. Two years before, he had been at the pinnacle of his career: he was completing work on the Dulwich Picture Gallery, built to house the art collection of Soane's friend Sir Francis Bourgeois, who had died in 1811. The building, lit with natural light streaming down from skylights – a feature of Soane's work, would be, in 1817, the first such gallery to open to the public in England. In addition Soane was now clerk of works at Whitehall,

---

* The relative social openness and mobility of English society astonished foreigners. It is remarkable how many of the innovators and entrepreneurs of the period had lowly, provincial social origins. This applied not just to Soane and Nash but to a host of others: Humphry Davy, a Cornish wood-carver's son; John Dalton, the developer of atomic theory, whose father was a Cumbrian weaver; Michael Faraday, son of a blacksmith; George Stephenson, son of a Northumbrian colliery fireman; Richard Trevithick, a Cornish miner's son; Thomas Telford, son of a shepherd in Dumfriesshire; Robert Owen, a Welsh ironmonger's son. Many were nonconformists, all were to a greater or lesser degree self-taught, and all came from outside the social hierarchy.

Westminster, St James's Palace and the Chelsea Hospital, and he was able to spend time developing his house on the north side of Lincoln's Inn Fields to accommodate his own growing collection of art and sculpture, including Classical statuary brought back from Greece and Rome. As a gratifying mark of his social respectability, he had also been elected a member of the Grand Lodge of London freemasons and appointed superintendent of the lodge's building works. Any pride in this, though, was dissipated by Soane's family troubles. He had hoped that his two sons, John and George, would follow him into the architectural profession and had pressed them to do so: John had done, without much success, but George could not be cajoled or bullied. He sponged off his exasperated parents until they refused to pay him any more and, in November 1814, had been imprisoned for debt and fraud. Finally, the boy's ailing mother, Eliza Soane, relented and paid his creditors so that he could be released from the King's Bench Prison in early 1815.

The way George repaid his parents, in September 1815, was to write two swingeingly critical – but anonymous – attacks on his father, his career, his personality and all his architectural works, in a Sunday newspaper called *The Champion*. They hit the old man directly where he was most vulnerable and sensitive: in his self-esteem and vanity. The articles compared the newly built clerk of works' house at the Chelsea Hospital to a grocery shop – 'a monster in the art of building' – and said the hospital infirmary was 'exquisitely ludicrous'. His father's Bank of England design contained 'extravagances which are too dull for madness and too mad for the soberness of reason'. Meanwhile the Lincoln's Inn house showed 'exceeding heaviness and monumental gloom… it looks like a record of the departed and can only mean that considering himself as defunct in that better part of humanity – the mind and his affections – he has reared this mausoleum for the enshrinement of his body'. Unfortunately, George knew his father well enough to know not only where his attacks would sting most, but also that the criticisms contained a grain of truth: the Lincoln's Inn house *was* gloomy and was being self-consciously designed for posterity. Of course Soane realized immediately who had written the diatribes. Eliza knew too: 'Those are George's doing,' she apparently said. 'He has given me my death blow. I shall never be able to hold up my head again.'

This unfortunately came to pass a few weeks later. Eliza collapsed, took to her bed and died within a day on 22 November 1815, apparently the victim of stress and debilitation caused by gall-stones. Soane, who had not been the most attentive of husbands, was suddenly devastated. 'Melancholy day indeed!' he wrote in his diary the following week. 'The burial of all that is dear to me in this world and all I wished to live for.' That Christmas he took refuge in the friendship of the painter J. M. W. Turner. He framed George's articles, labelled them 'Death Blows' and took steps to alter his will.

In the coming months he would design his wife's tomb and in doing so unconsciously create perhaps the most widely familiar of all his works. The tomb, in which he too would be buried more than twenty years later, sits in isolated splendour in St Pancras Old Churchyard, close to the railway line, rattled by trains heading into and out of the station. It is a strange, squat mausoleum without any religious iconography (Soane was an atheist): a square block of marble, surrounded by an Ionic pillar at each corner and topped with a shallow dome of Portland stone. If it looks vaguely familiar, it is because 108 years after it was built Sir Giles Gilbert Scott copied unmistakeable elements of the design to win a competition for what became the familiar red British telephone box.

7

'The age of surface'

— RICHARD BRINSLEY SHERIDAN

If the feckless poor needed to be kept under control, what of the feckless rich? This was the era of the dandy: the exquisitely dressed young men gambling their lives and fortunes away in pursuit of the deeply trivial, even at a time of national crisis. Young men with money to burn have always behaved badly, but for about the first twenty years of the nineteenth century the dandy, aided and abetted at least for a time by the Prince Regent, became a highly recognizable social figure. Dandies were objects of fascination and disapproval who have maintained a degree of period charm for two hundred years since, apparently giving the Regency a surface elegance and frivolity. They were womanizers and gamblers. Members of the sporting 'Fancy' who followed and bet upon horse-racing and boxing tended to be dandies, chancers and frauds, and they have, incongruously, left a perma- nent mark on men's fashion, in the shape of trousers, as opposed to breeches, and white tie and tails. The dandies were products of the prosperity engendered by the Napoleonic wars, who reaped the rewards of high agricultural prices on their families' lands and had nothing to do with their wealth except spend it. Earning an income or entering a profession was not necessarily work for a gentleman: far easier to borrow against capital, or mortgage future income to banks and money-lenders, trusting – and being trusted – to pay back regularly, with added interest, from their winnings. This was usually easier proffered than done and often ended in only one way, with a surreptitious night-time flit to France to escape creditors.

The term dandy encompassed ageing roués such as the playwright politician Richard Brinsley Sheridan; royal dukes and ordinary dukes – not only the Prince of Wales and Duke of York but also Bedford, Argyll and Rutland; aristocrats such as Lords Alvanley and Byron and Lord Frederick Beauclerk;* and young men on the make such as Scrope Davies, Tom Sheridan, Richard's son, and Frederick 'Poodle' Byng. They had their exclusive clubs, their card games – Faro and Macao the favourites – and their dances and balls; they had their mistresses and courtesans and their daily rituals which formed a rigid pattern in their lives. And their legacy was at least partly the prudish and moralistic reaction that characterized some aspects of Victorian life.

The leader of the pack was George 'Beau' Brummell, possibly the only person ever known to posterity for the stylishness of his neckwear (he would not have wanted it any other way); a man who for a period of about fifteen years – until he was forced to flee the country in 1816 to avoid paying his debts – exercised a strange level of influence over the *haut ton*. Brummell himself was not a member of the aristocracy but the son of a civil servant and grandson of a valet. His father, however, had amassed a fortune while serving first as secretary to Charles Jenkinson, father of the future Lord

---

* Alvanley, 1789–1849, was Beau Brummell's great friend. A contemporary portrait shows a plump figure trussed into a tight-fitting outfit, chest thrust out and looking somewhat like a pouter pigeon. He liked his food, once allowing his chef to spend £108 on buying the carcases of thirteen different sorts of rare game birds for a fricassee. It was said of him that he insisted on having a dish of cold apricot tart every day of the year – no mean feat in pre-refrigeration times – and that when he finished reading in bed at night he would hurl the candle to the floor instead of putting it out. If it remained alight, he would throw a pillow at it. Perhaps he was lucky to live as long as he did.

Liverpool, the government's patronage adviser (Jenkinson happened to have lodged with the Brummells when he first came to London), and then as private secretary to Lord North, prime minister at the time of the American War of Independence. Both were fruitful sources of contacts and patrons. The profits enabled him to retire to a country house at Donnington, the next village to Speenhamland just outside Newbury. Born in 1778, young George was sent to Eton and briefly to Oxford, before buying himself a cornetcy in the 10th Light Hussars, one of the most fashionable regiments in the army with a highly flattering figure-hugging uniform, from which he resigned when he learned that his unit was to be moved to deeply unfashionable Manchester. At the age of twenty-one he came into an inheritance from his father of £30,000 – worth several million pounds today – and he then descended on London society to set about spending it.

It seems Brummell had already made the acquaintance of the Prince of Wales – who was sixteen years older than he was – when he was a schoolboy at Eton. Perhaps it was his self-confidence and charm that appealed to the prince: 'He displayed there all that the Prince of Wales most esteemed of human things,' wrote Count Jules d'Aurevilly, one of Brummell's earliest and most admiring nineteenth-century biographers. 'A splendid youth enhanced by the aplomb of the man who has judged life and can dominate it, the subtlest and most audacious mingling of impertinence and respect and finally a genius for dress and deportment protected by a gift for perpetually witty repartee.' The prince, then in his most rebellious phase against his parents and the royal court, siding with the Whigs to annoy and discomfort his father, found a kindred spirit in Brummell. They shared common interests in fashion and fine living, in gambling and dining, and became close friends for twenty years until the dandy's barbed wit, insolence and irreverence went too far. The beau became a member of the prince's shadow court coterie.

This and other political contacts all helped Brummell to become what he most relished, the fashionable world's chief arbiter of taste. That taste was for simple, but stylishly tailored, conservatively toned menswear. There were blue tail jackets with brass or black buttons, white waistcoats, and tightly fitting, high-waisted buff-coloured trousers, held up by braces (another innovation) and worn with highly polished black boots or dancing pumps.* The *pièces de résistance* were white shirts and white, starched neckcloths: the sort of dress familiar from any Jane Austen film adaptation and, in modified versions, what English gentlemen have worn formally ever since. The whole ensemble was designed to show off the trimmest of figures and the shapeliest of calves to the finest advantage, and Brummell, tall, dark-haired and handsome, showed them off to perfection.

So precisely engineered were Brummell's dressing arrangements that visitors queued to watch him adjust his neckwear every day. It was quite a performance, for ablutions and dressing took several hours. First came shaving and body massage with a stiff brush, then a dentist's mirror wielded in order minutely to examine his face before removing any remaining stray bristles with a pair of tweezers. Then he got to the shirt, as his friend and biographer Captain William Jesse recorded:

> The collar, which was always fixed to the shirt, was so large that, before being folded down, it completely hid his head and face and the white neckcloth was at least a foot in height. The first

---

* A sprig called Captain Kelly, 'the vainest man in London', died because he insisted on trying to retrieve his immaculate boots from a burning building.

coup d'archet was made with the shirt collar which he folded down to its proper size and then, standing before the looking glass, with his chin poked up towards the ceiling by the gentle and gradual declension of his lower jaw he creased the cravat to reasonable dimensions.

If one of the creases got out of alignment, the whole procedure had to start again. This was what was required to be in fashion.

The starchiness of the linen was such that it was impossible to look sideways, so Brummell would ostentatiously ask a butler at dinner who was sitting on either side of him before starting to make conversation while staring straight ahead. It is little wonder that he gained a reputation for arrogance, not to say stiffness. With some awe, in a less fastidious, smellier age, it was also noted that Brummell changed his shirts several times a day and washed daily as well. In part this was all a reaction to the highly artificial fashions that preceded it: the extravagantly powdered wigs and coloured costumes of the epicene and affected macaronis of the mid-eighteenth century.* In part, too, it was a result of English fashion being largely cut off from the continent for twenty years after the French Revolution. It was a slightly military, notably restrained, theoretically less fiddly, noticeably more heterosexual direction for fashion to follow. But the style became everything for the dandies and Brummell's vicious tongue-lashings for those who deviated even marginally from it became famous, feared and repeated. One favourite sally was to ask an aristocrat whether he really thought the *thing* he was wearing was a coat, because it looked no more like a coat than a *cauliflower*. This was

---

* 'Macaroni' after the taste for pasta that fashionable young aristocrats brought back with them from their grand tours to Italy.

regarded as the height of wit, as was his assertion that he had never eaten a vegetable, except once – ah – he had tried a pea. Perhaps you had to have been there. Despite this, Brummell was considered both charming and amiable, but his cutting humour would precipitate his downfall.

The dandies' days followed a predictable and tedious routine. The Duc de Rochefoucauld, in exile during the 1790s, observed:

> The conduct of an Englishman's day in London leaves little time for work. He gets up at ten or eleven and has breakfast (always with tea). He then makes a tour of the town for about four hours until five o'clock which is the dinner hour; at 9 o'clock in the evening he meets his friends in a tavern or a club and there the night is passed in play and drink.

This of course only applied to gentlemen: mornings spent 'swarming' with other dandies; lounging in the park, going riding, shopping in Bond Street, or idling at the club. Some of them were even boy racers of a sort, tearing along the roads out of the capital, steering four-in-hand carriages in 'ungovernable phrenzy [sic]' between Hyde Park and Slough or out to Bedford, overtaking other drivers, overturning farm carts as they galloped past and, on occasion, lashing out with their whips to get menial folk out of the way. Their carriages were high-sprung, highly engineered affairs, some apparently with seats as high as a second-floor window. A few even dressed as though they were cabmen, 'coming coachy in fine style', though in liveried uniform of course. One apparently filed his teeth to points so he could whistle like a cabbie. Lord Petersham dressed all in brown and drove a brown carriage with brown horses, allegedly because he had once had a mistress called Brown; Lord Onslow dressed all in black, with a black carriage and black horses so it looked as though he was driving a hearse; and a chap called Cope was known as the Green Man because he always dressed in green, powdered his hair green, allegedly ate only spinach, and always carried with him a poodle dyed green. Other members of the hard-driving aristocracy were rather more fearsome, none more so than the Irish Barrymore family: the seventh earl was known as Hellgate, because of his reckless depravity; the eighth earl as Cripplegate, because he had a club foot; his younger brother, a clergyman, was Newgate, because he spent so much time in prison; and their sister was Billingsgate, because her swearing was worse than a fishwife's.*

Slumming it with 'the other half' – a phrase already in use – was quite fashionable. It occurred not only at sporting contests but elsewhere too, and was soon to be memorialized by the sporting journalist Pierce Egan with his two characters, the original Tom and Jerry. Egan's *Life in London or, The Day and Night Scenes of Jerry Hawthorne Esq., and his elegant friend Corinthian Tom, accompanied by Bob Logic, the Oxonian, in their Rambles and Sprees through the Metropolis* first appeared in 1820 in monthly instalments, costing a shilling and illustrated by Isaac Robert Cruikshank and his younger brother George. It was an instant popular success, spawning plays and sequels. Tom and Jerry amble through the capital getting into scrapes and brawls with the lower orders in various dives, the tales

---

* The dandies all had nicknames for each other. 'Poodle' Byng was so called because his tightly curling hair supposedly made him look like the dog. Thomas Raikes, the son of the philanthropic banker of the same name who promoted Sunday schools, was known as 'Apollo', not because of his great beauty but because, living in the family home in the City of London – way beyond the fashionable pale, in dandy terms – he rose in the East and set, once the clubs of Mayfair and Belgravia had closed, in the West. The City was far outside the dandies' milieu, which did not really extend beyond Bond Street and Park Lane: Brummell once promised to attend a dinner in Bloomsbury provided his coachman could find such a place.

all recounted in nonchalant and slang-laden prose: sprees and swells, flashes of lightning – gin – and jiggings with the girls. That did not mean that the class system was in any general way permeable, except under rare and special circumstances: making a large amount of money from trade helped, but did not entirely compensate for a lack of aristocratic breeding. Brummell got away with it, though he lacked a title, because he was rich and stylish and had known many of the other dandies since school days at Eton. It was, however, quite acceptable to mingle with the inferior classes (another phrase in contemporary use) around – or occasionally in – the boxing ring, on the cricket field, at the cock-fight, or indeed on the high road and in the street.

More sedately than the blustering, cursing, sweating four-in-hand racers, Brummell and his companions would gather at White's Club in St James's Street, sitting in the building's front bow window (inevitably it became the beau window) watching society passing by. London was at the heart of their milieu, but there were other places to visit for the Season: the spas at Bath ('probably the most dissipated place in the kingdom', according to the young American Benjamin Silliman) or Tunbridge Wells or the seaside at Brighton, especially when the Prince Regent was there.

Dandyism was not just for the young. A little way away in Piccadilly, the 4th Duke of Queensbury, now in his eighties and a roué of the old school, would sit in his window too and send his groom out to accost any passing female who caught his fancy and invite her in for an informal conjugal visit. Club membership was a mark of social acceptance: it was said that to be a member of White's, originally a Tory club, provided a young man with a cachet such as nothing else could give. The dandies might move on later to Brooks's, which was the Whigs' equivalent gathering place – Brummell was notionally a

Whig – for an evening's gambling for high stakes. A man could win, or lose, tens of thousands of pounds there in a sitting. In his memoirs Captain Rees Howell Gronow, who joined the dandies when he was not serving with the Guards, recalled how Lord Robert Spencer, brother of the Duke of Marlborough, ran through his entire fortune gambling, but was then allowed by Brooks's to set up as the banker in a faro game and won back £100,000: 'He retired, strange to say, from the foetid atmosphere of play with the money in his pocket and never again gambled.' Clearly Spencer was lucky – more so than George Harley Drummond of the banking family, who lost £20,000, gambling for the only time in his life, on a game of whist with Brummell at White's and was forced to retire from the bank as a result.

The accounts of the dandy Scrope Berdmore Davies were discovered in a trunk in a London bank vault in the 1970s and testify to his fluctuating fortunes. Scrope, four years younger than Brummell, was the son of a Gloucestershire vicar and a friend of Byron. He was educated at Eton and Cambridge but thereafter seems to have survived through gambling. His papers show him worth £22,000 in 1815, but just £5,000 the following year. In September 1817 he started with a credit balance of £13.12s.6d, then won 110 guineas on the 8th and 700 guineas on the 9th. But then two nights later he lost 1,050 guineas, then 995 guineas two nights after that, and 105 another two nights on. He subsequently won 270 guineas on 16 September, but by that stage he was more than £1,000 in debt. Constantly juggling such figures night after night – wins and losses of more money in an evening than a working man on a pound a week would earn in a lifetime – must have imposed a considerable strain. Scrope's losses were mainly at a briefly flourishing club called Watier's, of which Brummell was perpetual president; it had a French chef and served excellent food and wine as an attractive prelude to gambling.

As an alternative, there was Almack's in King Street, the most exclusive of the lot, which staged balls, not gambling. It was rather proud of twice turning away the Duke of Wellington, once for turning up a few minutes late and on another occasion for arriving wearing trousers rather than breeches (silk stockings, thin shoes and white neckcloths were *de rigueur* that year): 'hereafter no one can complain of the application of the rule of exclusion,' the club remarked. The duke was in good company because it was said that three-quarters of the aristocracy knocked on its door in vain. Its exclusivity was its attraction, for its food was meagre and mediocre and the décor of its ballroom unappealing. Those on its list were selected by a group of eagle-eyed arbiters of taste, all society women including Lady Castlereagh and Lady Jersey and also Princess Esterhazy and Countess Lieven, the wives respectively of the Austrian and Russian ambassadors. The attraction was the weekly ball held there on Wednesdays: 'we go to these assemblies to sell our daughters and to corrupt our neighbours' wives. A ballroom is nothing more or less than a great market place of beauty,' wrote one of those who got in. From 1814 London was flooded with eligible half-pay army officers released from military duties and, if they could not get into Almack's, there were plenty of other places in London where they could meet suitable young women, or gamble away their capital.

Now the waltz was the great craze following its introduction from Germany in 1813. Its shockingness lay in the gliding intimacy with which a couple danced – a man's arm around a woman's back – and the speed of the manoeuvring. Once the arbiters of taste at Almack's had accepted what had started as a Bavarian peasant dance, its social success was assured and everyone who was anyone had to learn how to do it. Thomas 'Apollo' Raikes, yet another Old Etonian, wrote in his memoirs:

No event ever produced so great a sensation in English Society…
in London, fashion is, or was then, *everything* [so] old and young
returned to school and the mornings which had been dedicated
to lounging in the parks, were now absorbed at home in whirling
a chair around a room to learn the step and measure of the
German waltz.

They also danced French quadrilles at Almack's, but only, it was said,
once Lady Jersey had mastered the steps herself.

∞

Eventually, the financial wind changed: agricultural prices fell, life
grew harder and more serious – and the Prince Regent changed his
political and personal allegiances. He cut dead his former friends
and forgot any personal, financial or moral obligations he might have
had to them. Among these was the Irish playwright Sheridan who,
as an MP, had loyally supported the prince's unpopular cause in
parliament for many years, and was now, by the end of 1815, nearly
destitute and ailing fast. During that August, the prince had seen
him only a few yards away as he was driving through Leatherhead
and said to his companion, 'There's Sheridan', but did not deign to
greet him. Even while Sheridan was dying upstairs the following
year, his London home in Savile Row was besieged by bailiffs, seizing
his furniture to pay his debts. 'There were strange-looking people in
the hall. The parlour seemed dismantled into which I was shewn,'
wrote William Smyth, Sheridan's son's former tutor, who visited
the old man at this time. 'On the table lay a bit of paper, thrown
carelessly and neglected. I took it up and it was a prescription.' At
the playwright's funeral in Westminster Abbey in July 1816, there
were four dukes, nine earls, three viscounts and the Lord Mayor of

London. 'Such a catalogue of mourners! And yet he was suffered to die in the hands of the sheriff,' his friend Samuel Rogers wrote to Walter Scott.

For Brummell himself, the fall was even more ghastly. There was one famous witticism too many for the Prince Regent, to precipitate his social decline. The pair had fallen out and in July 1813 Brummell did not include the prince on the guest list for a ball he was co-organizing with Lord Alvanley and other friends at the Argyle Rooms. The prince announced that he would attend anyway and, on his arrival, ignored Brummell, who turned to his companion and said, deliberately loud enough for the prince and everyone else to hear: 'Ah, Alvanley, who is your fat friend?' Perhaps it was that, or a tendency on Brummell's part to refer publicly to the prince's old flame and former wife Mrs Fitzherbert, who had grown plump in her mature years, as 'Benina' – a reference to the large porter known as 'Big Ben' at the prince's Carlton House home – that finally grated on the prince. In any case, after the scene at the Argyle Rooms they never spoke again. This was not, however, the cause of Brummell's clandestine flight from London society suddenly one night in May 1816 – that was a result of his pressing debts. The great dandy's money had finally dried up. That night, Brummell dressed carefully as usual, attended a performance of the opera at Covent Garden, and then slipped out before the end to take a cab to Clapham Common, where his own carriage was waiting to take him to Dover. There, he chartered a small boat to take him across the Channel to France and never set foot in England again. Soon Scrope Davies also ran out of money and would follow Brummell to the continent in 1820, living out his final thirty years in near-poverty in Brussels and Paris, though he would occasionally slip back quietly to England.

Brummell lived on in Calais and Caen for a further quarter-century, but his final years before his solitary death in 1840 were desolate ones. When the prince passed through Calais in 1821 – by then he was George IV – he spotted his old friend in the crowd, but made no attempt to meet him. Attempts by his former acquaintances to get Brummell work for a time as British consul in Caen did not last long. By then he was too far gone. Short of money and suffering from the final stages of tertiary syphilis, probably originally contracted in London, he became incontinent, his teeth fell out and he suffered dementia.* It was said that towards the end he would obsess once more about clothes, order candles and flowers for his room, and loudly announce the arrival of the by then long-dead Prince of Wales, the prince's mistress Lady Conyngham and others of his old coterie. His French biographer d'Aurevilly wrote a few years later:

> all the high personages of England for whom he had been the
> living law; and imagining them to appear as he announced them
> and changing his voice, he went to the doors to receive them:
> the open double doors of the empty salon through which, alas,
> no one was to pass on this or any other evening. And he saluted
> these chimeras of his imagination, offered his arm to the women
> of this company of phantoms he had called up and who would
> certainly not have cared to leave their tombs for one instant to
> attend the fallen Dandy's rout.

⊶⊷

* Syphilis and gonorrhoea were by no means uncommon in Regency London, or among the dandies: it is estimated that about 15 per cent of the general population of the city may have been infected by sexual diseases and that proportion must have been higher among Brummell's circle. To prevent syphilis you might try to wear a sheep-gut condom, but once you had the disease you might try treating it with mercury, a supposed cure that was almost as bad as the disease itself.

Dandification was accompanied by, but did not in any sense give impetus to, another phenomenon: the first stirrings of a new assertiveness by some women. The late eighteenth and early nineteenth centuries saw the emergence of women writers and campaigners. Mary Wollstonecraft, author of the philosophical and theoretical tract *A Vindication of the Rights of Women* (1792), the founding book of feminism, argued that women were not inferior to men but lacked only their education: '[Woman] was created to be the toy of man, his rattle and it must jingle in his ears whenever, dismissing reason, he chooses to be amused... I do not wish them to have power over men; but over themselves.' The Irish writer Anna Wheeler would also contribute a book called *The Rights of Women* and co-wrote the splendidly titled *Appeal of One Half of the Human Race, Women, Against the Pretensions of the Other Half, Men, to Retain them in Political and Hence in Civil and Domestic Slavery* (1825). Her co-author was a man, William Thompson, but Wheeler knew whereof she wrote, having endured marriage for a dozen years to a drunken and abusive husband. There was also Fanny Wright, the Scottish-born feminist, who would emigrate to the United States in 1818 at the age of twenty-three and become an abolitionist, and Eliza Macauley, an actor, socialist campaigner and polemicist – both these two were much influenced by the ideas of Robert Owen.

How widely such books were read at the time, outside radical and dissenting circles, is questionable, and certainly reforms to improve women's lives, marital and property rights, still less the vote, were a long way away. Most men would not have considered that their wives and female relatives were capable of the sort of political thought that would entitle them to suffrage – and, as wives were their husbands' chattels, part of his family entourage, it was for him to do their thinking for them. When the teacher Anna Laetitia Barbauld

1. George IV, as he wished to be depicted (by Sir Thomas Lawrence, 1822).

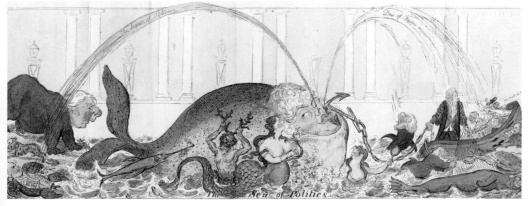

2. The cartoonist George Cruikshank preferred to depict George as the Prince of Whales – 'no fatter fish than he' – spurting water over his old Whig friends and casting a lascivious eye on his new mistress Isabella Hertford. Meanwhile the Tory prime minister Spencer Perceval – a few days from being assassinated – leads the prince by the nose.

3. General Andrew Jackson watches as British troops are repulsed from the American army's ramparts at the battle of New Orleans, 8 January 1815.

4. The dancing Congress: a French cartoon satirizes the rulers of Europe at Vienna, 1814–15. Britain's foreign secretary Viscount Castlereagh, second from the left, teaches assorted emperors and kings the steps, while the chief French negotiator Talleyrand (left) avoids the dance. The others, from left to right, are: Francis II of Austria, Alexander I of Russia, Frederick William III of Prussia, Frederick Augustus I of Saxony and an unknown Genoese delegate.

5. The Industrial Revolution bustles ahead: here a barge crosses the Barton aqueduct, a marvel of the age, over the River Irwell (in what is now Greater Manchester).

6. The crowded 'Red Rover' stagecoach heads for London from Southampton, c.1815.

7. The 'Newbury Coat': a publicity stunt for the coming age of mechanization. On 11 June 1811, Coxeter's Mill in Newbury, aided by a local tailor, transformed the wool from the backs of a pair of Southdown sheep into a coat for the back of landowner Sir John Throckmorton in just thirteen hours. The shorn sheep were fed to cheering townsfolk; but the Newbury woollen industry's days were numbered also.

8. Robert Owen's model community of textile mills, housing and shops at New Lanark, near Glasgow, c 1815.

9. The Quadrant of London's proud new Regent Street, designed by John Nash, the architect responsible for much of the layout of Regency London.

10. 'Gay Moments of Logic, Jerry, Tom and Corinthian Kate': a coloured engraving by George Cruikshank for Pierce Egan's *Life in London* (1821). Egan's monthly accounts of the 'rambles and sprees' of Corinthian Tom and Jerry Hawthorne in the dives of late Georgian London enjoyed huge popular success.

11. Joey Grimaldi, superstar, in his pomp before drink, overwork, injury and penury got to him.

12. George Wilson attempts to walk a thousand miles in twenty days, unaware that the magistrates will cost him his bet by stopping him after 751.

13. The dandy William Arden, 2nd Baron Alvanley – puffed up like a pigeon in the latest style – makes his way to White's Club.

14. Elizabeth Fry, a member of the Gurney banking family, worked to improve prison conditions. Her modest dress indicates her Quaker faith.

15. 'LA COTERIE DEBOUCHÉ', c.1825 – the courtesan Harriette Wilson happily accepts pay-offs from her former clients among the Regency great and good to keep their names out of her memoirs. 'Publish and be damned,' said the Duke of Wellington.

16. The fight of the decade: the Bristol butcher's son Tom Cribb meets the former American slave Tom Molineaux in a crowded ring.

17. A women's cricket match between Hampshire and Surrey, played at Stoke Newington, October 1811. Behind the bare-footed frolics portrayed by Thomas Rowlandson, a purse of 500 guineas was at stake.

18. Henri Philippoteaux's famous depiction of French cuirassiers charging a Scottish regiment's square at Waterloo. It is not an eyewitness depiction – the artist was only born in 1815 – but it gives a vivid impression of the terrifying chaos of the battle. Military historians have pointed out that cavalry did not charge squares directly, or get so close to them.

19. Viscount Castlereagh – depicted by Sir Thomas Lawrence, c. 1810 – stares haughtily from his portrait

20. 'Sidmouth on a crocodile rode by…': Henry Addington, 1st Viscount Sidmouth, home secretary in Lord Liverpool's administration from 1812 until 1822. His ruthlessness in cracking down on dissent in the aftermath of Waterloo earned him an unflattering reference in Shelley's radical poem *The Mask of Anarchy*.

21. Napoleon Bonaparte is transferred from the British warship HMS *Bellerophon* to HMS *Northumberland*, 7 August 1815, at the start of the journey to his final exile on St Helena. He would never threaten the peace of Europe again.

22. The caldera of Mount Tambora, formed during the catastrophic eruption of the volcano on the Indonesian island of Sumbawa, 10 April 1815. The eruption, the largest in recorded history, lowered the height of the mountain by nearly 5,000 feet and spread an ash cloud across the globe that turned 1816 into the 'Year without a Summer'.

published her poem 'Eighteen Hundred and Eleven' in 1812, specu-
lating that British imperial and commercial supremacy would be
superseded by America, her presumption was slapped down by John
Wilson Croker in an article in the *Quarterly Review*, not because her
ideas were wrong, but because she had them at all:

> she has wandered from the course in which she was respectable
> and useful and miserably mistaken both her powers and her duty
> in exchanging the birchen for the satiric rod... an irresistible
> impulse of public duty... [has] induced her to dash down her
> shagreen spectacles and her knitting needles and to sally forth
> in the magnanimous resolution of saving a sinking State by the
> instrumentality of a pamphlet in verse.

One can almost sense the chortles with which Croker wrote that.

There were other women thinkers and writers, though: Mary
Shelley, Wollstonecraft's daughter and author of *Frankenstein*;
Hannah More, the Somerset-based writer and evangelical anti-slavery
campaigner; the authors Jane Austen and Mary Russell Mitford; and
Fanny Burney, the playwright and author. Such women were often
skilled polemicists – writing was almost the only outlet for their views
and campaigns, apart from public speaking. They could get their
works published, which is the reason why their names have survived
and their words are still known. They were by no means all radicals.
Hannah More, aged seventy in 1815, was becoming steadily more
conservative ('I am sick of that liberty I once so used to prize'), writing
polemics against William Cobbett – who called her 'the old bishop in
petticoats' – and opposing both political reform and Catholic emancipation. She had, however, been an early supporter of the anti-slavery
movement, a close friend of Wilberforce and Thomas Clarkson, and

had set up a string of schools to teach the children of the Somerset peasantry. She did this in the teeth of opposition from local farmers and the Somerset clergy who, rightly, took More's initiative to be an indictment of their indolence.

All these women were outsold, however, by Mrs Radcliffe, whose thrilling gothic novels, full of rugged scenery, romantic heroines, brooding villains and merciless assassins, earned her a large and devoted following. They also earned her a huge advance of £800 for her final novel, *The Italian*, in 1797, at least ten times the advance any other novelist of the period received. Ann Radcliffe was still alive in 1815 but had given up writing fiction by then, perhaps because she was so rich that she didn't need to write any more, or possibly because she considered it unladylike. Indeed, there were many other novelists, poets and playwrights – an estimated thousand women from the 1780s to the 1830s – including Maria Edgeworth (*Castle Rackrent*), who was busy writing her historical novel *Ormond* in 1815, Amelia Opie, Joanna Baillie, Felicia Hemans ('The Boy Stood on the Burning Deck') and the lovelorn teenager Letitia Landon. Some of these highly educated, often multilingual middle-class women supported themselves and their families and relatives with their writing.*

Other women were writing about science. Jane Marcet's books, 'intended more especially for the female sex', included *Conversations on Chemistry*, which ran to sixteen editions in the half-century following its publication in 1806, *Conversations on Political Economy* (1816) and *Conversations on Natural Philosophy* (1819). Middle-class women might not yet be able to take an active part in political life, but they could read and perhaps had more time to do so than their husbands.

---

* Hemans, for example, spoke French, German, Italian, Spanish and Portuguese. More was proficient in French, Italian, Spanish and Latin and knew mathematics too.

There were social reformers such as Elizabeth Fry of the Quaker Gurney banking family, whose religious zeal felt only truly at ease when she was doing good works among the poor and in prisons: 'I felt quite in my element serving the poor and although I was much tired with looking about, it gave me much pleasure, it is an occupation my nature is so fond of… it brings satisfaction with it more than most things.' Elizabeth Heyrick, widow of a Leicester lawyer and a Quaker convert, was an ardent anti-slavery campaigner, arguing in a pamphlet that the male leaders such as William Wilberforce and Thomas Clarkson were much too moderate in accepting a gradualist approach to abolition: as the title of her pamphlet indicated, *Immediate not Gradual Emancipation* was her goal. She also had time and energy to campaign against animal cruelty, on one occasion rescuing a bull that was about to be baited by purchasing it.

For most women, though, life was a drudgery, of manual labour as hard as men's and of regular and repeated childbirth, producing a child a year, many of whom would not survive babyhood. Elizabeth Fry was not unusual in having eleven children, but was highly unusual in having ten of them survive into adulthood (and indeed old age). Much more common was the loss of small children to illness, still-births and the death of mothers in labour: an everyday risk that could destroy even the heir to the throne in a few excruciating hours. Then as now, less privileged mothers would be expected to keep working, though their earning capacity inevitably dropped off as more babies arrived. Estimates drawn from the reminiscences of contemporary writers show that, with just one child, four out of five mothers worked; with two, the proportion was more like three out of five; with three or more, only about half of mothers still went out to work; and once the figure went above eight, virtually none were able to do so. Then they would stay at home, or, if they were fortunate, persuade older daughters to help with the childcare.

Wives lost their property rights when they married, and a husband's violence, or abusiveness towards his wife, or his adultery, were not remotely considered grounds for divorce. A wife could not claim to be hurt by her husband's unfaithfulness, but her husband could claim damages as a plaintiff if his wife engaged in an affair of her own: 'The wound which a woman suffers by her husband's offence is only skin deep; but an unchaste wife, by her adultery, casts an indelible stain on her own offspring and her society is avoided by the chaste part of her own sex,' as a contemporary commentator wrote. The offence of adultery was known as 'criminal conversation' and, among the aristocracy, the damages to be paid to the wounded husband were usually reckoned at between £10,000 and £20,000. It was a system ripe for hypocrisy and mendacity: the husband would present his wife as an innocent victim of a foul seducer who had dismantled their happy and loving relationship, while the seducer/defendant would have to depict the woman, however much he loved her, as already debauched and corrupted before their affair had begun.

In Scotland there were additional complications as, although the law permitted divorce on the grounds of the husband's infidelity, it also forbade marriage between a couple previously caught in adultery. In 1810, when Lord Paget wished to divorce his wife and marry Lady Charlotte Wellesley, the wife of Henry Wellesley, the Duke of Wellington's brother and at that time a government minister, he and Charlotte moved to Edinburgh; he committed adultery with her, but she disguised herself as a courtesan and the couple allowed themselves to be witnessed in bed together. Thus the law was got round: Paget committed adultery, but not officially with the woman he wanted to marry. It is estimated that the cost to Paget of divorcing his wife, paying for the Wellesleys' divorce, paying damages and giving his first wife an annual pension of £1,000 for the rest of her life was £50,000 – 'a good and cheap bargain,' he said. The bad blood caused by this family feud may account for Wellington's famously insouciant response five years later at Waterloo, in the closing stages of the battle, when Paget, by then the Earl of Uxbridge, was hit by a cannon-ball: 'By God, sir! I've lost my leg!' 'By God, sir, so you have!'*Despite such astounding costs, criminal conversation cases seem almost to have been accounted fair game by some members of the aristocracy. Men could survive them with their reputations largely undamaged – it was noticed that there were several well-known adulterers in the Prince Regent's coterie (he was one himself, of course, as were his brothers); but for the women involved, such cases were social death, and however innocent they had been, they could expect a future of ostracism and banishment to the country. Divorce was expensive and required either a formal annulment or an Act of Parliament – and there were only about 300 such acts in the 150 years before the Matrimonial Causes Act was passed in 1857. Further down the social scale, husbands and wives were yoked together for life, or indulged in open marriages, for a wife would almost certainly lose her children in a settlement. The poor, who probably had not had a church wedding at all, might separate by mutual agreement or, informally, by a husband selling his wife at auction. This happened at Maidstone in January 1815, as reported by the *Morning Post*, when John Osborne sold his wife Mary and child to William Sergeant for one pound:

---

* Or maybe not. When Paget was given command of the cavalry at Waterloo, one of Wellington's aides reminded him of the scandal and added that Uxbridge 'had the reputation of running away with everybody he can'. The duke grunted: 'I'll take good care he don't run away with me. I don't care about anybody else.'

the business was transacted in a very regular manner, a deed and covenant being given by the seller... this document was witnessed in due form and the woman and child turned over to the buyer to the apparent satisfaction of all parties, the husband expressing his willingness to take his spouse again at any future period.

———

One way in which a beautiful woman of humble birth could fortuitously rise through society with luck, guile and nerve was by becoming a courtesan. Very many poor girls of course had to sell themselves as prostitutes from very young ages. For the courtesan it might be an insecure and transitory life and frowned upon by wives and moralists, but it was a career of sorts. The demi-reps, 'fashionable impures' or 'Cyprians', as they were known, had their own social gatherings and even an annual ball, and their liaisons were widely known and gossiped about. They could be seen in their own boxes during the season at the opera, they were set up in their own establishments by their wealthy suitors, in Belgravia or, if slightly less esteemed or with stingier admirers, in Somers Town, and they occasionally even got to marry an aristocrat. Of the courtesans, the best known of the period was Harriette Wilson, who with her sisters Amy and Sophia became known as the three Graces. Harriette, Amy and Sophia were the daughters of a Swiss watch-mender named Dubochet and his wife Amelia, who supported the household by mending stockings – something that was possible while living in Queen Street, Mayfair in those days. The daughters inevitably caught the eyes of passing aristocrats – that was possibly the intention as they sat in their parents' front window every day – and by the time she was fifteen Harriette had become the mistress of Lord Craven. 'Whether it was love, or the severity of my father, the depravity of my own heart, or the winning arts of the noble lord which induced me to leave my paternal roof and place myself under his protection does not now much signify,' she wrote in the first sentences of her memoirs. 'Or if it does, I am not in the humour to gratify curiosity in this matter.'

Harriette was not accounted a particular beauty, though since the descriptions tended to be written by her rivals or former suitors, elements of sour grapes may have crept in. She was, it was said, 'far from beautiful, but a smart, saucy girl with good eyes and dark hair and the manners of a wild schoolboy', and what she clearly had was wit and feistiness. She seems to have gone through the ranks of the English aristocracy like a dose of salts: after Craven, there was Lord Frederick Lamb, brother of the future prime minister Lord Melbourne (and possibly Melbourne himself), the Dukes of Argyll, Beaufort and Leinster, Lord Ponsonby (her one true love), Lord Byron, the Marquesses of Worcester, Anglesea, Bath, Headfort and Sligo, the Duke of Wellington and quite a few others. Harriette charged them astronomic sums – sometimes £200 a visit – and her sister Amy claimed to have required £100 from a Mr Hart Davis for the privilege of allowing him to stroke her arm ('Pray send your patting men to me,' said the sisters' friend and rival Julia Johnstone). Harriette herself changed her lovers as easily as her shoes, wrote Johnstone sniffily. At one time or another, she had hopes of marrying Ponsonby or Worcester (whose father the Duke of Beaufort packed him off to the Peninsular War to avert such a catastrophe), and indeed Harriette and Amy's sister Sophia Dubochet managed to bag Lord Berwick in marriage. But Harriette's most celebrated coup came when she needed money in 1825 and decided to kiss and tell about her lovers in her memoirs. By then she was living in Paris – her looks had faded and she was down on her uppers. As she prepared to spill the beans, she first wrote to everyone she had ever been connected with, making them an offer: £200 to keep their name out of the book. Her standard letter is a model of its type:

> Do just as you like. Consult only yourself. I get as much for a small book as you will give me for taking you out, or more. I attack no poor men because they cannot help themselves. Adieu! – Mind, I have no time to write again, as what with writing books and altering them for those who buy out, I am done up – *frappé en mort*. What do you think of my French?

Many paid up – though Wellington famously replied in red ink 'publish and be damned' – but those who did not found themselves written up in breathless prose of a sort and in a style that would not have disgraced the *News of the World* a century and a half later. The book was a sensation. Published in instalments, it went through thirty-one editions in its first year and netted Harriette £10,000, though her publisher Stockdale went bankrupt defending his company against libel actions.

8

'Lombard Street to a China orange'

— PIERCE EGAN

Besides being a nation of shopkeepers, Britain was certainly a sporting nation by the start of the nineteenth century. Many country games – such as football matches between whole villages – had been played for generations. Fishing and fox-hunting were common pursuits for the gentry, but by 1815 three competitive sports in particular had emerged and were being organized on something like a professional basis: cricket, horse-racing and boxing. All three allowed a degree of social interaction between classes. The city swell, the dandy and the country gentleman – colloquially known as members of the Fancy – could mingle with the *hoi polloi* at the ringside or beside the track and would often employ them, or even compete with them on the field of play. And the matter which greased the working and prompted the promotion of all three activities was gambling.

Betting on results or even on phases of play was an obsession with the sporting public. Men – it was almost always men: women attended sporting events, but on sufferance and under suspicion of being prostitutes – could win, and correspondingly lose, huge sums of money. Captain Barclay was a celebrated sporting gentleman, well known on the hunting field, on the grouse moor, in the boxing ring and on the cricket pitch; when, in the summer of 1809, he took on the challenge of walking a thousand miles in a thousand hours, he did so for a bet of a thousand guineas. For six weeks, all day, every day, he trudged a half-mile-long course at Newmarket to a marker post and then back, a route lined with illuminated gas lamps for the night-time hours. Barclay, who was in the army and had inherited a landed estate in Scotland near Aberdeen, prepared meticulously. He was used to walking long distances for bets. Pedestrianism, or 'fair heel and toe' walking, was becoming a popular betting sport,* and none was more accomplished than he: twice previously he had walked 100 miles in nineteen hours, but this was entirely different in scale. He carried a brace of loaded pistols and was accompanied by the former champion boxer John Gully at night to ward off dirty tricks. The technique was to walk back-to-back miles at night to give himself an hour and a half's sleep in between bouts. He walked through the summer heat and through rainstorms, through an injured ligament and through toothache, and by the time he had walked his thousand miles, he had lost thirty pounds in weight. But he finished on the afternoon of 12 July 1809, to the cheers of a large crowd and, presumably, the scowls of those who had made the bet that he could not manage it. *The Times* devoted a lengthy report to the feat and said he completed the marathon 'with perfect ease and great spirit'. A thousand guineas was the equivalent of a workman's pay for twenty years, and if the rumours were correct that his winnings on the side from other bets amounted to sixteen times as much, he was set up for life – or at least until he lost his next rash big bet. Barclay (his

---

* 'Fair heel and toe' meant that the heel of one foot could not leave the ground until the toe of the other touched down. It was the precursor of modern road-walking, though often it took place over poor tracks: Barclay was canny in undertaking his walk on a grass path, which he had had cut especially short, on Newmarket heath. Such strategies were fair game: the Earl of March, who bet that he could deliver a message fifty miles in under an hour, secured it in a hollowed-out ball and employed twenty cricketers placed in a circle half a mile in circumference to throw it to each other in turn: 100 laps did the trick.

full name was Robert Barclay Allardice – he tacked on his mother's more aristocratic surname to his father's) was a canny manipulator, well versed in trickery; a photograph taken much later in life shows a shrewd and calculating, weather-beaten man dressed as a member of the Regency Fancy should be, in a flowery waistcoat.

As it was, Barclay headed for Deal to rejoin the army, which was about to embark on the disastrous Walcheren expedition (see page 46) to block access to the port of Antwerp. Barclay was serving as an aide-de-camp to his relative the Marquis of Huntly, colonel of the 92nd Regiment, and it was fortunate that the invasion was delayed by bad weather for a week, otherwise he would have had to abandon the bet and return to the colours. Barclay's financial coup was far from exceptional for the period. Gully, the son of a debt-ridden Bristol butcher, would go on to win a half-share of £60,000 when St Giles, the horse he owned with his business partner, won the Derby in 1832.

Tattersall's, the bloodstock auction house and club which coordinated the horse-race betting industry, was said to have paid out £300,000 in winning bets after the 1816 Derby. Men would bet on anything: 'Hellgate', the carriage-racing 7th Earl Barrymore, who was said to waste £300,000 a year himself in gambling, in 1788 apparently accepted a bet of a thousand guineas from the 5th Duke of Bedford to eat a live cat (in the end he couldn't face it and denied he had ever accepted the challenge), while an Irish labourer reputedly ate five live fox cubs for £50.

As Barclay's precautions for his long walk showed, where such sums were involved, corruption was rife. In 1811 a groom named Daniel Dawson was hanged for pouring arsenic into the drinking trough of a rival trainer and killing four horses as a result, though the gentlemen bookies who induced him to do it went unpunished. But it was not necessary to kill rivals' mounts, for it was easy to nobble horses or to run ringers at a time before photography and routine veterinary testing, when individual horses were hard to identify and each local racecourse operated independently with its own rules. Poorly paid stable boys and jockeys could be bribed and horses might be fed opium balls or even lead shot to slow them down. Conversely, it was not illegal to feed horses stimulants such as cocaine to make them run faster, or to stage false starts to wind or exhaust the other horses in a race. By 1815 two of the classic races, the Oaks and the Derby, were well established, having been run at Epsom for more than thirty years, but most race meetings were local, since the horses had to be walked from their training stables to courses, and races were largely unregulated.

In boxing, too, there was sharp practice. Contests were held on the fly, in the open air, in obscure spots such as farmers' fields, with locations and meeting points spread in advance by word of mouth. The sport was technically illegal – counting as a 'riotous assembly' – and local magistrates or constables might intervene, if they had not been bribed, causing contests to be moved even at short notice to a new location in a neighbouring jurisdiction. Even so thousands, sometimes tens of thousands, attended matches. Such ploys could scarcely be secret since local roads would suddenly be crowded with hundreds of coaches, wagons and barouches, with many more people coming on horseback or on foot, seeking the field in which the match would take place. Since forthcoming contests were freely discussed in the press and in boxing pubs such as the Horse and Dolphin in London's Leicester Square, owned by the black trainer Bill Richmond, or Tom Cribb's pub, the Union Arms in Panton Street, it was not hard to find out what was going on. Indeed, in the journalist Pierce Egan, the sport had its first and perhaps greatest-ever chronicler. Egan, who has claims to be the first sports reporter, wrote thrillingly – demotically and graphically – about boxing and its fighters, creating a florid, conversational and colourful style that has been emulated by sports writers ever since.

The illegality of the fights did not prevent royalty and senior members of the nobility from attending. The Duke of Clarence, later William IV, was a regular and could be seen cheering on his favourites, as when Cribb – known as the Black Diamond from his previous, muscle-building trade as a coal haulier – fought Richmond at Hailsham, Sussex in October 1805. It was said that the duke, who had ridden over from Brighton, could be seen standing up in the stirrups, waving his whip and shrieking with pleasure: 'his language garnished with many a pleasant "God dammie".' The Prince Regent, too, followed contests and won £3,000 on his own account when the English hero Jem Belcher beat the Irish champion Andrew Gamble on Wimbledon Common in 1800. It was a match watched by many Irish spectators, who had backed their champion heavily and were not amused when he gave in easily. Egan, whose family background was Irish, noted ruthlessly:

The Paddies had not been so neatly cleaned out… it proved a most woeful day for the Irish indeed… Andrew's name had hitherto been a tower of strength; he was the tight Irish boy and the darling of his country – but alas! The scene was changed; he was now called a cur, an overgrown thing, a mere apology and was in danger of being tossed in a blanket by his enraged and disappointed backers. Gamble from this defeat lost the warm hearts of the Paddies ever afterwards. The evident superiority of Belcher completely frightened all Gamble's courage and science out of him.

Such bare-knuckle contests were fantastically bloody and could last for many rounds until one of the boxers submitted or failed to step up to the mark drawn in the centre of the ring, or his seconds conceded defeat by throwing in a towel. The fighters were allowed to grapple, gouge and throw each other and rounds lasted until one was felled, so could last for seconds or minutes. It was not uncommon for matches to go to forty or fifty rounds and last for well over an hour until both boxers were scarcely capable of continuing or even seeing their opponents through the gore dripping down their faces. Although they trained with mufflers (primitive boxing gloves), they fought with bare fists, which were capable of causing terrible wounds (and damaging the hands of the puncher). Blood was copious with boxers slithering about on grass or boards made slippery from the rain and the bleeding wounds they had inflicted on each other. Often they fought on even if they had been blinded or had their arms and ribs broken. A flavour of what Egan called 'milling' is evident in his account of a fight between Henry ('Hen') Pearce, known to aficionados as the Game Chicken, and John Gully on the same bill as Cribb versus Richmond, shortly before the battle of Trafalgar. We join it some way in:

18th round, – Torrents of blood flowing from Pearce – no fighting – and Gully slipped in making play… 20th. – One of the Chicken's eyes so much swelled that he could scarcely see out of it and the blood flowing from him copiously; Gully followed the Chicken around the ring, several blows exchanged when they closed and fell… 37th–43rd, – The Chicken displayed a manifest superiority: their figures were bloody in the extreme; but Gully was literally covered from the torrents that flowed down from his ear… his head was truly terrific and had a giant-like appearance from being so terribly swelled and the effect was most

singular, for scarcely could his eyes be seen. 44th, – The Chicken
with considerable science and force planted his favourite hit on
Gully's throat, when he fell like a log of wood…

By the fifty-ninth round Gully's friends intervened and stopped the
fight. The contest had lasted an hour and ten minutes. It was not
surprising that boxers sometimes died during or after these contests
– perhaps the surprising thing is that so many survived at all, though
many succumbed young to poverty, disease or alcoholism. Pearce,
already suffering from tuberculosis, would be dead within four years;
Gully would live to a ripe old age, invested wisely and at one stage
became a Tory MP.

The most epic contests of the age, though, were between Tom
Cribb, the butcher's son from Bristol, and Tom Molineaux, a black
boxer and former slave from America who had come to Britain to
seek his fortune. Molineaux lived up to the boxer's stereotype – he
was hard living, loving and drinking – and had caused his trainer Bill
Richmond no end of headaches as he pummelled his way to challenge the English champion. Cribb, overconfident and overweight,
scarcely bothered to train, but in their first match, held in a field
near East Grinstead, Sussex in driving rain in December 1810, Molineaux might well have won but for a stoppage engineered by Cribb's
second. Joe Ward accused his man's opponent of hiding stones in his
fists – an unlikely charge in a bare-knuckle fight but one which took
a quarter of an hour to sort out, by which time Cribb had recovered
from being knocked insensible and Molineaux was shivering with
cold. On several occasions when it seemed the white man might lose,
the crowd burst into the ring to halt the contest: Molineaux had to
fight their racism as well as his opponent. The referee, Sir Thomas
Ap Rhys, who had also bet on a Cribb victory, apparently whispered

into his ear the encouraging suggestion, 'For God's sake Tom, don't let the nigger win for Old England's sake', and he duly triumphed in the 39th round. Even the Prince Regent apparently thought that the result was a fix: 'Molineaux beat Cribb! Curse me if he did not.'

There was a rematch in Leicestershire the following September for which Cribb trained hard under the tutelage of Captain Barclay, while Molineaux, confident that he had the beating of his opponent, continued down the slippery slope of dissipation. Cribb's training on Barclay's Scottish estate would sound familiar to modern boxers, but was then regarded as unusual and eccentric, even underhand: the captain put his charge through a strict diet, early-morning runs, lengthy walks – thirty miles a day – sweats in heavy blankets and weight training, with the result that he lost thirty-seven pounds in two months.

On the morning of the match, Cribb's breakfast was two boiled eggs, while Molineaux's consisted of a whole roast chicken, an enormous apple pie and several pints of porter. By the time he clambered into the ring he was in no fit state to fight anyone, let alone Cribb, who was itching to prove his superiority properly. This time the fight lasted only eleven rounds, in the course of which Molineaux flailed wildly and furiously against the stolid Cribb while being taunted by the crowd. Cribb himself was injured over his eye early in the fight, but was bled by Gully, his second, who slit open the bruise with a cut-throat razor and squeezed out the blood. Even half-blinded, Cribb managed to shatter Molineaux's jaw, after which the fight was over. It was, said Egan, 'Lombard Street to a China orange,* Molineaux was dead beat.'

---

* In betting terms, the heart of the City of London's traditional banking centre to something essentially worthless.

The crowd at the fight was estimated at 20,000; the historian Fred Henning wrote that it was:

> as well-framed and supported a circle of pedestrians as were, perhaps, ever witnessed, notwithstanding the great distance from the metropolis: the first row of these, as usual upon these occasions laying down, the second kneeling and the rest standing up. Outside again were numerous horsemen, some seated while others more eager stood circus-like on their saddles. These were intermixed with every description of carriage, gig, barouche, buggy, cart and wagon. The display of sporting men, from the peer on the box of the four in hand to the rustic in clarted shoes, made as fitting a picture as the Fancy can well conceive.

Molineaux would be dead within a few years. His last fight was in 1815 and he died three years later, aged thirty-four, penniless, alcoholic and alone in a regimental barracks in Galway, having been reduced to fighting all-comers at Irish country fairs. Cribb, taken up by the Fancy and several aristocratic backers, retired to become a trainer and publican and died many years later. His last appearance in a ring was at a benefit evening in 1814 for several of the crowned heads of Europe, who were attending the celebrations in London following the initial defeat of Napoleon. On this particular evening, almost exactly a year before the battle of Waterloo, Lord Lowther opened his house in Pall Mall to Tsar Alexander of Russia, King Frederick William of Prussia, Prince Metternich, the Duke of Wellington and Marshal Blücher, and the boxing was laid on as entertainment. The exhibition of sparring, so popular with the royalty that it was repeated two days later, had an ulterior purpose – to show off British manliness and pluck, though the cream of British boxing talent by this time was growing old: Gentleman John Jackson, whose physique was described as the finest in England, was forty-six, Tom Cribb was nearly thirty-three, and Bill Richmond was fifty-one. Egan wrote:

> The set-tos in general were excellent, but the sparring of Jackson was particularly admired... The Champion of England (Cribb) occasioned a general *stare* among the spectators and the veteran Blücher eyed him with more than common attention. The royal guests expressed their satisfaction at the treat they had experienced and... complimented his lordship as the patron of so manly and characteristic a trait of his country.

If anything could demonstrate the acceptability of such a sport – even though it was technically illegal – this performance was it.

Most boxers were members of the working class, though not all. Captain Barclay was also a fighter in a gentlemanly sort of way, and as many as a third of the peerage was said to work out at Gentleman Jackson's boxing gym in Old Bond Street – among them the young Lord Byron, who had sparring lessons from Jackson. Even the Prince Regent apparently sparred there at least once and invited Jackson, a London builder's son, to punch him. But, as always, fighting offered the possibility of a way out of poverty for men who took it up. The most successful boxers, such as Cribb, would be fighting for purses of 500 guineas: ten times the annual wage he might have expected when he was a butcher's apprentice or coal porter in the London docks. The black fighters Richmond and Molineaux faced racism and name-calling, but at least they were not slaves as they would have been had they stayed in Virginia and were generally respected for their fighting qualities. Richmond had his pub and training business, an avenue that would have been open to his protégé had he not frittered his talent away. Fighters from other backgrounds were also able to flourish: Daniel Mendoza, who fought Jackson for the championship of England, was Jewish, as was Ikey Pigg, another man who fought Cribb. Mendoza would end his days in poverty, but not before he had tried training, running a pub and appearing in panto-mime. In 1814, in emulation of the Marylebone Cricket Club (MCC) and the Jockey Club in their sports, the gentlemen who followed boxing established a regulatory body of their own, the Pugilistic Club, to set the rules. They even agreed their own uniform as a first priority: blue coats and yellow waistcoats with buttons engraved with the letters PC. Attending the inaugural dinner were Captain Barclay, of course, and Lord Byron; Sir Harry Smyth took the chair and the Earl of Yarmouth made a speech about sportsmanship. The profes-sionals Cribb, Gully and Jackson were also invited, but not to speak.

All Regency sport, however bizarre, was a vehicle for betting and financial gain. Rowlandson has a cartoon of a cricket match between barefooted women's teams from Hampshire and Surrey, their skirts hitched up in a most daring fashion, played in Stoke Newington in October 1811 for a purse of 500 guineas. As throughout its history, cricket was not immune from either betting or cheating. Indeed, both seem to have flourished in a sport which had yet to acquire the trap-pings of a Victorian moral code and the pretentions of superior virtue. The days of the national supremacy of the club from the Hampshire village of Hambledon were over after the 1780s – though that club had drawn its players from right across the county – and the game was soon widespread in both England and the colonies. Hambledon, it was said, never played a major match for less than £500. Cricket, transported across the world by mainly military expatriates, was first played in Australia in 1803, India in 1804, the West Indies in 1806 and South Africa in 1808. The game was no longer played just by rustics but had been taken up by the public schools (or rather by their pupils, since games did not yet feature on the curriculum) and by the aristocracy, some of whose members sponsored teams even if they were not themselves enthusiastic participants. Although some thought it unseemly that lords and gentlemen, clergymen and lawyers should associate themselves with butchers and cobblers, wrote John Nyren, the early cricket writer whose father had played for Hambledon, they were quite capable of playing in 'the style in which we were always accustomed to impress our aristocratical playmates'.

It was a game the aristocracy thought they could play in the company of menials, for it required no physical contact and could be conducted under their authority. They played it under all conditions. In June 1815 a team of Guards officers whiled away the time waiting for the advance of Napoleon by arranging at least one game in a clearing in the Forest of Soignes between Brussels and Waterloo.* By the first years of the nineteenth century the Mary-le-Bone gentlemen's cricket club had been founded and was playing on the first of the grounds created for it in north London by the professional cricketer employed to bowl at the members, a Yorkshireman called Thomas Lord. His first ground was in Dorset Square, but development of the

---

* The Royal Brussels Cricket Club cheekily dates its foundation to these matches. The team flourishes still, nowadays made up of expatriate Anglophone British and Irish European Union officials, young Pakistanis, Australians, South Africans and New Zealanders living in Belgium, even the odd Belgian and a smattering of journalists – of which the author was one when he was the *Guardian*'s European Affairs Editor in the late 1990s. Its ground is at Ohain, just off the lane that Blücher's troops marched down to get to Wellington's assistance, and fielders standing at deep mid-on can, if their attention strays, see the Lion Memorial commemorating Waterloo sitting on top of its artificial mound in the distance. The 'Royal' in the title, incidentally, was granted by King Baudouin of the Belgians in the mid-twentieth century.

area forced a move, first in 1808 further north to the Eyre Estate. Then, when that land was required for the building of the Regent's Canal, in 1811 Lord took his turf – literally, to enable the noblemen and gentlemen of the MCC 'to play on the same footing as before' – slightly further north again to land in St John's Wood, where Lord's cricket ground remains to this day. The first match was played in 1814, when the MCC beat Hertfordshire by an innings and twenty-seven runs. That the ground remains where it is, though, is not down to Lord, who eventually wanted to sell it for building land to pay off his debts, but to William Ward, a director of the Bank of England, who bought him out for £5,000 in 1825 and preserved the land for cricket.

The MCC, invested with the wealth, influence and authority of its aristocratic members, essentially seized control of the conduct of the sport. It wrote the laws of the game (cricket enhances its *amour-propre* by insisting it is governed by laws, not just rules) and oversaw its running. Thus its aristocratic members prescribed, in 1809, the weight of a cricket ball and the width of the bat, and in 1817 they widened the wicket and increased its height. The club's membership did not mean that the behaviour of even its most aris-tocratic players was necessarily pristine, or even altruistic. The first great player of the period, Lord Frederick Beauclerk, a younger son of the 5th Duke of St Albans, entered holy orders and became the rector of that city, but spent a considerable part of his time throwing his weight around on the cricket field. He even boasted that he expected to make £600 a season in bets on matches. As John Major writes in his history of the game, Beauclerk was seen as 'avaricious, ill-tempered, hypocritical and a gamester adept at sharp practice'. He was a batsman of skill and he also bowled, though he could be put off his stride by cunning opponents such as the Yorkshireman Squire George Osbaldeston, an all-round sportsman fit to rival Captain

Barclay, who could provoke the reverend clergyman into losing his temper and so forfeiting control. John Nyren has a graphic picture of him bowling to the 'unadulterated rustic' stonewalling batsman Tom Walker, known as 'Old Everlasting' for his defensive play: 'Off went his lordship's white hat – dash upon the ground (his constant action when disappointed) calling him at the same time "a confounded old beast". "I don't care what ee zays," said Tom.'

There were also professional players such as William Lambert, an all-rounder who in 1817 became the first batsman to score two centuries in the same match – and the same year was warned off the ground at Lord's for allegedly selling a match by deliberately underperforming at the behest of bookmakers. There were those who said that it was Beauclerk's revenge for Osbaldeston and Lambert's cunning victory against him in a single-wicket contest six years earlier (both Beauclerk and Osbaldeston were allowed a professional on their side and the match was played for a stake of fifty guineas). Osbaldeston, who resigned his membership of the MCC in a fit of pique over another row, found Beauclerk's Christian charity did not extend to allowing him back into the club when he subsequently applied to rejoin. Such contretemps were common, especially with money at stake – and not just in betting. Thomas Lord could expect crowds of up to 5,000 for big matches at his ground and, charging sixpence a time for admission as well as providing refreshments, could make tidy sums of money. The affluent middle classes were also taking an interest: Ward, the banker who saved the ground (and once scored 278 in an innings there), was not an aristocrat, nor was Edward Budd, the second-best batsman in the country after Beauclerk, nor Ben Aislabie, a wine merchant who became the MCC's first secretary in 1822.

True ferocity could be found in the rat pits and the bull-baiting and cock-fighting taverns of London, where men would bet on how quickly terriers could kill a mound of rats, or dogs torment and bring down a bull (and how many would be gored, tossed or savaged in the process). In the rat pits in the back rooms of pubs, sacks of live rats would be upended into a circular wooden arena surrounded by a wall three feet high – higher than a rat could jump – and a dog would be let loose on them. The rats were garnered from sewers or brought in from the countryside, for farm rats were esteemed more cunning and less smelly and disease-ridden: the best specimens sold for a shilling each, the worst for half a crown a dozen. Fighting terriers were the dogs of choice and were timed as they went about their killing. The champion was a hulking dog called Billy, which once killed 1,000 rats in fifty-four minutes at the Cockpit tavern in Westminster. Billy was a twenty-six-pound bull terrier, but even a miniature terrier might be bred to be ferocious enough to slay at will: a five-pound black-and-tan terrier called Tiny, which wore a woman's bracelet as a collar, managed to polish off 200 in a session.* Such ghastly events were not just attended by lowlifes: the Duke of Wellington and Lord Byron were among those who might be present. Jimmy Shaw, a former prizefighter who kept a rat pit at his pub, told the Victorian journalist Henry Mayhew in the 1850s: 'Bless you, I have had noble

---

* The author can appreciate the fierceness of rat-killing dogs as – purely in the interests of journalistic inquiry – he once accompanied a party of rat-hunters on a night out at a poultry farm in the West Midlands, where more than 700 rats were killed by a pack of the men's Jack Russell terriers. They were allowed to eat the first ones they killed, but after they were satiated, they carried on slaughtering the rats for fun. One of the dogs, placed at my feet as I cowered against a barn wall four feet from the battery cages, killed eighteen rats as they were driven out from the trays beneath the chickens. A quick bite to the neck and a flick of the corpse over the dog's shoulder disposed of them instantly. Not one of the rats touched me, though they formed a neat heap at my feet.

ladies and titled ladies come here to see the sport – on the quiet you know.' Sporting gentlemen might bring their dogs to compete; Mayhew spotted a sign outside a Soho pub: 'Rats always on hand for the accommodation of Gentlemen to try their dogs.'

Nor was it just vermin that were killed for sport. Bulls were still baited in many places – the practice had formerly been justified as a means of tenderizing the meat – and bulldogs were specifically bred to go for the animals' throats and snouts and to hang on. The adult bulls would be tethered to a post, sometimes with a length of chain so that they could move around a small radius, and pepper would be blown into their nostrils to enrage them before the dogs attacked, either singly or in groups. The 'best' sport was if a bull managed to catch and toss a dog with its horns, and again gentlemen were invited to bring their dogs along to test them. In Bethnal Green on a Sunday it was customary for men to club together to buy a bullock from the drovers bringing cattle in for the market on Monday at Smithfield. They would push peas into its ears and poke it with iron rods until the poor animal was so maddened that it would charge down the Bethnal Green Road, surrounded by a screaming crowd of as many as 2,000 men and boys, dodging its horns, who were desperate to see what it did. At Christmas 1818 the hunt was especially rough as two people, one a milkmaid, were tossed and gored by the animal and fighting broke out between opposing gangs of men in the pursuit. On that occasion special constables joined in, trying to prevent the fighting, only to be turned on and attacked with sticks and stones themselves. This was accounted unusual because normally the constables kept out of it. When the local vicar complained to the magistrate Joseph Merceron, he was blandly informed that there was 'no kind of amusement' he was so fond of as bullock-hunting and that when he was younger he had generally been first in the chase.

Such cruel practices would eventually be outlawed, along with cock-fighting and dog-fighting, in 1835, though it had taken parliament more than a third of a century – almost as long as banning slavery – to do so, since the first attempt to legislate in 1802. The main campaigners against animal cruelty were evangelicals such as William Wilberforce – sparing time from leading the fight to end slavery – and the Irish MP Richard Martin, facetiously nicknamed 'Humanity Dick' by the Prince Regent and much mocked for his feverish opposition to the ill-treatment of donkeys, horses and cattle. Martin eventually managed to get the Cruel Treatment of Cattle Act passed in 1822, but that specifically excluded bulls. Both he and Wilberforce were founder members of the Society for the Prevention of Cruelty to Animals,* but both were dead by the time the cruelty act was finally passed. The clinching argument for MPs was not cruelty but that baiting animals was a public nuisance.

———∞∞∞———

By 1815 Captain Barclay was having troubles of his own and he was certainly not fighting Napoleon, having retired from the army after the Walcheren expedition so he could devote more time to sport. Not only was his financial situation rocky – his annual income of £7,000 meant it was hard to keep up with the extravagance of his cronies in the Fancy, particularly with his penchant for lavish bets; but by the end of the year he had also made his sister's seventeen-year-old maid Mary Dalgarno – a woman half his age – pregnant, and she was demanding marriage. He took her south, well away from her home and his estate near Aberdeen, to his country seat in Oxfordshire, where she was presented as his wife, but she was soon demanding

* It became the Royal Society by permission of Queen Victoria in 1840.

that he should honour his rash promise and indeed marry her. The captain was famous by now: his strenuous training methods which had served Cribb so well before the second Molineaux fight made him not only a celebrity athlete, but also a national role model for physical fitness. *The Sporting Magazine* suggested his sort of training could win the war: 'We freely avow that we think Captain Barclay's desire to establish a regular system of manly corporeal exercises, similar to those of the Palaestrae and Gymnasia of the Greeks and of the Circus and the Campus Martius of the Romans, is a laudable and patriotic ambition.'

Possibly even more vexing to Barclay than the demands of his young partner was the fact that his great walking record had been beaten. There was now something of a craze. In 1815 Josiah Eaton, a baker, walked one mile every hour for 1,100 hours at Blackheath – and he was ten years older than the captain. Then, the next year, Eaton did it again: only this time, to make it more gruelling, he started each mile within twenty minutes of finishing the last. Three months later, he set out to walk 2,000 half-miles in 2,000 successive half-hours – and he nearly did it too, giving up just a mile short of his goal. Meanwhile another man, George Wilson, poor and emaciated, set out to walk 1,000 miles in twenty days. He attracted large crowds, but the magistrates put a stop to his endeavour after sixteen days and 751 miles – as a non-gentleman, Wilson could not be allowed to flout the law against riotous assemblies. Nor was pedestrianism the only activity in which feats of stamina were attempted: a Scottish clergyman promised to try to read six chapters of the Bible every hour for 1,000 hours, and someone else vowed to eat a sausage every hour for the same length of time – though he had obviously not trained seriously enough as he gave up after just three.

Over the coming years, the boxing craze would wane, following the retirement of Cribb and Jackson and controversies such as the death of a Scottish boxer and Barclay protégé called Sandy McKay who was harried into fighting a much more experienced Irish fighter named Simon Byrne and died from the pummelling he received. Barclay fled and only narrowly escaped prosecution for manslaughter, probably through the expedient of paying a bribe. Although the captain lived into the 1850s, by the time Victoria came to the throne, his high-stakes world of the Fancy was no more.

9

'Bards, that erst sublimely told'

—JOHN KEATS, 'ODE TO APOLLO' (1815)

The year 1815 was probably a time that Lord Byron would have preferred to forget. It was three years since he had, in his own words, awoken one morning and found himself famous, following the publication of the first two cantos of his epic poem *Childe Harold's Pilgrimage*, which had sold out in three days. The handsome, charming and dashing young aristocrat was suddenly invited to all the best parties, was lionized by society and found himself being swooned over by half the young women of London. Perhaps he was the first true literary celebrity.

The Duchess of Devonshire recorded: '*Childe Harold* [was] on every table and [Byron] courted, visited, flattered and praised wherever he appears.' The noble lord, then aged twenty-four, was not immune to such celebrity, energetically bedding actresses, society women and young men with enthusiasm. Lady Caroline Lamb, the woman who famously described him as 'mad, bad and dangerous to know', was one of the more persistent in the queue. Then there was his married half-sister Augusta Leigh with whom he had a passionate affair which may well have resulted in the birth of her daughter Medora in 1814. In that year Lady Caroline's mother-in-law, Lady Melbourne, probably anxious to avoid scandal and save her son's marriage, steered Byron towards her twenty-two-year-old niece Annabella Milbanke.

Byron was intrigued by her intelligence and sparkiness, even her interest in mathematics, especially when she rejected his first proposal of marriage. But he was not besotted and seems to have been rather stampeded into proposing again, then being accepted and finding himself betrothed. 'I was the fashion when she first came out,' Byron wrote. 'I had the character of being a great rake and was a great dandy – both of which young ladies like… She married me from vanity and the hope of reforming and fixing me.' Poor Annabella really was not his type, physically or spiritually (neither was anyone else in the long run: his infatuations rarely lasted more than three months); Lady Caroline Lamb wrote gleefully that he would 'never be able to pull with a woman who went to church punctually, understood statistics and had a bad figure'.* Byron made his way slowly and reluctantly up to the Milbankes' family home in County Durham in the autumn of 1814, making a lengthy stop at Augusta's home outside Newmarket in Cambridgeshire on the way, and arrived on New Year's Eve to find wedding preparations in full swing. They were married on 2 January 1815 at Annabella's parents' home, but already the signs were bad. As Fiona MacCarthy, Byron's biographer, remarks:

> What was lethal in Byron was his emotional duplicity. The language of love came all too easily to the great amatory poet and he seems to have been writing himself into a temporary belief in his own sincerity. Love *in absentia* was one thing. It was the reality of love with a complicated, well-bred, intellectual female,

---

* Annabella was supposedly on the dumpy side, though a portrait shows her looking vivacious and attractive as a young woman. A photograph of her taken in old age depicts a plainly disappointed and glum figure in a mob cap, definitely not looking like someone who might have enjoyed sexual ecstasy with the most handsome man of the century.

the face-to-face demands, the challenges, the suffocating cosiness, that Byron could not bear.

During the ceremony Byron grimaced when he had to say the words about all his worldly goods, and when he wrote to Lady Melbourne the following day, he remarked unromantically: 'so there's an end of that matter and the beginning of many others… the kneeling was rather tedious and the cushions hard.' His wedding present to his wife was a collection of his own poems and he referred to their subsequent holiday as a treaclemoon. 'Good God, I am surely in hell!' he exclaimed while lying in bed on their wedding night, loudly enough to wake up his bride.

Once they got to London, after a stay with Augusta Leigh in Cambridgeshire ('We can amuse ourselves without you,' he told his bride), they took on a house much larger than they could afford in Piccadilly Terrace near what is now Hyde Park Corner. The bored and negligent husband resumed his round of social engagements. He met his publisher John Murray regularly, went to parties, became involved with the running of the Drury Lane Theatre, and cheered on his old hero Napoleon from afar. The emperor's escape from Elba thrilled Byron and lifted his spirits. The poet had been a long-time enthusiast: 'It is impossible not to be dazzled and overwhelmed by his character and career,' he wrote. He received reports from his close friend John Cam Hobhouse, who stayed in Paris throughout the Hundred Days, the period between Napoleon's return and the battle of Waterloo. Both were stunned and disillusioned by the defeat, and Byron wrote a poem, 'Napoleon's Farewell', which was published in the *Examiner* accompanied by a self-protective disclaimer from the editor. Byron wrote:

Farewell to the Land, where the gloom of my Glory
Arose and o'ershadowed the earth with her name –
She abandons me now – but the page of her story,
The brightest or blackest, is filled with my fame.
I have warred with a world which vanquished me only
When the meteor of Conquest allured me too far;
I have coped with the nations which dread me thus lonely,
The last single Captive to millions in War.

Support for Napoleon was a distinctly minority view by then, though some, including the Anglo-American painter Benjamin West, the president of the Royal Academy, shared it. How extraordinary, the painter Robert Smirke remarked, that 'men who professed themselves advocates of liberty should be so warped in their opinions'.

At the same time that he was expressing such lofty sentiments about Napoleon, Byron was in turns brutally ignoring or verbally abusing his now pregnant young wife. He also engaged in a brief affair with an actress called Susan Boyce – 'she was a transient piece of mine,' he wrote later to Hobhouse. When Annabella gave birth to their daughter Augusta Ada that December, his behaviour towards her grew worse. There was, in her words, 'the strongest expression of aversion and disgust', so much so that early in the New Year she left for her parents' home, convinced that her husband was insane, taking the baby with her. When her father Sir Ralph Noel* wrote to Byron that February demanding a separation on the grounds of his daughter's personal safety, the poet appears to have been surprised and wrote that he was 'ignorant of any particular ill treatment' on his

* Noel had changed the family name in order to receive an inheritance under the terms of the will left by his wife's brother, Viscount Wentworth.

part. But the veiled threats of exposing him as a homosexual – the London gossip was already getting around: 'reports abroad of a nature *too horrible to repeat*' – grew more pointed. Sodomy was a crime still punishable by execution – at least in the case of the lower orders such as rank-and-file soldiers, rather than aristocrats – and Byron insisted he had never done anything illegal like that *in England*. A separation was agreed and in April 1816 Byron left the country forever. He never saw England or his wife and daughter again.

Back in April 1815, while he was still the toast of the town, Byron had met another, equally famous, literary lion at the office of his publisher John Murray in Albemarle Street. Sir Walter Scott had come south for the summer and the two became friends – improbably, because Scott was a high Tory while Byron was a radical who had written critically of Scott's poetry in the past. That summer, however, they met several times: both shared a fascination for history and the dramatic and romantic, as well as their experience of literary fame. Murray's son, also named John, watched the two men clumping down the stairs of the house together: 'Lord Byron's deformity in his foot was very evident, especially as he walked downstairs. He carried a stick. After Scott and he had ended their conversation in the drawing room, it was a curious sight to see the greatest poets of the age – both lame – stumping downstairs side by side.'*

Scott, an Edinburgh lawyer, had become famous as a poet, but the previous year had published his first novel, *Waverley*, to huge acclaim. Generally regarded as the first historical novel in English, it was set sixty years earlier, at the time of the Jacobite rebellion, and concerns

---

* Scott had had childhood polio; Byron is now thought to have had dysplasia at birth, a failure of his lower right leg and foot to form properly. He was, understandably, extremely sensitive on the subject and it probably accounts for his determined development of physical prowess, through energetic swimming, boxing and cricketing.

a young English officer who falls in love with a Highland chieftain's daughter and defects to the other side. Scott's character creation and plotting and his variations of narrative style – third person, first person, different speech patterns to distinguish and delineate cast and caste – were also innovations and much copied as the nineteenth-century novel evolved through the work of writers including the Brontës and George Eliot. What appealed to the Regency readership, though, was not only a fast-moving and dramatic plot, but also a rich cast of exotic Scottish characters, all set against the romantic and sublime backdrop of the remote and rugged mountains and glens. Some of the language now seems clotted and the characters' speech both arch and convoluted, but to nineteenth-century readers it appeared authentic and lyrical, and on publication the book was a great success, even though – or possibly because – its author was supposedly anonymous.

Scott kept his name off the title pages of all his novels, originally because *Waverley* was an experiment that could be disowned if it was unsuccessful, and also because he thought it was unseemly for a lawyer to be writing fiction; but a third – and more public – reason he gave was that he had turned to writing fiction once Byron's talent for poetry had supplanted his own. Nevertheless, it was pretty generally known that Scott had written it, and he immediately followed up his success with a second novel, *Guy Mannering*, written in six weeks in the autumn of 1814 while he was still working as a lawyer and published within a few weeks the following February. Scott's biographer, the novelist John Buchan, who knew a thing or two about fast-moving plots, describes this novel as carelessly written, crudely conceived and casually told, with perfunctory love-making, a wooden hero, and much coy and cumbersome writing, but he was nevertheless a fan of its sheer narrative skill, and it too was an immediate bestseller. When he headed south with his family in March 1815 after the Edinburgh legal term had finished, Scott was a literary sensation: 'Make up your mind', a friend wrote to him, 'to be stared at only a little less than the Czar of Muscovy and old Blücher.' He was invited to meet anyone who was anyone; the Prince Regent, a fan of his writing, threw dinner parties for him and called him Walter – and then there was Byron. They probably steered clear of politics and were full of mutual esteem for each other's work: 'Byron's countenance is a thing to dream of,' Scott told a friend.

⸺∞⸺

In 1815 Jane Austen was at the height of her literary powers. She finished writing *Emma*, her comic masterpiece, at her home at Chawton in north Hampshire on 29 March and spent much of the rest of the year trying to get it published. Her previous publisher, Thomas Egerton, seems to have procrastinated, probably about payment, even though he had seen *Sense and Sensibility* and *Mansfield Park* sell out, and later in the summer her brother Henry took it to John Murray instead. Murray bought the copyrights to the three novels from Egerton for £450 and published *Emma* that Christmas. Meanwhile, wasting no time, Jane Austen started writing *Persuasion*, the last novel she would complete, on 8 August 1815.

By the time *Emma* was published, Austen knew that she had a royal fan in the Prince Regent. That November she was in London, seeing Murray and, more importantly, helping to nurse Henry Austen through a serious illness at his home in Hans Place in Knightsbridge. One of Henry's doctors was a royal physician and told her how much the prince enjoyed her work – indeed, he kept copies of all her novels in each of the royal residences. The next day, James Stanier Clarke, the royal librarian, called on her to tell her that she was welcome to visit the Prince Regent's residence at Carlton House, where he would show her round. When she did so the following week, she was told that she had permission to dedicate her next work to the prince. Clarke wrote to her on 16 November 1815: 'It is certainly not *incumbent* on you to dedicate your work now in the press to his Royal Highness; but if you wish to do the Regent that honour either now or at any future period I am happy to send you that permission.' That heavy hint was the equivalent of a royal command, of course, and even though *Emma* was already at the printer's, the addition was made and the frontispiece of the first edition of the novel is extravagantly dedicated to the prince, the wording seemingly at Murray's suggestion:

To HIS ROYAL HIGHNESS **THE PRINCE REGENT**,
THIS WORK IS BY HIS ROYAL HIGHNESS'S PERMISSION,
MOST RESPECTFULLY DEDICATED,
BY HIS ROYAL HIGHNESS'S DUTIFUL AND
OBEDIENT SERVANT, **THE AUTHOR**.

Austen's name did not appear on the title page of this or any of her other works at the time of their first publication, though her fame was beginning to spread and her name was known, rather to her consternation. It was about now that she turned down a chance to meet the French literary celebrity Madame de Staël – perhaps just as well, as de Staël had declared Austen's work vulgar and provincial. Austen would have preferred something slightly less obsequious for the dedication to the Prince Regent, for whom she had scant respect, but she was not going to turn down the royal invitation. She was accordingly teased by her friend Martha Lloyd, who later married her brother Frank, that she had done it for money. Published in three volumes, priced at twenty-one shillings, *Emma* received slightly dismissive reviews ('there was no story in it,' wrote Maria Edgeworth, and even her publisher Murray wrote to his most successful author, Scott, saying: 'It wants incident and romance, does it not?'), but the first print run of 2,000 copies sold out anyway. Scott, who had been a little ambivalent about her writing when she was alive, wrote in 1826:

> That young lady [had] a talent for describing the involvements and feelings and characters of ordinary life, which is to me the most wonderful I have ever met with. The Big Bow-Wow strain I can do myself like any now going; but the exquisite touch which renders ordinary common-place things and characters interesting from the truth of the description and the sentiments is denied to me.

Austen would probably have been happy with that.

The Prince Regent himself did not bother to reply, or to offer personal thanks, for the dedication, but Clarke eventually did so on his behalf some months later, and pronounced himself a fan of her work too: 'Your late works, Madam… reflect the highest honour on your genius and your principles. In every new work your mind seems to increase its energy and power of discrimination… accept my best thanks for the pleasure your works have given me.' The librarian seems almost to have stepped out of an Austen novel himself, in turns obsequious and pompous. He probably had a middle-aged crush on Jane and could not help suggesting improvements and ideas for new plots, such as 'the Habits of Life and Character and Enthusiasm of a clergyman' – someone just like himself, for example – with animadversions on the iniquities of the tithe system for clerical stipends.

By 1816 Clarke had been appointed chaplain and private secretary to Prince Leopold of Saxe-Coburg-Saalfeld, Princess Charlotte's impecunious German suitor and future husband. He also took the liberty of suggesting a possible future plot to the novelist. Clarke thought 'an historical romance illustrative of the august house of Cobourg would just now be very interesting' and could be dedicated to his new employer. Fortunately, Jane Austen had other ideas – her nephew later said she must have thought it ludicrous – and wrote back gently but firmly:

> You are very kind in your hints… but I could no more write a romance than an epic poem. I could not sit seriously down to write a serious romance under any other motive than to save my life… No, I must keep my own style and go my own way; and though I may never succeed again in that, I am convinced that I should totally fail in any other.

She settled down to finishing *Persuasion* in 1816 instead, but it and *Northanger Abbey* and indeed the fragments of other novels such as *Sanditon* would not be published until after her death at the age of forty-one the following year. In her lifetime, Jane Austen's literary efforts earned her less than £800.

⁂

Across London in 1815 nineteen-year-old John Keats, the son of a London innkeeper, was starting to write poetry, including the lines in his 'Ode to Apollo' celebrating the release of his hero Leigh Hunt from prison (see pages 71–2). He was enrolled at Guy's Hospital that October as a student, training to become a doctor or surgeon, and his literary life would be squeezed into the following five years.

At that time, too, Percy Bysshe Shelley, three years older than Keats, wrote *Alastor, or The Spirit of Solitude*, the epic poem that would be published early in 1816. The death of Shelley's grandfather in January 1815 had given him a measure of financial security because he inherited more than £7,000 and was granted an allowance of £1,000 a year, enabling him to pay off his debts and take a house in Hans Place at least for the time being – a few months before Jane Austen arrived in the same street to nurse her brother. Of more pressing concern was his tangled private life. Estranged from his teenaged wife Harriet, who had given birth to one child and was pregnant with another, he had eloped in the summer of 1814 with Mary Wollstonecraft Godwin, fleeing to the continent in the company of her half-sister Claire Clairmont. By 1815 they were back in London. Shelley's relationship with his wife was embittered by his spiteful letters to her, blaming her for the breakdown of their marriage, and complicated by his estrangement from his own family and hers. His Whig MP father hated his avowed atheism as much as his political radicalism, and he was also understandably disapproved of by Mary's father, the philosopher William Godwin, who was Shelley's intellectual mentor. Little is known of what was happening to Shelley and Mary during the first few months of 1815 because the pages of their respective journals are missing. There seem to have been further fallings-out, both with Claire, with whom Shelley may have had an affair, and with his friend Thomas Jefferson Hogg, who apparently took the poet's belief in free love too far by trying to seduce Mary.

By August 1815 Percy Bysshe and Mary were renting a cottage near Windsor and hiring a wherry with friends to row up the Thames to Lechlade and back. The idyllic trip in hot weather that September seems to have fired Shelley's imagination for an altogether longer voyage, made possible by the newly interconnecting canal system.

'We had in the course of our voyage conceived the scheme… of going along a canal which joins the Thames to get into the Severn and so also follow up that river to its source,' wrote Shelley's friend, the novelist Thomas Love Peacock, who had originally organized the trip:*

> Shelley also proposed in his wildness that there should be no halting place even there; he even proposed by the help of divers canals and rivers to leave North Wales and traversing the inland counties to reach Durham and the Lakes, so on to the Tweed and hence to come out at the Forth, nor rest until we reached the Falls of the Clyde, when by the time we returned we should have voyaged two thousand miles.

Unfortunately, the party could not manage the £20 sailing fee to use the Severn Canal and the voyage instead petered out when their wherry ran aground, surrounded by weeds and cattle, as the Thames narrowed to no more than a stream on the Gloucestershire border, and they had to turn back. Shelley seemingly babbled of even more exotic trips 'up and down some mighty stream which civilisation had never visited, or long since deserted: the Missouri and the Columbia, the Oronoko and the Amazon, the Nile and the Niger, the Euphrates and the Tigris… under the overcanopying forests of the new or by the long silent ruins of the ancient world'. So wrote Peacock, fictionalizing

---

* Peacock was Shelley's closest friend at this time: a budding satirical novelist himself, he had supported the poet in his estrangement from his wife and became manager of his business affairs. Peacock wrote his first, brief novella, *Headlong Hall*, at this time; little read now, it makes up for what it lacks in dramatic tension or plot development with an extended series of wry philosophical and political dialogues between its characters. He would soon abandon novel-writing for a long career in the East India Company's revenue-collection department in London.

his friend in his much later novel *Crotchet Castle*. In the meantime the Thames trip seems to have fired Shelley's inspiration for *Alastor*, the brooding, introspective tale in blank verse of how a poet leaves his alienated home to pursue his vision of ideal love across Persia to India, dogged by an evil spirit of solitude.

The idyllic journey up the Thames was probably one of Shelley's last abiding memories of England. The following year his wife Harriet committed suicide, enabling him to marry Mary, and within a couple of years they would move abroad to Italy where, in 1822, an altogether shorter boat trip would cost him his life.

The young radicals were not the only poets active in England at that time, of course. The previous generation was still publishing, or, in Samuel Taylor Coleridge's opium-addled case, trying to do so, in Calne, Wiltshire, where he was dictating a semi-biographical exposition of what poetry should be about. His former friend William Wordsworth, the pioneer of the new romantic sensibility in poetry, was now in his forties and eking out his meagre income – he reckoned that in the previous twenty years his poetry had earned him a total of £120 – by becoming the government's distributor of stamps, to authenticate and tax documents, for Westmorland. This in itself earned him £200 a year, but involved a great deal of travelling around the Lake District, appointing sub-distributors and collecting payments, and it coincided with his middle-aged drift towards conservatism. The man who had once welcomed the French Revolution was now also earning a little extra money by keeping the local aristocratic Tory family, the Lowthers, abreast of any potential radicalism in the area. Wordsworth's friend Robert Southey was also in the pay of the government. He had become Poet Laureate in 1813 when Walter Scott had turned down the post. Southey needed the payment that came with the role, although it amounted to only £90 a year and a butt of sherry. He would hold the royal appointment for thirty years.

Both men were accordingly ridiculed for venality. Leigh Hunt wrote: 'Mr Southey and even Mr Wordsworth have both accepted offices under the Government of such a nature as absolutely ties up their independence.' Both were also felt to be past it as poets, though Wordsworth had another third of a century to live. When he published his 420-page-long poem *The Excursion* in 1814 – another rumination on a poet's lonely wanderings, but this time, unlike Shelley's, with pessimistic conservative musings on the decline in religious faith and the loss of public virtue – the work was lambasted. Famously, the *Edinburgh Review's* assessment began, 'This will never do', and added that while there were occasional good lines that sparkled like gems in the desert, they were merely an 'intimation of the great poetic powers that lie buried in the rubbish that has been heaped around them'. Wordsworth's next effort in 1815, *The White Doe of Rylstone*, which he thought one of his best, got even worse treatment in the same influential journal, probably by the same reviewer, Francis Jeffrey: 'This we think has the merit of being the very worst poem we ever saw imprinted in a quarto volume.' Despite their political and personal differences, however, both Wordsworth and Southey praised Byron's work, as did Coleridge, and the younger man acknowledged their influence on his writing. All three of the seniors would outlive the younger generation of poets – Byron, Keats and Shelley – by decades.

For the painter John Constable, who turned thirty-nine the week before the battle of Waterloo, 1815 was a year of further frustration. Professionally he was still denied associate membership at the Royal Academy – he had applied every year since 1810 – and personally his relationship with the love of his life, Maria Bicknell, whom he had first met fifteen years before and had proposed to in 1809, was proceeding with glacial slowness. Maria's father, the Admiralty solicitor Charles Bicknell, who was also an adviser to the Prince Regent, clearly saw the artist as a dubious prospect and probably a social inferior, as he was the son of a Suffolk mill owner. In 1815 Bicknell finally allowed Constable to visit the family home in Spring Gardens Terrace, central London, as 'an occasional visitor' – this was in addition to the loving correspondence that he had been carrying on for years with his daughter. Maria too was frustrated. 'From being perfectly wretched I am now comparatively happy,' she wrote to Constable, conveying the news that he could come to see her. 'I cannot tell you what I felt last Tuesday when you left us at the door now to be no longer closed, is it not delightful?' They would finally be married without ceremony at St Martin-in-the-Fields in London in October 1816, having overcome the doubts of Maria's father and grandfather, the rector of East Bergholt, after Constable received a legacy following the death of his father. The great paintings – *Flatford Mill*, *The Hay Wain*, *The Corn Field*, *The Leaping Horse*, *Hadleigh Castle* and *Salisbury Cathedral from the Meadows* – were still to come, the latter two after Maria's death from tuberculosis in 1828.

In the spring of 1815 both Constable's mother and Maria's died, and it is a measure of the painter's ambitious determination that he did not return home to East Bergholt to attend Ann Constable's funeral because it coincided with admissions day for the Royal Academy's summer exhibition. He spent that summer in London, earning money by assisting a painter called George Dawe with a portrait of the actress Eliza O'Neill – Constable painted the landscape in which she posed as Juliet. Then, after meeting Maria for a Sunday outing to Putney, he returned home to Suffolk for much of the rest of the year. There he painted *A Cottage in the Cornfield* and other scenes of harvest time. Outside events, though, did impinge on the rural idyll: his cousin Captain James Gubbins of the 13th Dragoons was killed at Waterloo and his body was never found.

10

'Hearts beat high to tread the paths of Glory'

— RECRUITMENT POSTER FOR
THE 7TH LIGHT DRAGOONS, 1814

In 1815 the British army was at its greatest manpower strength. Officially, 233,852 officers and men were under arms, the equivalent of perhaps one family in five having a serving member, yet it struggled to reach the troop level the government had promised the continental allies in Vienna. At the battle of Waterloo, the Duke of Wellington's army of about 68,000 men contained only about 25,000 British troops.* Of that number less than a quarter, approximately 7,000 men, were veterans who had fought in the Peninsular War. The rest had had to be recruited fresh, either from civilian life or from the county militia and yeomanry regiments. About 30,000 troops were hurriedly raised and marched to the Kent coast to join the transports at Deal. Wellington said that it was 'an infamous army, very weak and ill-equipped and a very inexperienced staff', as he tried to force the government back in London into sending more men in the weeks before the battle.

Finding enough troops to keep the army up to strength during the prolonged Napoleonic wars had been a constant struggle, and new arrivals had never kept up with the losses through death in battle, or

---

* The rest of its manpower was scattered around the empire, the West Indies, Canada and on the islands of the Mediterranean.

from sickness and epidemics, injuries and wounds, desertions and captures. The best year, 1808, had seen 15,308 men recruited, but even the smallest depreciation in numbers, which had occurred two years previously, had exceeded 16,000. The shortfall was made up by recruiting foreign troops and mercenaries: they had formed 11 per cent of the army's strength in 1804 and by 1813 the proportion had risen to more than 20 per cent. There were Dutch, Belgian, Swiss, Polish, Hungarian, Greek and Italian soldiers in the army's ranks, many Germans and even a French unit, the Chasseurs Britanniques, made up of emigrés and royalists whose families had fled the revolution (though this last was disbanded in 1814).

When it came to home-grown troops, the regular army had a reservoir of local parish and county militia units to draw on and, from 1803, it had been allowed to recruit from these part-time units. Previously this poaching of men had supposedly been illegal (though it went on frequently) and it was resented by the militias, which then had to make up the shortfall in their own numbers to compensate for the manpower they had lost to the army. Militias were needed to keep the peace in their own areas and did not serve beyond them, still less abroad.

If recruits were needed, men serving in the militia would be offered bounties to swap to the regular army, and if that did not produce the desired numbers, harsh measures might be adopted to make them feel that joining the regulars would be an easier life. One contemporary wrote:

> The Militia would be drawn up in line and the officers, or non-commissioned officers, from the regiments requiring volunteers would give a glowing description of their several regiments, describing the victories they had gained and the honours they

had acquired and concluded by offering a bounty. If these inducements were not effective in getting men then coercive measures were adopted: heavy and long drills and field exercises were forced upon them: which became so oppressive that to escape them, the men would embrace the alternative and join the regulars.

If all else failed, recruitment to the army was sometimes by ballot (for limited service for a term of three years) but those whose names were drawn could buy themselves out if they had the means to do so: £20 or £30 for a substitute to be called in their place. For the very poor there was no escape. The Dorset shepherd boy Benjamin Harris related this in his memoirs after his twelve years' service, mainly as a rifleman in the Peninsular War:

> My father tried hard to buy me off and would have persuaded the sergeant of the 66th that I was of no use as a soldier for having maimed my right hand (by breaking a forefinger as a child). The sergeant however said I was just the sort of little chap he wanted and off he went, carrying me (amongst a batch of recruits he had collected) away with him.

Why would men swap from the infantry militia or the yeomanry to sign up as a volunteer for prolonged periods – up to twenty-five years – in the regular army?* There were many reasons, not least the sense of adventure: 'the apparent freedom, the frankness and gaiety of an open-hearted soldier's holiday life,' as one sergeant of the 43rd put

---

* The yeomanry was recruited from a slightly higher social class: at this time at least the yeoman farmers, minor landowners and squires and tradesmen. They were mounted troops and generally brought their own horses with them.

it in his memoirs – a glitter unknown in any other profession. Then there was the excitement of the drum-beat and the trumpet-call, the scarlet (or green or blue) uniform, and the chance to fire a musket or wield a sabre for the country's honour. As one Chelsea pensioner wrote in his memoirs forty years later:

> It was in the month of January 1806 that, happening to be on a stroll through Westminster… I was attracted by a huge placard on which was emblazoned the figure of a light dragoon, mounted on a dashing steed and brandishing a sabre. I felt a tap on the shoulder and looking round I was accosted, with a wink meant to be particularly knowing, by a swaggering blade of a light horseman in full fig of the very costume which I had been admiring.

For many, therefore, this was an adventure, or an escape from destitution and unemployment. For others the bounty they received was an obvious attraction. This varied according to the shortage, or the difficulty of recruiting in a particular area at any given time: up to twenty guineas or more a man, with bonuses paid to the recruiting party and maybe two guineas to the 'bringer' – the person who had brought the volunteer along (often the landlord of the pub where he had been drinking).

The historian Kevin Linch, in his history of the army during this period, says: 'There is no escaping the fact that money played a very large part in the decision to enlist.' Soldiering became for some a more attractive option the longer the Napoleonic wars went on: the length of the conflict increased inflation and raised prices, but civilian pay in many industries did not keep up. At least as a soldier there was food, accommodation, some basic medical care and even the chance of a pension if one served and lived long enough. Linch's researches show that in 1808 an infantry recruit would commonly receive £16.6s cash in hand for enlisting for an unlimited period, eleven guineas for a short term, but by 1813 the bounties had gone up to £23 and £16.14s respectively. Then, after the war ended in 1814, the money was slashed to four guineas for the cavalry and six guineas for the infantry, only to rise by half again the following year when troops were urgently needed. Not that the men or their families saw much of this money: there were stoppages after they had been recruited for drink and clothing, and it might take some time for them to arrive at their unit's depot while more recruits were enlisted, so that there would be more spending on the way. It was the lump sum that was the potential appeal – theoretically more than six months' wages for a labouring man; families received separate payment if their husbands were in the militia but not when they were in the regular army, so a cash sum in advance was welcome. Their wages once enlisted were generally a shilling a day – less than a labourer but more regular and fewer outgoings – though there were deductions from this to pay for uniforms and rations. The pay rate remained the same from 1797 until 1870.

Some 'volunteers' for the regulars made a habit of signing up, receiving the bounty, then absconding and signing up again elsewhere to repeat the process. One of Rifleman Harris's first duties on joining the 66th Regiment was to be a member of an execution party near Portsmouth, shooting a man who had deserted sixteen different times after receiving a bounty:* 'He made a short speech to the parade, acknowledging the justice of his sentence and that drinking and evil company had brought the punishment upon him,' Harris wrote. When the volley did not finish the man off and he was

---

* Despite the risk, others managed to get away with it many more times than this: one Thomas Hodgson had been executed in 1787 after admitting to forty-nine desertions, which had netted him 387 guineas.

still lying on the ground twitching, four riflemen were ordered to step forward, put their muskets against his head and fire again.

The army also raised volunteer units in times of national emergency such as the Napoleonic wars when invasion was threatened. These were usually recruited by local aristocratic landowners from among their tenantry, or in cities by organizations such as trade guilds or magistrates, and they served strictly within their own local areas: the Hitchin volunteers, for instance, would defend no more than a three-mile radius around their Hertfordshire town. Often their uniforms were quite fancy, but their limitations of service were such that they were regarded as – and were – no more than weekend soldiers. The glamour of such uniforms, with their gold braid and high boots, was a distinct attraction to landed gentry and the professional classes. Linda Colley points out that nearly half of all the MPs sitting in parliament in the Napoleonic era served in militias and a fifth of all MPs joined the regular army. She writes in *Britons*: 'Never before or since have British military uniforms been so impractically gorgeous, so brilliant in colour, so richly ornamented or so closely and cunningly tailored… the higher his rank the more dazzling his uniform was likely to be. In every sense he was dressed to kill.'

The regular army recruited heavily in Scotland and Ireland, less heavily in Wales, where there was a language (and religious nonconformist) barrier and only one distinctively Welsh regiment to inspire Welshmen to join up. In 1815, 58 per cent of the rank-and-file recruits were English, 10 per cent Scottish (two years earlier the proportion had been nearly 20 per cent) and 32 per cent Irish. Recruitment rose in periods of economic hardship: while agricultural prices and consequently wages were high in southern England, fewer men came forward. When weavers were becoming unemployed in Nottinghamshire, recruitment among them went up: the 3rd Foot Guards marched into the county recruiting in 1811 and filled their ranks with unemployed stocking weavers from Nottingham. In 1807 and 1808 in Lancashire there were strikes by cotton weavers and half the men who joined the army from the area at that time were refugees from the mills. Many of the men who joined up were literate, but many were also escaping, from prison sentences or home circumstances. Some were pious (Wellington was suspicious both of Catholics' loyalty and Methodists' potential radicalism), but many more were rough and potentially violent men, especially when in drink. The Irish in particular gained a reputation as fearless fighters but also for being nearly uncontrollable if they were inebriated. Rifleman Harris called an Irish militia group 'as reckless and devil-may-care a set of men as I ever beheld, either before or since'. But they died in their ranks at Waterloo: the 27th (Inniskilling) Regiment, standing stoically in their infantry square in the centre of the allied line for hours under cannon-fire and cavalry attack, suffered 66 per cent casualties that day, the highest in the army: 'it may literally be said, lying dead in square,' as Sergeant Major Edward Cotton of the 7th Hussars described it.

To keep the troops in order, their punishments were harsh even in peacetime: flogging was common and executions not unknown. Their training, too, in camps at Shorncliffe near Folkestone in Kent or at Brighton was gruelling and tedious – repeated drills and, for the cavalry, long hours caring for their horses. Recruits might even be joined by young officers, who had purchased their commissions but were entirely ignorant of the disciplines they needed to learn. Lieutenant John Cooke of the 43rd Regiment wrote that they had to

> drill with a squad composed of peasants from the plough and other raw recruits, first learning the facings, marchings and the companies' evolutions. That being completed, the officer put on

cross-belts and pouches and learnt the firelock exercises; then again he marched with the same; and when it was considered that the whole was perfect, with and without arms, they began to skirmish in extended file and last of all learned the duties of a sentry and to fire ball cartridge at a target.

Generally such training took six months, with four one-hour drills every day. The 43rd was the Monmouthshire Light Infantry Regiment, one of the units with most casualties at the battle of New Orleans. Whether young aristocratic officers of more elite regiments had to undergo the same basic training may have been more doubtful: the Royal Military College was first established for officer training in 1801 (based at Sandhurst in Berkshire from 1812) but attendance was not compulsory.

The Duke of Wellington's remark about his men being the scum of the earth – made in a speech in 1831 – is well known, but it actually came in a passage extolling the troops who had fought for him:

A French army is composed very differently from ours. The conscription calls out a share of every class – no matter whether your son or my son – all must march; but our friends – I may say it in this room – are the very scum of the earth. People talk about enlisting from their fine military feeling – all stuff – no such thing. Some of our men enlist from having got bastard children, some for minor offences, many more for drink; but you can hardly conceive such a set brought together and it is really wonderful that we should have made them the fine fellows they are.

Virtually all the officers serving in the British army at this time were drawn from the aristocracy and landed gentry, certainly in the higher ranks, and many bought their commissions. Wellington was himself the son of an Irish peer and had originally bought his way in, becoming a lieutenant colonel at the early age of twenty-five because of it, and he had on his staff at Waterloo the sons of earls, lords and Scottish lairds, with only a scattering of men whose parents were from the professional classes. The duke was prepared to defend the practice of buying and selling officer ranks because, he said, 'it brings into the service men of fortune and character – men who have some connection with the interests and fortunes of the country', and – given the number of mercenaries in the ranks – this was to a certain extent true. More common were officers drawn from the local squirearchy: the class of relatively poor and honourable men, 'the sons of valiant squires', in the words of the Prince de Ligne, 'who were themselves accustomed to country life and the hunt. From the age of twelve they conditioned themselves to hardship, sleeping in the woods with their dogs, arresting poachers and fighting every now and then with some neighbour's son over the possession of a hare.' Scottish and Irish officers from the clan lairds or the small tenantry were often even more impoverished and, like the rankers, joined up as a means of escaping their surroundings. As Sir Walter Scott told Wellington: 'Scotland is a breeding, not a feeding country and we must send our sons abroad, as we sent our black cattle to England… we have a strong tendency to put our young folks all to the sword.'

The English squires' sons could generally stump up the cash – or had a wealthy local patron to do so for them – to buy a cornetcy or an ensign's junior rank in a cavalry or an infantry regiment. These cost several hundred pounds, depending on the fashionability and desirability of the regiment. An energetic trade in officer ranks certainly went on, as subalterns purchased promotion from officers who were retiring and selling their ranks, or swapped regiments to get on more quickly. The British army, however, never became aristocratically hidebound, with only those with noble rank allowed to become officers, as happened in other continental countries and Russia, for the British aristocracy was much smaller than that of most other countries. Especially at time of war, there could be promotion on merit when the demand for officers exceeded the supply. The military historian Richard Holmes calculated that, in the 200 years before the reforms of 1870 abolished the practice, about two-thirds of army commissions were purchased, but that during the last few years of the Napoleonic wars shortages meant that as many as four-fifths were obtained by other means: by seniority, battlefield gallantry, distinguished service or patronage. It was possible, very occasionally, for men who joined up as privates to become junior officers after many years' service – and the reverse was also true: some officers who left the service were known to have signed on subsequently in the ranks to fight in another regiment.

Holmes cites the case of John Shipp, a parish orphan, who enlisted in the 22nd Foot in 1797, distinguished himself during a siege in India in 1805, was subsequently commissioned without purchase in the 65th Regiment, then moved as a lieutenant to the 76th and sold his commission to pay off his debts on his return to England. Afterwards he enlisted in the 24th Dragoons, rose to the rank of sergeant major, was commissioned into the 87th Foot, then in 1823 fell out with his major and was court-martialled. Another case was Charles Cureton, who joined the Shropshire militia as a lieutenant in 1806, deserted by faking his own drowning after getting into financial trouble, re-enlisted under a false name as a private in the 16th Light Dragoons, was spotted by Wellington's military secretary Lord Fitzroy Somerset, who took him onto the headquarters staff, and was then commissioned into the 40th Foot. Cureton exchanged into the

20th Light Dragoons in October 1814 and by 1846 had ended up as a colonel in the 16th Lancers – a varied and meandering forty-year military career.

Officers in the ordnance and technical regiments – the Royal Artillery and the Royal Engineers – did not purchase their commissions but, with advancement dependent on the Buggins' turn of seniority, promotion was slow compared with the cavalry or infantry. Sir George Wood, who commanded the artillery at Waterloo, had still only reached the rank of major by 1836.

Once in the service, troops could generally expect a career that would take them abroad for prolonged periods – to India or the Caribbean for years on end – and there was a lot of foot-slogging in a campaign such as that in the Iberian peninsula.* Battles tended to be quite short (Salamanca, Wellington's greatest victory in Spain, was over in forty minutes, though there were 13,000 French casualties and 5,000 British and Portuguese). Although the main battle of Waterloo was over in a day, it was an unusually prolonged and intense combat. And of course the risk of death, either in battle or, more likely, from disease, was ever present during a campaign. A soldier had to hope for a quick end if he was wounded since medical attention was likely to be rudimentary. With luck he might survive an amputation, without anaesthetic, of an injured arm or leg, but a severe head or stomach wound would invariably be fatal. A battle won might produce some spoils or financial bounty, usually paid years afterwards, but a battle lost would be grim. The dead would be thrown into pits together, with little chance of their relatives discovering their fate, and the wounded might be left at the side of the road, a prey to looters and bandits who

---

* The Light Infantry famously marched forty-two miles in twenty-eight hours through the heat of the Spanish high summer to reach the battle of Talavera in July 1809.

would probably take the opportunity to finish them off as they stole their money, weapons and anything else of value that they could root out. It would be an ignominious, forgotten end.

In Brussels in the spring of 1815, once he had assumed charge of the British, Dutch and German army, Wellington divided the force at his disposal into three corps. The Prince of Orange was given command of one, as a sop to the Dutch royal family's pride; the second, under the British general Lord Hill, was made up of two Dutch and two British divisions; and Wellington himself commanded the reserve of two further British divisions, the corps of Brunswickers and a Nassau contingent. Nearby on the borders of Holland and Germany was the separate Prussian army led by the seventy-three-year-old Marshal Blücher. Other allied armies were scattered around Europe. There was an Austrian army in northern Italy, in case Napoleon attacked there, and a further German army, made up of more Austrian troops, Bavarians and Württembergers, along the Rhine. The Russian army was held in reserve in Poland.

Wellington interspersed veteran troops with newly recruited units and soldiers, such as the British, whom he considered reliable, next to those he suspected to be of doubtful loyalty or steadfastness. The Prince of Orange's division was similarly a mix of regular battalions and militia. The army was, says J.W. Fortescue in his history, a subtle mix. The first plan was to mount an invasion south with the Prussians to capture Paris, but this really depended on what direction Napoleon took: if he headed north first, the allies had to stand firm together and not allow themselves to be divided. As it was, Wellington had to defend the ports of Antwerp and Ostend, which were not only the source of his supplies and reinforcements from England but also the escape routes back across the Channel if things went wrong. The army needed to be salvaged to keep order back home if the government fell, as was bound to happen if the French were victorious. He and Blücher met at Tirlemont (modern Tienen, in Belgium) on 3 May to discuss strategy and to divide up their respective areas of responsibility: the Anglo-Dutch-German army to the south and west of Brussels, the Prussians further to the south and east. They also swapped liaison staff to aid communication and understanding. Fortunately, Wellington and Blücher got on: 'He was a very fine fellow and whenever there was any question of fighting, always ready and eager,' said the duke later. 'If anything, too eager.' It might have been a different matter had Blücher's second-in-command Augustus von Gneisenau been in charge of the Prussians – he appears to have had an antipathy towards the British ever since fighting alongside them during the American War of Independence nearly forty years earlier.

It was a delicate diplomatic tight-rope that Wellington had to walk, not to upset the Dutch or the Prussians, or to provoke possible defections to the French. Thus, perhaps over-sensitively but from fear of appearing too triumphalist, he stopped the Italian soprano Madame Angelica Catalani from singing an encore of 'Rule Britannia' when she gave a concert in Brussels, just by glaring at the officers shouting for her to sing it again. Fanny Burney, the writer, who was watching, wrote: 'he instantly crushed it by a commanding act of disapprobation and thus offered me an opportunity of seeing how magnificently he could quit his convivial familiarity for imperious dominion, when occasion might call for the transformation.'

Wellington's other task was to maintain morale during the ten weeks the army waited for Napoleon to make a move. Brussels was full of British families, including wives of the officers and potential sight-seers. There were balls: 'the Duke during this period was forever giving balls… and very agreeable they were,' wrote the Whig diarist and politician Thomas Creevey, who spent the whole period in Brussels. There were also horse-races and fox-hunting in the Forest of Soignes. Local farmers objected to the British officers chasing through their growing crops in the open country further south, where the battle would take place. Cricket matches were arranged and picnics held for the officers, though Wellington quietly urged the Duchess of Richmond not to stray too close to the French border when she held hers: 'You'd better not go. Say nothing about it but let the project drop.' The duke had sent his wife Kitty home from Paris to England before Napoleon's arrival in March, but there were plenty of English women in Brussels to keep him amused, including Lady Shelley and twenty-two-year-old Lady Frances Wedderburn-Webster, whose philandering husband would later sue a newspaper for suggesting his wife had had an affair with Wellington.

But it was how his largely untried, amalgamated army would react to an all-out assault by the French that concerned Wellington most. Creevey came across the duke walking in the park a couple of weeks before the battle. There had been some discussion of politics back home and Wellington had expressed his relief that there was now cross-party support for the campaign against the French, Creevey asked him how he thought things would go. Creevey reported that Wellington 'replied: "By God! I think Blücher and myself can do the thing… do the business." Then he pointed to a British infantry soldier standing nearby, gawping at the statuary. "There," he said, "it all depends upon that article whether we do the business or not. Give me enough of it and I am sure."'

And so the army, gathered in the flat Flanders countryside around Brussels in the early summer of 1815, waited to see which way the great Napoleon would come. All they knew was that come he would.

11

'A damned nice thing'

—DUKE OF WELLINGTON, QUOTED BY THOMAS CREEVEY

With four continental armies ranged against him and having been made a public outlaw at the Congress of Vienna, Napoleon realized there was no chance of being able peacefully to resume his dictatorship of France. If he ever seriously believed that had been an option, the degree of hostility that there was to him in the country showed that the previous status quo would never be a possibility now. He had to take on and defeat the European powers once again and would have to attempt to do it one by one because he did not have the troops or resources to beat them if they all combined. The allied armies in Belgium were the nearest and most obvious targets, and if he could destroy first one and then the other, he might once again be in a position to impose terms, or negotiate a settlement subsequently with the Austrians and Russians. The Anglo-Dutch army and the Prussians could be defeated in turn. Blücher's force was centred forty miles to the east of Wellington's, so Napoleon planned to head for the gap between them. This would prevent them uniting and actually drive them apart: the Prussians towards Germany and the British back to the Channel ports.

It seems such an obvious strategic move now that it appears odd that Wellington thought that the French might try to circle round his right flank, across western Belgium, cut off the line of retreat and seize Brussels behind the back of the allied forces, since this would have driven the two allied armies together rather than prising them apart. But it was a move the duke had to consider, especially as one of his priorities was preserving the British army and its escape route. Encirclement would have destroyed his forces and ultimately renewed the threat of a French invasion of Britain. As it was, Napoleon was so skilful in disguising his intentions – false information was spread, the French frontier sealed, and communications across northern France restricted – that his 70,000-strong army reached the Belgian border in early June before the allies were really aware that it had left Paris. Now the question was which direction it would take: if westwards through the southern Belgian town of Mons, then Napoleon would be intending the encircling strategy; if eastwards through Charleroi, then he would be heading for the gap. Since both towns are less than thirty miles south of Brussels, even at the slow pace of early nineteenth-century armies there would be little time to manoeuvre to face the threat.

The forward line of Wellington's troops – unreliable and inexperienced Dutch and Belgian troops – were stationed near Mons; Blücher, raring for a fight – he was not known as Marschall Vorwärts (Marshal Forwards) for nothing – was concentrating north of Charleroi near the village of Ligny. The duke reckoned he could get his orders circulated to his commanders within six hours and his army into position within forty-eight, but that depended on good intelligence. Messages about the French deployment were taking up to ten hours to get back to Brussels. If Napoleon came through Charleroi, Wellington's strategy was to hold him at a crossroads called Quatre Bras about ten miles further north and six miles north-west of the Prussian army. It was directly on the road to Brussels, but the fall-back position was another eight or nine miles further north, still on an open plain just south of the village of Waterloo. He had made a note of the site some months before: it was open farmland on a slightly rising slope with a crest on the reverse side on which troops could gather – a good vantage from which to deploy the army.

Wellington was told that Napoleon had crossed the frontier on the afternoon of Thursday 15 June, but he and his staff still did not know quite where. The army was ordered to stand to in readiness but could not yet advance. A small group of French officers defected to Blücher's forces, but any intelligence they brought with them seems to have been slow to be passed on. In the circumstances, to avoid panic, the Duchess of Richmond's famous ball, immortalized by Lord Byron and later Thackeray in *Vanity Fair*, went ahead as planned in a former coach-builder's workshop – a barn-like room that was the most convenient space available that evening in Brussels. Wellington had reassured the duchess that she could give her ball 'with the greatest safety, without fear of interruption'. How far joy was unconfined that night, however, or whether a thousand hearts beat happily, is hard to know – Byron was not there* – but there probably was some frenetic excitement and apprehension about the battle everyone knew must be imminent. Later in the evening Wellington himself took a break from the laborious work of preparation and issuing instructions to drop by. Many of his officers were there too, so it was a convenient place to give orders. It was at the ball that he was told that Napoleon's troops had swept through Charleroi earlier in the day, and so the French direction finally became clear. Soon officers started clattering off into the night to prepare to march their troops at first light to cover the twenty miles to Quatre Bras, and Wellington asked his host, the Duke of Richmond, for a map.

* He was in London, worrying about the financial affairs of the Drury Lane Theatre whose board of management he had recently joined and arranging with his lawyer to draw up his will.

In later years the Iron Duke always insisted that he had not been taken by surprise, but his reported remarks as he pored over the map – 'Napoleon has humbugged me, by God. He has gained a 24 hours' march on me' – have a ring of likelihood about them. He then retired to his hotel to snatch a couple of hours' sleep before heading south himself.

By that stage Brussels was already waking up to the sound of clattering hooves, wagons and rattling gun-carriages, as parts of the army moved out down its cobbled streets. Wellington himself must have proceeded at a fast trot that morning, for he was at the crossroads by ten o'clock, probably in better shape than some of his officers who had gone there straight from the ball and would die that day still wearing their dancing pumps. On this Friday morning, even before the allied army had assembled, Napoleon had divided his forces. It must have been an act of supreme confidence – he did not rate Wellington or the British troops – but it also indicated that his plan to beat the allied armies in turn had been abandoned and he had decided to take on both at once. He turned the bulk of his forces towards the Prussians at Ligny while ordering Marshal Michel Ney to lead the remainder and force open the road to Brussels at Quatre Bras. Ney, however, had only just joined the army: he had arrived in a farm cart to join his old chief the day before and did not even have a horse, so he had not seen the lie of the land, nor had he been involved in planning the strategy, nor was he fully informed about it. Napoleon had relatively few of his former marshals available for the campaign. Nearly half of them had defected to the king or made themselves unavailable, and Alexandre Berthier, his long-serving chief of staff, had been frustrated in his attempt to join the emperor's campaign and had then died suddenly, falling out of an upstairs window a fortnight earlier. Had he been pushed or, less likely, committed suicide?

It did not matter: Napoleon had lost his most vital aide and his replacement, the bumbling Nicolas Soult, was no substitute.

Had Ney been able to attack at once that Friday morning at Quatre Bras, he would have won easily: he had more than 40,000 men against the 6,000 Dutch troops who were already there, with the British still rushing to join them. But, not realizing the numbers, he delayed the attack until mid-afternoon. In the meantime, Wellington had time to ride over towards Ligny to consult with Blücher, who was himself facing imminent attack from Napoleon. They promised to come to each other's aid in the coming battles, though in the event Wellington was not able to do so.

It was a sweltering hot afternoon as the armies finally clashed, increasingly close and humid until a thunderstorm drenched the troops in early evening. Some soldiers were driven nearly mad with thirst that afternoon, having had no time to fill their water bottles before their early march. Wellington himself was almost captured by French cavalry as he rode back towards Quatre Bras, and old Blücher was unhorsed and ridden over as his cavalry charged the French. The Prussian army was battered by artillery fire. Blücher did not believe in the Wellingtonian strategy of shielding his troops from cannon-fire on reverse slopes: 'My men like to see the enemy,' he explained. Wellington replied: 'If they fight here they will be damnably mauled', and he was right. The Prussians were also pummelled by cavalry charges and the steady advance of the crack troops of the Imperial Guard until they finally buckled and gave way as night fell.

There were four armies engaged that afternoon and the French had the better of it. They had inflicted heavy casualties, especially on the Prussians, who had lost 16,000 men, but had been mauled themselves and had not finally broken through to Brussels. At the much smaller battle at Quatre Bras, Ney had been too cautious in pressing his attack: unlike Napoleon, he had had experience of Wellington in the Peninsular War and may have overestimated the British strength. Crucially, too, the French first corps under General Jean-Baptiste d'Erlon had spent the afternoon trooping fruitlessly between the two battlefields without engaging at either: Napoleon had called for it to reinforce his attack at Ligny but then Ney had called it back to help at Quatre Bras. It might have made the difference in either battle, but played no part.

Wellington's army was able to retreat to the fall-back position in front of Waterloo, having sustained about 5,000 casualties. Ligny and Quartre Bras were major engagements – there were more British casualties in the latter than at Salamanca or Badajoz in Spain – but they would be overshadowed by the battle two days later. Blücher's Prussians also fell back, but they did so, crucially, not eastwards away from the British army as Napoleon had expected and hoped, but north to the village of Wavre, east of Brussels, which meant they were still in touch. This was Gneisenau's doing, as the elderly Blücher was still being patched up, but if the Prussian deputy commander thought it was a first stage to disengaging their army from the British prior to moving east towards the German border, Blücher, once he had been found lying in a pile of straw in a cottage at Mellery, soon disabused him. The old general was determined to keep in contact with Wellington and not abandon the joint effort, even though Gneisenau and other officers believed they had been let down that day. Wavre was only seven miles from Waterloo across undulating country and farm tracks, and from there the two armies could come together against the French. The duke later described the Prussian decision as the decisive moment of the century. Had the Prussians headed back towards their homeland, Napoleon would have won.

The Prussians were bitter for many years that they had not been assisted by Wellington at Ligny, believing he had broken his word about coming to their aid – the controversy still splutters occasionally among German historians – but both armies were hard pressed that day. Wellington had only promised them that he would send help to the Prussians if he was not being attacked himself. But he was. Importantly, the allies had buckled but not broken: the British and the Prussians were still in touch and the French had not got between them – they lived to fight another day. 'Old Blücher's had a damned good licking,' said Wellington on receiving news of the battle. 'As he has gone back we must go back too. I suppose in England they will say we've been licked. Well, I can't help it.'

Had the fighting resumed immediately the following day, the outcome might still have been different, but both Ney and Napoleon appeared exhausted and lassitudinous, and they were slow to issue orders or follow up either the Prussians or the Anglo-Dutch army, which were both able to fall back largely unmolested. During the retreat the Prussians lost 9,000 Rhineland troops, who abandoned them and fled, and it may have been the sight of these men in the distance leaving eastwards that convinced the emperor that the whole Prussian army had disintegrated. Napoleon accordingly decided to turn his main attention to Wellington's army, but detached 30,000 troops under Marshal Emmanuel de Grouchy to harry the Prussians and keep them away. He demanded that Ney should resume the attack at Quatre Bras, but by the time the marshal got round to doing so, Wellington was gone. Napoleon was by now furious with his subordinates, particularly Ney, to whom he stormed: 'France is lost.' More heavy rain slowed the French advance as they came close to the English rearguard – so close that the British artillery officer Captain Cavalié Mercer caught a glimpse of the great Napoleon himself, sitting on his white horse, caught in a shaft of sunshine on the crest of a hill, staring at the retreating allied army. Then the storm broke, the pursuit became bogged down and the day was lost. Wellington was even able to take lunch at a tavern in Genappe on the way to Waterloo. Ney was not the man he used to be, Napoleon complained later – but that weekend, neither was he. The emperor was slow and distracted: maybe suffering from the debilitating effects of piles, or possibly gall-stones, or a pituitary disorder. Eight miles further north, the Anglo-Dutch army was now positioned behind the ridge at Mont-Saint-Jean, south of Waterloo. Furthermore, and again crucially, they had occupied two strategically placed farmhouses in front of their line: ancient, thick-walled Belgian farmsteads with courtyards – Hougoumont on the far right of the line and La Haye Sainte in the centre. Both these would hold up the French attacks all through the following day's battle.

That night the duke was accosted by the Earl of Uxbridge at his quarters in the village of Waterloo to ask what his plans for the battle were. If Wellington had been incapacitated the following day, Uxbridge, in charge of the cavalry, would have taken over command, so he needed some idea, but the duke was not going to give him any. Was this again a slight residue of the divorce action a few years earlier when Uxbridge – then Paget – had eloped with Wellington's sister-in-law? Or was it simply that the duke was habitually used to keeping his cards close to his chest? Wellington asked who he thought would attack first in the morning. Bonaparte, Uxbridge replied. 'Well, Bonaparte has not given me any idea of his projects,' snapped the duke, 'and as my plans depend on his, how can you expect me to tell you what mine are?' For the allies it would be a defensive battle. Then, more gently he added: 'There is one thing certain, Uxbridge: that is that whatever happens, you and I will do our duty.'

At some point during the night Wellington received assurances that the Prussians would come to the aid of the British, for Blücher had overruled Gneisenau, who was still not sure that the perfidious 'master knave', as he called Wellington, would stand and fight. Outside the duke's headquarters the rain poured down throughout the night, soaking the troops on both sides, making the farmland on which they were to fight boggy, and delaying the start of the battle the following morning. 'It would be impossible for anyone to form any opinion of what we endured this night,' wrote Sergeant William Wheeler of the 51st Regiment in a letter a day or two after the battle. The gin they had bought with money dropped by a fleeing Belgian helped him and his colleagues a bit, but:

> being close to the enemy we could not use our blankets, the ground was too wet to lie down, we sat on our knapsacks until daylight without fires, there was no shelter against the weather: the water ran in streams from the cuffs of our jackets, in short we were as wet as if we had been plunged over head in a river. We had one consolation, we knew the enemy were in the same plight. The morning... broke upon us and found us drenched with rain, benumbed and shaking with the cold... if I had not had a good stock of tobacco this night I must have given up the ghost.

The battle of Waterloo on Sunday 18 June 1815 has probably been more written about – analysed, debated, imagined, re-imagined, rhapsodized, criticized and pored over – than any other single day's conflict in history. It was a battle as devastating as it was decisive: a single, agonizingly intense day, which changed the course of European history for decades to come. Before it, Europe had been at war almost continuously for twenty-five years; after it, the nations

of the continent were at peace for half a century. We know minute
by minute how the action developed and, perhaps more than any
battle before and most since, how the men who took part felt about
it. Many of the survivors wrote their memoirs or told their tales later
to their families, or to journalists, or to ghostwriters. It was the most
vivid and memorable day of their lives and, however long they lived,
they could not forget it: what it was like to be there, what it sounded
like and what they saw. The battle shut off all arguments about
whether it should have been fought at all, about rights and wrongs
and whys and wherefores: Napoleon was beaten now and forever
and that was an end of his great adventure. He would never be able
to come again. The Duke of Wellington ensured that those who had
fought with him that day should all receive a medal – the first time
such a recognition of a single day's fighting had ever happened – and
most of them wore theirs for the rest of their lives. For the next four
decades, the ageing duke kept a sovereign in his pocket to give to any
veteran soldier he saw wearing the medal. Officers and men formed
a band of brothers. All this was in the knowledge that the outcome
could have been very different if other things had gone only slightly
differently – if it had not rained overnight, if Napoleon had not
delayed his attack, if Hougoumont and Mont-Saint-Jean had fallen,
if the British infantry squares had broken, above all, if the Prussians
had not turned up to swing the battle. It was, as the duke famously
said afterwards, a close-run thing and indeed his aphorisms form a
running descant to the day.*

Wellington himself was up by 3.00 a.m. at his lodgings in Waterloo,
writing instructions and letters; one was to his young friend Lady

---

* In Sergei Bondarchuk's epic *Waterloo*, filmed in the Ukraine in 1969, a smirking
Christopher Plummer playing the duke says virtually nothing else.

Wedderburn-Webster in Brussels, promising to give her the earliest information of any danger: 'at present I know of none'. By 7.00 he was dressed, in blue frock-coat, white breeches, a black cocked hat, and a short blue cloak which he would put on and take off repeatedly through the day as showers gusted across the battlefield. As he rode out of the village on his horse Copenhagen, accompanied by his staff officers, he was spotted by Ensign Gronow, the dandified Welsh Guards officer, who said that the cavalcade came on at high speed, all 'as gay and unconcerned as if they were riding to meet the hounds in some quiet English county'. The entourage was heading out to inspect the battlefield and the deployment of the sodden and mud-covered troops, from right to left, starting at Hougoumont, where the duke ordered extra loopholes to be made in the walls surrounding the farm's orchard, right across the front of the line, two-and-a-half miles away, to inspect the Dutch cavalry. By 11.00 a.m. he was back at the centre of the line, still giving instructions and exuding calm confidence.

This contrasted with Napoleon, who rose later and disdained the concerns of his generals who had actually fought the British before, as he had not. He was impatient and brusque. There were ninety chances in their favour and not ten against, he told them. When his brother Jérôme told him that a waiter at the inn in Genappe where Wellington had had lunch the day before had reported that English officers had been talking about the Prussians joining forces with them, the emperor dismissed it as nonsense. It would be impossible for at least two days, he said. Instead of recalling de Grouchy and his 30,000 troops from their pursuit of the Prussians, Napoleon ordered them to keep on their trail. The British were bad troops, he told his generals, and Wellington was a bad general – it would be a picnic: 'Ach, those English – now I've got them.' He rode out to parade on his white horse along the front of the French line to inspire his troops' confidence and was greeted with cheering and shouts of *'Vive l'empereur!'* It must have been a considerable spectacle for the British, Dutch and Belgian troops watching from the slope opposite: one of the last occasions on European soil when both sides went into combat wearing an array of bright uniforms – red, grey and green, blue and white; black bearskins and gold braid; standards and regimental colours waving and the sun coming out to reflect off breastplates and scabbards. All this was accompanied by the cheers of men, the hoarse shouted orders of officers and sergeants, drum-beats, fifes and pipes, beating out the *pas de charge* on the French side, the wail of bagpipes rising from the Scottish regiments on the British. All day long, for hour after hour, there would be the deafening roar of the guns too: 'so loud and continuous that you could hardly hear what was said by the person next to you', according to a surgeon of the 15th Hussars. Private Charles O'Neil of the 28th Regiment wrote in his memoirs years later: 'The continued reverberations of pieces of artillery, the fire of the light troops, the frequent explosions of caissons blown up by shells, the hissing of balls, the clash of arms, the roar of the charges, and the shouts of the soldiery, produced a commingling of sounds whose effect it would be impossible to describe.'

Even by the standards of the time, despite the open fields of corn and rye, this was a claustrophobically small battlefield: barely three square miles with nearly 150,000 men engaged and more than 400 cannon deployed – 246 on the French side, 156 for the allies. Soon their smoke would obscure the field, like a London fog, causing some to remember the battle taking place in semi-darkness. Europe was going to war in the old style one last time.

Before the guns opened up, a watery sun was coming out, but instead of opening fire immediately, it took the French artillery until late morning to begin the assault. Was it because the mud made their cannon unmanoeuvrable, or because Napoleon was so confident of victory and so relaxed about the unlikelihood of the Prussians being able to regroup and return? The delay may have cost him victory. Even though some of the Nassau troops ran away and the Belgians declined to follow the English and lie down to form a smaller target, the opening barrage was heavy but ineffectual. It must, however, have been terrifyingly noisy: a great deafening ripple of crashes and roars from the enemy guns and then the reply from the allied side – in Sergeant Wheeler's words, 'dupping [sic] about like hail... devilish annoying'. Facing such a cannonade and canister required steady nerves: the balls bounced erratically across the ground and could be seen coming, but even though slowed down they were red-hot and could still bowl through a phalanx of men, taking heads and limbs with them. But the ground was very soft following the rain and the cannon-balls tended to sink rather than bounce or skim.

The French infantry were sent against Hougoumont first and were repulsed by the Scots and Coldstream Guards units inside the farm, as they would be throughout the day. The farm compound stood halfway between the British and French lines, in front of the allied army's right flank. The French needed to capture it in order to open up the battlefield, but also in the hope that Wellington would have to weaken the centre of his line to reinforce it. The sturdiness of the defence, however, meant that he did not have to do so. By contrast, the French had to devote increasing numbers of men in a series of vain attempts to seize it. The fighting around the farmhouse and its courtyard was ferocious all day: guardsmen firing through the loopholes they had made in the walls and from the windows of the building and French troops lapping around the outside looking for a way in. They initially found one surprisingly easily: the double doors of the main gate had been left open and a number of French troops poured through, but by a huge effort nine guardsmen, led by their enormous commander Lieutenant Colonel James Macdonnell ('You don't know Macdonnell,' the duke had said when his decision to put him in charge had been queried), managed to close the entrance and bar the gates. Had they failed, Hougoumont would have been lost and the army's right flank exposed. The success of Waterloo depended on the closing of the gates, the duke said later. As it was, every French soldier who had got inside was killed, except for an unarmed fourteen-year-old drummer boy.

Now, with fighting still continuing around the farmhouse, further across the field the battle entered its second phase as Napoleon ordered the 16,000 men of d'Erlon's corps forward to smash against the centre of the allied line – d'Erlon's troops, making up a quarter of Napoleon's army, being the ones who had trudged back and forth between Ligny and Quatre Bras two days before. Their attack, made in huge, parallel, tightly packed columns of men, took them more than a thousand yards across open ground, slithering through the muddy fields, trampling chest-high ripening corn and up the slope remorselessly towards the allied army. The crops at the start of the battle were high enough to disguise the French attacks: they got within forty feet of the allied line at one point before being spotted. As the day went on, however, the crops were trampled down until they were 'the consistency of an Indian mat', as one officer wrote later. Now, as d'Erlon's columns came on, one of the columns diverted to attack the farm at La Haye Sainte – which the French did not, however, capture at this time, thanks to the firepower of the German Legion troops inside its walls. The other columns withstood heavy fire as they plodded onwards. A Dutch-Belgian brigade broke and ran in front of them, but then the French soldiers were hit by a volley fired at a hundred yards' range by British troops of Sir Thomas Picton's division. Picton was a grizzled, irascible Welsh career soldier in his mid-fifties: Wellington called him 'a rough, foul-mouthed devil'. He had not wanted to take part in the campaign at all and had in fact broken two ribs at Quatre Bras, though he had not told anyone. Leading his men, wearing a civilian coat and a top hat because his uniform had not arrived, Picton was swearing and shouting at them to charge the French when he received a bullet between the eyes – there is some suggestion that he was the victim of friendly fire or even a bullet fired deliberately by his own men – and toppled off his horse as they charged past him. The general was the most senior British officer to die in the battle.

Three Highland regiments surged into the attack on d'Erlon's massed columns, and then the Scots Greys, Royals and Inniskilling Dragoons and the Household Cavalry – Life Guards and Horse Guards – slammed down the battlefield, scattering the French infantry and swamping the cuirassiers' cavalry beyond them. They struck the French breastplates with their swords, it was said, like the noise of a thousand coppersmiths. The cavalry were swept up in a wave of excitement and exhilaration as they stormed through the French troops. They swept down the hill, across the sunken, hedge-lined track which crossed the battlefield, on into the French lines far beyond, ignoring or not hearing the bugle calls summoning them to stop and return. 'I felt a strange thrill run through me,' wrote Corporal Dickson of the Scots Greys, and so did his horse Rattler. 'I am sure my noble beast felt the same, for, after rearing a moment, she sprang forward, uttering loud neighing and snorting and leapt over the holly hedge at a terrific speed.' They hacked and carved their way through: Life Guardsman Shaw cleaving a skull so that the man's face 'fell off like a bit of apple'; Sergeant Charles Ewart carving two men down to the chin with his sabre. Watching from his vantage point behind the

French troops, even Napoleon was impressed: 'Those terrible grey horses,' he murmured, 'how they fight.' Two French eagle-topped standards were captured in the onward rush. 'On to Paris!' someone shouted. And then they found themselves surrounded by fresh French lancers and cuirassiers, circling, prodding and carving at them as they struggled to regroup. Wellington's cavalry had been undermined by its own impetuosity and inexperience, and nearly half – more than 1,000 out of 2,500 horsemen – did not make it back to their own lines. The duke must have been exasperated. It was what he always feared would happen with cavalry: running away with themselves, led by Uxbridge, the man who had run away with his sister-in-law. They had crushed the French infantry attack, but at a terrible cost.

By now it was about 3.00 p.m. and the French had neither broken through nor captured either of the farmhouse strongholds in front of the British position. Hougoumont was in flames, set alight by howitzer shells. The wounded of both sides, who had been laid down in the farm barn, burned to death where they lay or were smothered by smoke. Wellington sent a message ordering the defenders to hang on as long as possible. On the far side of the battlefield, however, there were now more encouraging signs: the first Prussian troops were starting to appear in the distance.

All this time the British and Brunswicker infantry in the centre of the allied line were coming under sustained French artillery bombardment, heavy and ferocious, in a bid to break them. The cannon were beginning to tell, swathes now being cut into the line which had edged forward in the combat onto the down slope. The firing was intense and inescapable: 'We had nothing like this in Spain, sir,' one veteran gasped to his officer. 'Never had the oldest soldiers heard such a cannonade,' wrote General Charles Alten, commander of the King's German Legion. The Irish troops of the 27th Regiment, the

Inniskillings, who had only arrived that morning after an arduous day without rest or food covering the allied retreat from Quatre Bras, had spent the first few hours of the battle resting behind the lines. They were now in place in the centre of the allied position and were particularly badly hit, by artillery fire and the musketry sniping of French skirmishers lurking in the standing corn between the lines. They waited stoically in position all the rest of the afternoon and by the end of the day had lost 450 men killed and wounded out of 750, with only one officer of eighteen unhurt. Even lying flat on the ground, faces in the mud, did not stop casualties.

In the distance, through the smoke, it seems the French commanders started to see men being helped back up the ridge. They thought the British were done for, as had happened so often in Napoleon's battles against European troops in the past. They believed that they were on the verge of breaking the allied line and smashing through. Now was the time to attack. Within a few minutes the allied troops, who in fact were still standing stolidly, could see the French cavalry massing in the distance, ready to charge. The allied artillery was ranged along the front a few yards ahead of the infantry and they awaited their moment. Then Ney – or someone else, for it has never been established quite who – launched the first of what became a series of increasingly desperate massed French cavalry charges against the centre of the allied infantry line.

The attack started with an advance on La Haye Sainte, the farmhouse situated in front of the centre of the allied lines. Once that citadel cracked, the whole of the Anglo-Dutch centre would be vulnerable: it could be raked with fire from behind the farmhouse walls and attacks would be launched from the cover of the farm, which would no longer form a bottleneck, obstructing the thrust of the French advance. How much of a bottleneck was clear as the cavalry charged past, for over the course of the next three hours approximately 10,000 horsemen – eighty squadrons – and forty horse-artillery teams had to squeeze, one after another, through the 1,000-yard gap between the farm and the burning Hougoumont in the distance. It was ground that was getting progressively more churned, waterlogged and congested, covered with wounded, dead and dying men and horses. To start with, just as had happened an hour before to the British cavalry, the French cuirassiers, then the lancers and dragoons, sensing an advance was imminent, grew restive and excited, edging forward, their horses pawing the ground. It may even have been, as the historian Andrew Roberts suggests, that the general, impatient shuffling forward developed into a charge almost of its own volition. Exhilarated, even laughing, assured that the British were in retreat and could be caught on the run, they were therefore knocked back to be hit at short range with a round of grapeshot and canister from the cannon just in front of the British lines. A few moments later they discovered that the redcoats and the black-uniformed Brunswickers had formed infantry squares. After the initial fire, the cannon had been temporarily deserted as the artillery men took cover in the squares, and the attacking cavalry were then struck by successive volleys of musket-fire. They had been misinformed. There was no retreat. It must have come as a shock in their last seconds before the buffeting blows of shot and musket-ball struck them like a punch, winding them and lacerating their bodies and those of their horses. The remaining French cavalry surged onwards, lapping around the massed ranks of the British infantry with their bristling bayonets, seeking a way in, or a way through the squares. But there was none.

Every time the cavalry wheeled away, the French cannon bombardment started again and the British artillery men, who had raced from their guns inside the nearest square, rushed out to fire back. The infantry square was vulnerable to cannon-fire but almost impregnable to cavalry unless a gap opened up.* Horses would not charge directly against men, especially, as here, where the front ranks were kneeling, their muskets pointing upward from the ground to form a wall of spikes. Drawn up in two or three ranks, firing volleys – one rank firing, then reloading, while the next rank fired over their heads – the infantry produced formidable firepower over short ranges, and with the French so close, a few yards distant, the muskets did not have to be accurate to cause carnage. The heavy musket round shot might not be able to hit a designated target above ten or twenty yards, but it could punch a hole through a steel breastplate. Facing packed ranks of charging horsemen required steadiness and courage in troops who were mainly enduring their first battle that day. But they were given courage and confidence by the square formation, surrounded and sustained by colleagues and friends and with men behind guarding their backs. In the middle of the square stood the officers and the standard-bearers, maybe a chaplain and a medical orderly, and the drummer boys to pass round the ammunition and water. Into the square, too, were carried the wounded and the dying, the beaten earth becoming slithery with blood. The noise and the cries and the stench of gunpowder must have been nearly overwhelming, had it not been for the remorselessness of the French attacks. Soon every face was blackened with the discharge of powder from the muskets. Captain Gronow, who was inside one of the Guards' regimental squares, wrote later in his memoirs:

---

* 'Square' is a slight misnomer since it might be and often was a somewhat different shape: oblong, or even triangular, but always with the same principle of troops facing outwards, their backs covered behind them. Private Charles O'Neil wrote that the squares were not quite solid, but several ranks deep, 'arranged like the squares of a chessboard; so that if any of the enemy's cavalry should push between the divisions they could be attacked in the rear as well as in the front'.

Our squares presented a shocking sight. Inside we were nearly suffocated by the smoke and smell from burnt cartridges. It was impossible to move a yard without treading on a wounded comrade, or upon the bodies of the dead; and the loud groans of the wounded and dying were most appalling. At four o'clock our square was a perfect hospital, being full of dead, dying and mutilated soldiers. The charges of cavalry were in appearance very formidable, but in reality a great relief, as the artillery could no longer fire on us; the very earth shook under the enormous mass of men and horses. I shall never forget the strange noise our bullets made against the breastplates of Kellermann's and Milhaud's cuirassiers, six or seven thousand in number, who attacked us with great fury. I can only compare it with a some-what homely simile, to the noise of a violent hailstorm beating upon panes of glass.

The artillery did great execution, but our musketry did not at first seem to kill many men, though it brought down a large number of horses and created indescribable confusion. The horse of the first rank of cuirassiers, in spite of all the efforts of their riders, came to a standstill, shaking and covered with foam, at about twenty yards distance from our squares and generally resisted all attempts to force them to charge the ranks of serried steel… In the middle of our terrible fire, their officers were seen as if on parade, keeping order in their ranks and encouraging them. Unable to renew the charge but unwilling to retreat, they brandished their swords with loud cries of '*Vive l'empereur!*' and allowed themselves to be mowed down by hundreds rather than yield. Our men, who shot them down, could not help admiring the gallant bearing and heroic resignation of their enemies.

The French cavalry regrouped and charged again and again, maybe fourteen times in all – people lost count – over the course of the next three hours, until the survivors and their horses were blown and could no longer falter forward through the mud. The charges did not work: the squares did not cave in and the French neglected either to launch the infantry with the cavalry, or, seemingly, to attempt to spike the cannon while they circled the squares. The British artillery teams emerged from inside the formations each time the French horses retreated and started firing again until the next attack.

Throughout the afternoon the Duke of Wellington, seated on Copenhagen, was traversing the allied lines with his staff, issuing orders, exhorting and praising the troops, seemingly missing very little, keeping an eye on Hougoumont, now well ablaze, and anxious for the arrival of the Prussians, who were starting to pour onto the eastern end of the battlefield, overrunning the French-held village of Plancenoit, then losing it to a counterattack, then winning it back again. Occasionally during the French charges he took refuge in an infantry square, at other times he could be seen near a battered elm tree close to the centre of the British line. He was lucky to survive the day unharmed. Several of his staff were killed or wounded beside him: Lord Fitzroy Somerset's right arm was hit by a bullet while he was touching the duke with his other arm, and Wellington's American-born friend Colonel Sir William De Lancey, the army's deputy quartermaster, was talking to the duke when he was struck in the back by a ricocheting cannon-ball and flung many yards over his horse's head.* Wellington was running so short of aides that twice he commandeered civilians who had been watching the battle to carry

* Somerset survived the amputation of his arm – he called for the limb to be brought back after it was hacked off so that he could retrieve his wedding ring – to become (as Lord Raglan) a notably inept British army commander in the Crimean War forty

messages for him. One, a London commercial traveller, had allegedly chosen a quiet moment to ask whether he had any orders for his firm – clearly no time like the present – only to be told: 'No; but will you do me a service? Go to that officer and tell him to refuse a flank…'

Wellington was contemptuous of Napoleon's tactics as charge after charge was repulsed, almost as if professionally he had expected something more imaginative: 'Damn the fellow,' he said to one of his colleagues. 'He is a mere pounder after all.' He raised morale by his presence even when his message was uncompromising. Taking refuge in the square of the 73rd Regiment during one charge, Wellington asked General Sir Colin Halkett how he was getting on. Halkett replied: 'My Lord we are dreadfully cut up. Can you not relieve us for a little while?' The duke replied: 'Impossible.' 'Very well, my Lord, we'll stand until the last man falls.' He nevertheless shored up Halkett's battered infantry square by moving an adjacent Guards regiment closer. At one point the duke asked his aide-de-camp the time and, told it was twenty minutes past four, replied: 'The battle is mine and if the Prussians arrive soon, there will be an end of the war.'

At last, sometime about 6.00 p.m., the French launched a combined cavalry and infantry attack, again marching in columns through the debris-strewn cornfields into what one of their generals described as a hail of death. Now, too, they made a renewed effort to capture the farm of La Haye Sainte in the centre of the battlefield. The defenders, of the King's German Legion, had resisted all day, but armed with rifles rather than muskets, they were fast running out of ammunition and had not been resupplied. Finally the French broke into the farmyard and the German troops tried to fend them off with

---

years later, somewhat confused to be allied at last to the French. De Lancey died of his internal injuries eleven days after the battle.

bayonets. At about 6.30 the farmhouse was finally captured; the 376 troops who had manned it at the start of the day were reduced to just forty-one by the time it fell. At last the centre of the allied line was open to a full French assault. It was the crisis point of the battle for the allies. Ney sent forward a swarm of skirmishers and sharpshooters who could not be cleared because there was no British heavy cavalry left to charge them down. The exhausted troops began to crumble and Wellington was forced to make repeated appeals for the line to remain steady. The Prussians were not yet in position: night or they must come, he said. Under the pressure of the bombardment, five battalions of inexperienced Brunswickers started to give way. Near the battlefield the oncoming Prussians paused, believing the allied line was retreating, only, fortuitously, to be urged forward by Baron von Müffling, the duke's Prussian liaison officer, who galloped across shouting that they must come to the rescue at once. All the allied reserves that were still available to fight were now deployed to hold the line. One French push might have forced the allied front to cave in and Napoleon still held the veterans of the Imperial Guard in reserve. They had always been used to seal his victories at the end of a battle. Now he declined to use them to press home the advantage immediately. At this moment Napoleon contemptuously turned down Ney's anguished appeal for reinforcements to renew the attack. 'Troops? Where do you expect me to find them? Do you expect me to make them?' Elizabeth Longford says that, with these words, Napoleon threw away his chance of victory.

Instead of pushing forward, the French paused, allowing the allied line to stabilize. And then, finally, at about seven o'clock the 6,500 men of the Imperial Guard were led forward to La Haye Sainte by the emperor himself, mounted on his white horse. With shouts once more of 'Vive l'empereur!' they began to move steadily and remorse-lessly across the battlefield to the beat of drums. Napoleon stopped at the farm and Ney took over command for the last few hundred yards, during which his fifth horse of the day was shot from under him, leaving him to stagger forward on foot in his tall cavalry boots. Up the slope the Guard came: two long, formidable columns, eighty men wide, in full ceremonial dress – high bearskins, blue uniforms. 'We saw the bearskin caps rising higher and higher as they ascended the ridge… and advanced nearer and nearer to our lines,' wrote Captain Gronow. As cannon-fire and canister-shot raked their ranks, they closed up and still came on. In front of them, lying down behind the crest, was the first brigade of Foot Guards, with Wellington behind them, watching for the moment. At sixty yards' range he shouted to the Guards' commander: 'Now Maitland. Now's your time!' They stood up and for the first time the Imperial Guard faltered in surprise. Lieutenant Captain Harry Weyland Powell wrote:

> Whether it was from the sudden and unexpected appearance of a Corps so near them which must have seemed like starting out of the ground, or the tremendously heavy fire we threw into them, La Garde, who had never before failed in an attack, suddenly stopped… the effect of our fire seemed to force the head of the column bodily back.

The British front rank's first volley knocked over 300 men at about thirty yards, then came the second volley. The French were so tightly packed that they could not get out of the way and suddenly they were retreating. Now they were being hit by volleys from the 52nd Regiment opposite their line as they fell back. The French chas-seurs accompanying the Imperial Guard also faltered and suddenly the British and Dutch troops were among them, charging with their bayonets and driving the retreat into a rout. Gronow wrote:

> It appeared that our men, deliberately and with calculation, singled out their victims; for as they came upon the Imperial Guard our line broke and the fighting became irregular. The impetuosity of our men seemed almost to paralyse their enemies: I witnessed several of the Imperial Guard who were run through the body apparently without any resistance on their parts. I observed a big Welshman of the name of Hughes, who was six feet seven inches in height, run through with his bayonet and knock down with the butt-end of his firelock, I should think a dozen at least… This terrible contest did not last more than ten minutes, for the Imperial Guard was soon in full retreat, leaving all their guns and many prisoners in our hands.

There was no pause here as the French had had a few minutes before as Wellington urged his troops forward: 'Well done! Go on. Go on. Don't give them time to rally – they won't stand.' Now the Prussians too were pouring onto the east side of the battlefield. 'Oh damn it! In for a penny, in for a pound,' the duke is said to have exclaimed, and waving his hat three times towards the French, he ordered the army into the attack. With whoops and cheers of relief they moved forward and the French crumbled before them. The shock of the Imperial Guard's retreat – the shout went up, *'La Garde recule!'* – demoralized the troops behind them. Napoleon himself tried to rally the survivors into forming squares, but now the allied artillery was up and at sixty yards' range poured more shot remorselessly into their ranks. Did General Pierre Cambronne shout *'merde!'* when called upon to surrender? He denied it later, having survived the onslaught, but now even the Imperial Guard was in full flight. Napoleon himself had to abandon his carriage, leaving behind his solid gold travelling case, leather bottles full of rum and Malaga, a million francs' worth of diamonds and a cake of Windsor soap. The carriage would eventually be bought by Madame Tussaud's waxworks. Within days he would abdicate and soon after would surrender finally to the British.

After his twilight meeting with Blücher in the blood-soaked surroundings of the farmhouse at La Belle Alliance, south of the battlefield, which had been Napoleon's headquarters throughout the day, the Duke of Wellington headed slowly back across the fields to his lodgings in Waterloo. The pursuit of the French was left to the Prussians, whose lancers bore down on the retreating enemy, spearing them as they fled. The British and Dutch troops were exhausted after the nine hours' battle, and many lay down among the piles of dead and dying to get some sleep. Wellington arrived back in Waterloo at about 11.00 p.m., gave his horse Copenhagen a consoling pat on its hindquarters – and nearly received a kick from the exhausted animal for doing so. He fell asleep on a camp-bed because his aide-de-camp Alexander Gordon was dying in the duke's own bed after having his leg amputated.

Four hours later, at three o'clock the following morning, the duke was woken by a doctor bringing him the casualty list, including the names of many of his staff. He burst into tears and uttered the famous phrase that next to a battle lost, the greatest misery was a battle won. Several variations were quoted later as Wellington tended to recycle his bon mots. Then he had a cup of tea and some toast and sat down to start composing his dispatch to the war minister Lord Bathurst. It is a remarkable document in the circumstances, precisely and for the most part accurately detailing, from memory, the tumultuous events of the previous four days. Nevertheless, it was controversial, as parts of the battle seemed to be downplayed and some of the heroism undervalued. Wellington paid due respect to Blücher and the Prussians: 'I should not do justice to my feelings... if I did not attribute the successful result of this arduous day to the cordial and timely assistance I received from them' – timely assistance rather than vital contribution; but this was the start of a rather consistent downgrading of the role played by foreign troops in the allied army. The duke's wounded and dead officers were much in his mind as he wrote and, detailed by name, they form a core part of the narrative. In later years Wellington conceded that he should have given more praise, but dressed as he was in his battle-stained uniform and not having had a chance even to wash following the fighting, he managed to write what is for the most part (as one of the British troops later said) a dispatch of 'noble simplicity, perfect calmness and exemplary modesty'.

Later that day, back in Brussels, the duke saw Thomas Creevey and gave him a brief account of the battle, containing some of his most famous aphorisms, which the politician noted down. Creevey and his family and the rest of the expatriate community in the city had had merely fragmentary accounts of what had happened only twelve miles to the south on the previous day and were still not aware of the extent of the victory. 'It has been a damned serious business,' the duke told him. 'Blücher and I have lost 30,000 men.* It has been a damned nice thing – the nearest run thing you ever saw in your life.' Then finally he burst out, 'By God! I don't think it would have done if I had not been there.'

The first news of the battle reached London two days later, on the following Tuesday. It came from a messenger taking the tidings

---

* An understandable overestimate: the true figure was nearer 23,000.

specifically to the financier Nathan Rothschild, whose command of the news meant the family was in the know in advance of everyone else in the City, and was able to make some profit – or at least recoup costs – by manipulating shares which plunged on the uncertainty of the battle's outcome. Rothschild was said to have put on an especially gloomy face at the Exchange to give the impression that there was bad news. The message was anyway confused, but the man was then sent on to the government. When questioned by John Croker, the secretary to the Admiralty, there seemed to be some doubt about what he was saying and the prime minister Lord Liverpool initially refused to believe it. Finally Croker asked the messenger how the French king Louis XVIII had received the news at his exile in Ghent: 'His Majesty embraced me and kissed me!' the man replied. Still cautious, Croker demanded: 'How did the King kiss you?' 'On both cheeks,' he was told. That seemed authentic enough. 'My Lord, it is true,' Croker told Liverpool. The government nevertheless did not publicize the news.

Official confirmation came a day later on the Wednesday evening as a blood and dust-stained Major Harry Percy, one of Wellington's few aides-de-camp uninjured in the battle, arrived with the duke's dispatch. It had been an epic journey. Becalmed in the Channel, Percy had had to be rowed to the Kent coast, where he commandeered a carriage in Broadstairs. With the two captured French eagle standards fluttering out of the window, he had careered up to London, arriving in eight hours at eleven o'clock at night. The first stop was Downing Street, but the prime minister was not there, so he was directed on to Grosvenor Square, where the cabinet was having dinner at the home of Lord Harrowby, the Lord President of the Council. Percy announced the news with the cry 'Victory, Sir! Victory!' By now a crowd was gathering outside and Harrowby went to a window and read the dispatch to them. Now Percy clattered on to St James's Square, where the Prince Regent was attending a ball. The ladies were asked to leave the room while the casualty list was read out. The prince burst into tears: 'It is a glorious victory and we must rejoice in it,' he said. 'But the loss of life has been fearful and I have lost many friends.' The news was not altogether welcomed by a Mrs Boehm, the hostess of the party: 'All our trouble, anxiety and expense were utterly thrown away,' she wrote. 'I shall always think it would have been far better if Percy had waited quietly till the morning instead of bursting in on us as he did with such indecent haste.' Outside, as the news spread, the crowd started cheering. By morning the dispatch was in *The Times* and stagecoaches decorated with oak leaves were fanning out across the country bearing the news. But it would be many months before those at home could cheer the duke in person – he headed calmly back to Paris, resumed his ambassadorship and did not return to London for another year.

There was a considerable crowd of British civilians in Brussels during and after the battle. Some such as the Duchess of Richmond and Fanny Burney were accompanying their husbands; others, including the Creeveys, were there for the benefit of their health. Even though they were within twelve miles of the battlefield and must have been able to hear the cannon firing – and to see the wounded arriving back in the city – they could not be sure who had won until the following day. Some even fled northwards on hearing rumours that the French were at the gates. Thomas Creevey himself wandered towards the battle in the afternoon to see if he could find out what was happening: 'a curious busy scene it was,' he wrote, 'with every kind of thing upon the road, the Sunday population of Brussels being all out in the suburbs… sitting about tables drinking beer and smoking and making merry as if races or other sports were going on'. Later that evening his spirits were raised by seeing a line of French prisoners, but then he came across Thomas Legh, a young Tory MP who had been watching the battle and told him that everything was going as badly as possible – and that he was keeping his horses by the front door of his lodging so that he could escape if Napoleon won. Wounded British officers told him that the battle was lost, so Creevey returned home phlegmatically: 'With this intelligence I returned to Mrs Creevey and my daughters between 8 and 9, but I did not mention a word of what I had heard, there being no use in my doing so.'

It was not until the next morning when Creevey saw the duke – who was clearly quite happy to chat informally to a Whig MP – that he discovered the outcome of the battle. On the following day Creevey became one of the first civilians to visit the battlefield, where there were still piles of dead and wounded men lying in heaps:

It was a distressing sight, no doubt, to see every now and then a man alive amongst them and calling out to… give them something to drink. It was a curious thing to see on each occasion the moderation with which the soldier drank and his marked good manners. They all ended by saying… 'Mon général, vous êtes bien honnête'… I rode home with Hume, the physician at headquarters, who said there were 14,000 dead on the field and upon my expressing regret at the wounded people being still out, he replied: 'The two nights they have been out is all in their favour… they will have a better chance of escaping fever this hot weather than our own people, who have been carried into hospitals the first.'

The Radicals at Westminster were demoralized by Wellington's victory and they were about to lose their leader. As the military campaign reached its climax in June, Samuel Whitbread's weight had ballooned, he was suffering from blinding headaches and insomnia, and his mood was swinging between agitation and despondency. He told his daughter he hoped that he would have a fit of apoplexy – a stroke – and that it might take him off. He was becoming paranoid and worried obsessively about money problems because he had invested heavily in the Drury Lane Theatre, which was struggling financially following its rebuilding after the disastrous fire in 1809 (see page 124). In the Commons his speeches became rambling and incoherent. Then, on 6 July, a fortnight after the battle, he slit his throat. He was fifty-one. 'It is no slight homage to his character that at a moment when the grief of everybody seemed to be engrossed by some loss in the battle of Waterloo that his death should have made so deep and so general an impression,' wrote the Whig magnate Henry Holland to his colleague, the future prime minister Earl Grey. 'The truth is that with all his failings – and some he had – he was not only an able and honest, but a most useful public man.'

12

'Complete darkness covered the face of the day'

— COMMANDER OF THE EAST INDIA
COMPANY SHIP *BENARES*, 1815

Two months before the great battle of Waterloo, thousands of miles away in the Indonesian archipelago, a natural event occurred which had more profound and disastrous effects across the world, scientists now believe, than anything else that happened all year. On the evening of 5 April 1815 the inhabitants of Java, Bali, Lombok and the chain of Sunda Islands started to hear distant explosions that sounded like cannon-fire. The crackling sound could be heard in Batavia – modern Jakarta – nearly 800 miles away and people in Sumatra 1,800 miles off thought they were hearing gunfire. The noise was so extreme that at least in one place troops were mustered to defend the port from pirates, and in another boats were launched in case there was a ship in distress offshore. The sounds were not caused by human agency, however, nor even by divine intervention, as some inhabitants thought, but by what was the start of the largest volcanic eruption in the last 10,000 years. Mount Tambora on the island of Sumbawa was starting to blow its top off, and when the caldera finally collapsed five days later, it shot its summit nearly thirty miles into the atmosphere.

That we know as much as we do about what happened when Tambora erupted is almost solely due to Sir Thomas Stamford

Raffles. A great name in British imperial history, Raffles was the founder of Singapore, and was at that time serving as lieutenant governor of Java, which the British had seized from the French (who had taken over the island from its Dutch colonists after Napoleon occupied the Low Countries) four years earlier in 1811. Raffles heard the noise at his residence just south of Batavia at the far end of Java and commissioned reports of what was going on from local district officers and Royal Navy ships in the region. It is their contemporary eyewitness accounts, published in his memoirs, which form the core of our descriptive knowledge of the eruption. Raffles wrote:

> The first explosions were heard on this island… they were noticed in every quarter and continued at intervals until the following day. The noise was, in the first instance, almost universally attributed to distant cannon… On the following morning however a slight fall of ashes removed all doubt as to the cause of the sound; and it is worthy of remark that as the eruption continued, the sound appeared to be so close, that in each district it seemed near at hand… From the 6th, the sun became obscured; and it had every appearance of being enveloped in fog: the weather was sultry and the atmosphere close and still: the sun seemed shorn of its rays and the general stillness and pressure of the atmosphere foreboded an earthquake. This lasted several days, the explosion continued occasionally, but less violent and less frequently than at first. Volcanic ashes also began to fall but in small quantities and so slightly as to be hardly perceptible in the western districts.

This continued until 10 April, seemingly little different from previous eruptions in the region, but on that evening the explosions became louder and more frequent, as Raffles describes:

The air became darkened by the quantity of falling ashes… and many said they felt a tremulous motion of the earth… The explosions were tremendous, continuing frequently during the 11th and of such violence as to shake the houses perceptibly; an unusual thick darkness was remarked all the following night and the greater part of the next day. At Solo on the 12th at 4pm objects were not visible at 300 yards distance. At Gresie it was dark as night the greater part of the 12th April.*

Although no one would know of it in the west for months, the explosions created a natural disaster around the world. About 12,000 local people of the islands in the Flores and Bali Seas are thought to have died as a result of the initial eruption – smothered in ash and molten lava or drowned in the tsunami it caused – but perhaps another 60,000 around the world died of famine and disease as the cloud sent up by Tambora spread across the planet during the course of the coming two years. The resulting ash in the atmosphere, obscuring the sun, created what became known as the 'Year without a Summer' in 1816, when icy temperatures ruined harvests in Europe and North America, leading to food riots and migrations, caused floods in China, and provoked a new form of cholera to emerge in India which would eventually send waves of epidemics across the northern hemisphere for decades to come. It would take another century and a half for scientists and volcanologists to link Tambora's eruption to the Year without a Summer, but the consensus now is that that is what caused it.

As a measure of its scale, the explosion is thought to have been four times greater than that of Krakatoa, the volcano further along

---

* Solo is now known as Surakarta, a city about 300 miles east of Jakarta, so about 500 miles west of the volcano; Gresie, now Gresik, is about 400 miles away.

the chain of islands west of Java, which erupted in 1883. Krakatoa became known because by the time of its eruption the world could be speedily informed by telegraph, photographers could record the devastation, and there were more Europeans in the vicinity to record what they saw and what happened. It is estimated that there were about five million people living on the Indonesian islands in 1815; now there are more than 140 million, four million of them on the nearby tourist island of Bali, so if ever Tambora explodes again, the world will know of it in seconds, and tens of millions, rather than tens of thousands, will be affected. In 1815 Tambora ejected 100 times more ash than the eruption of Mount St Helens in the northwestern United States managed in 1980: perhaps as much as 24 cubic miles were shot into the air. Before the eruption started, Tambora was an estimated 14,100 feet high; by the time it finished a fortnight later, that had been reduced by a third and the mountain was (and is) 9,350 feet high. The ash buried Sumbawa three metres deep and covered other islands up to 800 miles away.

Even though there were few European witnesses in 1815, Raffles's correspondents, closer to the blast than he was, provided for him graphic first-hand accounts of the darkness that followed the eruption, the rain of ash and pumice, and the tsunami that inundated the surrounding islands. His agent in Gresie wrote:

I am universally told that no one remembers nor does their tradition record so tremendous an eruption. Some look upon it as typical of a change, of the re-establishment of the former government; others account for it in an easy way, by reference to the superstitious notions of their legendary tales and say that the celebrated Nyai Loroh Kidul has been marrying one of her children, on which occasion she has been firing salutes from her supernatural artillery. They call the ashes the dregs of her ammunition.

On the morning of 13 April, two days after the main eruption, the East India Company's cruiser *Benares* set sail from Macassar on Sulawesi island, about 300 miles north-east of Sumbawa, to investigate the noise. Its captain assumed that the noise of explosions must be coming from pirate ships, though it was loud enough – 'like three or four cannon fired together' – to shake his ship and rattle the nearby houses in the port. 'Some of them seemed so near that I sent people to the masthead to look out for the flashes.'

The unnamed captain submitted an extensive report to Raffles on his return, reprinted at length in the memoirs. As they set off:

the face of the heavens to the southward and westward had assumed a dark aspect and it was much darker than before the sun rose... The ashes now began to fall in showers and the appearance was altogether truly awful and alarming... complete darkness covered the face of the day... I never saw anything to equal it in the darkest night; it was impossible to see your hand when held up close to your eyes. The ashes fell without intermission and were so light and subtile [*sic*] that they pervaded every part of the ship.

By the morning pumice stone lay in heaps a foot deep on the deck. With the true instincts of a nineteenth-century explorer, he recorded:

Though an impalpable powder or dust when it fell, it was, when compressed, of considerable weight; a pint measure weighed twelve ounces and three-quarters: it was perfectly tasteless and

247

did not affect the eyes with painful sensation, had a faint burnt smell, but nothing like sulphur; when mixed with water it formed a tenacious mud difficult to be washed off.

The *Benares* reached Sumbawa on 18 April, a week after the main eruption, sailing through heaps of floating pumice. Offshore there was a three-mile-long floating bank of pumice, rocks, trees and logs that had been shivered from their trunks. The ship passed within six miles of the volcano, which was still shrouded in smoke. Incredibly, the crew found people alive about forty miles eastwards, including the Resident there, though the houses had been destroyed. Meanwhile, other British ships were on their way and Raffles dispatched a Lieutenant Owen Phillips to the island with a supply of rice – inadequate as it would turn out – for the survivors. He arrived on 23 April, a fortnight after the eruption, to find corpses still floating in the water and an epidemic and starvation among the survivors onshore: 'The extreme misery to which the inhabitants have been reduced is shocking to behold,' he wrote:

There were still on the roadside the remains of several corpses and the marks of where many others had been interred; the villages almost entirely deserted and the houses fallen down, the surviving inhabitants having dispersed in search of food. Since the eruption a violent diarrhoea has prevailed which has carried off a great number of people. The rajah of Saugar came to wait on me… The famine has been so severe that even one of his own daughters died from hunger.

The rajah told Phillips that the sea had risen twelve feet and flooded the rice fields, destroying the crop. The terrified local people endured four days of eruptions, and as the wind and ash died down, whole settlements were destroyed. Those who were left were trading horses and buffaloes for half a rupee's worth of rice or corn.

The ash cloud thrown up by the Mount Tambora eruption of 1815 spread across the northern hemisphere and the following year produced extraordinary weather patterns, which had striking and unforeseeable human effects. The Year without a Summer – 'Eighteen Hundred and Frozen to Death', as American farmers came to know it, or the 'Year of the Beggar' in Germany – turned out to be cold, wet and windy: the sun hidden behind lowering clouds, warmth not getting through to ripen the crops. There were strange events that people had never experienced before: snowfalls in mid-summer and hailstorms battering down the wheat harvest before it could be gathered in.

In England, where political and social stability meant there was a long history of meticulous daily recording of weather readings, amateur meteorologists put July 1816 down as the coldest in 192 years. They had noticed something strange in the sky as early as the autumn of 1815: 'Fair, dry day,' wrote Thomas Forster in Tunbridge Wells, 'at sunset a fine red blush marked by diverging red and blue bars.' *The Times* recorded the melancholy effects dispassionately, not as weather reports, however, but for their effects on agricultural prices. On 11 September 1816 it reported: 'Very little corn is yet reaped and that little is too green… without warmer weather and sunshine, it must prove a bad sample', and it quoted a farmer named Humphrey Harris, from Devon, who had said that the harvest was the worst and latest he had known in fifty-three years – a month or six weeks later than normal and the crop much diseased by canker. A few days later, on 16 September, snow was said to have fallen around Maidstone in Kent and the frost was so heavy that the ice had a thickness of a half-crown coin. At Buxton in the Derbyshire Peak District the hills were already covered in snow in the second week of September and the paper said: 'Even in the South the severity of the weather has been beyond all former experience.'

On 10 October the paper remarked: 'Corn dealers are now raising the price of corn rapidly on the ground of the badness of the harvest so they will probably make the bad harvest answer better to themselves than a good one.' In a period when most people lived much closer to subsistence and hunger than their descendants, shortages and price rises could have a devastating effect: they were not the only cause of the post-war discontent and political agitation, but they were certainly one of them and not just for the peasantry – impoverishment had a knock-on effect. John Tuke, a land agent in East Yorkshire, was reported as saying as much at the end of September that year, just as the quarterly rents were falling due and the Michaelmas hiring fairs were approaching:

> A considerable proportion of farmers are in great arrears and have no stock either in corn or cattle to enable them to pay their rents and must of course be sold up. Neither the dealers in cattle or in other articles of the produce of the land, nor the farmers, can obtain the bankers' notes or draft on credit, therefore fairs and markets are heavy and dull and the farmers are prevented from making their payments. A great many of the labouring poor are out of employ, the farmers are not willing to employ more than are absolutely necessary and in some places the farmers are compelled by the overseers to take them by turns for a week at a time.

That November a dust cloud settled over Chester, causing impenetrable darkness at noon; then a few days later the fog was succeeded by two feet of snow. No wonder people wondered what they had done to incur God's wrath.

The artist J. M. W. Turner was in Yorkshire in 1816, undertaking a lucrative commission to provide drawings of the Richmond area for his patron Thomas Whitaker. He had hoped to travel in Europe that September, but many of the routes were already impassable and he had to revise his plans. 'Rain, rain, rain,' he wrote to his fellow painter James Holworthy in the second week of that month. 'Day after day, Italy deluged, Switzerland a washpot, Neufchatel, Bienne and Morat Lakes all in *one*. All chance of getting over the Simplon or any of the other passes *now* vanished like the morning mist.' His journey across Europe would have to wait for the following year. It seems likely that some of the spectacular red and black sky effects in Turner and Constable's paintings were inspired by what they saw in this period, and in Germany at this time Caspar David Friedrich painted a sky with a chromatic density in his painting *Ships in the Harbour* that can have come only from witnessing the dust effects caused by a volcanic eruption. Certainly, the pioneering London meteorologist Luke Howard noted that the sun set 'fiery red and much enlarged' on 27 December 1817.

The bad weather and the unripening crops that autumn caused food shortages across England, prompting bread riots in East Anglia – five rioters were hanged after blood was shed during a riot in Ely – and strikes and disturbances in industrial cities such as Birmingham that caused alarm to the authorities. The price of wheat, bolstered by the protective Corn Laws, rose to 111 shillings a quarter and the cost of a loaf to more than a shilling – a tenth of a labourer's average weekly wage. There were disturbances randomly right across the country as starvation occurred, even in rural areas and small country towns. In Somerset coal miners went on strike and in Bideford in

Devon there was an attempt to stop ships carrying grain to London from leaving the harbour. But it was the demonstrations in the cities that alarmed the authorities most: riots in London, Birmingham, Walsall, Nottingham, Preston and Newcastle; in Merthyr Tydfil, where local employers tried to reduce wages just as food prices were increasing; in Glasgow and in Dundee, where 100 shops were looted – word spread fast. The demonstrators' cries for help to relieve starvation quickly turned political: if the current government could not give them food, or ease their plight, perhaps another one would. Their banners read: 'Bread or Blood'. Calls for a provisional government scared ministers. Hospitals filled up as a result of a typhus epidemic – in Edinburgh the authorities commandeered the Queensberry House barracks as a fever hospital when the Royal Infirmary could take no more patients.

In Ireland the constant rain caused floods and the ruin of the potato crop: the first of a series of famines that would sweep the rural country over the coming thirty years. On 19 October 1816 *The Times* printed a gloomy report from a correspondent in Westport, in the far west of County Mayo, which invoked the Almighty:

> From the present state of the harvest and constant rains with which we are deluged, I see nothing before us but the prospect of the most grievous of all earthly calamities – famine. There is not in this extended county 100 acres reaped – the heavy crops all so floundered and rotted that no change of weather at this advanced season can render them productive – add to which a complete failure in the potatoes. God is powerful and can by a miracle save his creatures from destruction but without such we see nothing for it but the desolation of the land.

The food shortages led to a typhus epidemic in Ireland which killed 65,000 people over the course of the next two years – an event observed by the government's Irish secretary, Robert Peel, in Dublin. When the potato famine struck again in 1845, the memory of the earlier disaster was still in his mind and precipitated the political crisis that followed his decision to repeal the Corn Laws.

Typhus swept across the continent in 1816. The grape harvest in the wine regions of Switzerland was the latest in eighty years, but worse than that, the country experienced its worst famine in half a century: the price of grain tripled and the supply of potatoes ran out by August. The famine grew so bad that cantons sealed themselves off, refusing to export even to their neighbours.

It was in a villa by Lake Geneva that summer that the teenaged Mary Shelley began writing *Frankenstein*: 'It proved a wet, ungenial summer and incessant rain often confined us for days to the house,' she recalled years later. 'Have you thought of a story? I was asked each morning, and each morning I was forced to reply with a mortifying negative.' Then she had an idea about reanimation: perhaps a corpse could be revived? Her imagination fired up and unable to sleep that night, she discerned a waking dream:

> I saw – with shut eyes but acute mental vision – ...the hideous phantasm of a man stretched out, and then, on the working of some powerful engine, show signs of life, and stir with an uneasy, half vital motion. Frightful must it be; for supremely frightful would be the effect of any human endeavour to mock the stupendous mechanism of the Creator of the world... I could not so easily get rid of my hideous phantom; still it haunted me. I must try to think of something else. I recurred to my ghost story – my

tiresome, unlucky ghost story! Oh! If I could only contrive one which would frighten my reader as I myself had been frightened that night!

In France, still recovering from the prolonged Napoleonic wars, there were food riots too. Meanwhile, across the Atlantic in New England, farmers recorded their experiences: weeks of icy blasts and frosts in May, culminating in six inches of snow in June as far south as the Massachusetts state line, and heavy frosts in July and mid-August. In Vermont that autumn, countryfolk were reduced to eating nettles and hedgehogs. What made the experience even more bizarre was that the freeze was interspersed by hot sultry days, so it was hard to tell what to expect: heavy overcoats and mittens, or shirt-sleeves. Unsurprisingly, the local clergy resorted to prayer: the Rev. Thomas Robbins of South Windsor, Connecticut, who was also a farmer, found himself oppressed by anxiety for his crop and preached the week after the June storm from the passage in Luke's gospel on the fruitless fig tree. His colleague Calvin Mansfield in North Branford recorded in his diary: 'Great frost – we must learn to be humble.' The ruination caused by the weather caused some farmers to sell up and start the journey westwards, into the Midwest and Indian territory.

Tambora's aftershocks rippled widely and unpredictably across the world. The cause was unknown and unknowable: at best the working-out of a divine providence, not the result of an unknown exploding mountain on an island in a distant sea half a world away.

13

'Emotions both of rage and fear'

—LORD BYRON, *THE CORSAIR*

There had been political protests and civil unrest in Britain periodically for centuries, but the four years following the battle of Waterloo and the end of the Napoleonic wars produced successive waves of working-class discontent which terrified the government and local magistrates. They thought something akin to the French Revolution was being sparked among the disaffected stocking weavers of Nottinghamshire or the cotton spinners of Manchester – a threat they partly magnified, but a real fear nonetheless – and to combat it they introduced repressive legislation, endorsed draconian punishments, including executions, and infiltrated working-class groups with spies and *agents provocateurs*.

The first bout of unrest in the period came in 1811–12 with the Luddite movement, a protest started by stockingers in the Midlands against the mechanization of their industry following the introduction of weaving frames. It was an economic rather than a political protest: they feared – rightly – that the machines would mean lower wages and bring more unemployment. The demonstrators targeted employers they did not like, broke into their factories and demolished their machinery. The outbreaks spread to the silk, cotton and woollen mills of Derbyshire, Lancashire and Yorkshire, where the looms and shearing frames which spun and trimmed the cloth were destroyed. The groups, usually coming by night, sometimes signalled their imminent arrival with letters signed by the eponymous Ned Ludd, who supposedly resided like Robin Hood in Sherwood Forest. Even individual framework knitters might be threatened unless they offered financial support: 'Ned Ludd's compliments and hopes you will give a trifle towards supporting his army as he well understands the art of breaking obnoxious frames,' read one missive in December 1811. 'If you comply with this it will be well, if not I shall call upon you myself.'

The spring and summer of 1812, with bread prices at their height, produced real terror for isolated rural factory owners, some of whom took to sleeping in their mills armed with muskets and surrounded by the more loyal and robust members of their staff or by heavies brought in from nearby towns. The machine-breakers did not stop at vandalism: some started robbing their victims and one particularly unpopular mill owner named John Horsfall – who had incautiously boasted about riding up to his stirrups in Luddite blood – was shot from his horse and murdered on his way back from the Huddersfield woollen exchange. He was not the only fatality: two protesters died after an unsuccessful attempt to attack the heavily protected Cartwright's mill at Rawfolds near Cleckheaton. By late summer the government had called up militia units from across the country to protect property, stem the violence and arrest the ringleaders – or anyway such sympathizers as they could find – and the disturbances were contained. The West Kent militia was sent north to patrol in the Leeds area; there were troops of dragoons from the regular army in Halifax, Burnley and Bradford; 3,000 men were called up in the West Riding to cross the Pennines into Lancashire (how many turned up is uncertain); and 1,000 troops were supposedly billeted in the pubs of Huddersfield. The government passed laws against machine-breaking and there were mass arrests: sixty-four men were put on trial in York in January 1813, and although thirty-seven were acquitted, seven of the rest were transported for seven years for administering or swearing illegal oaths of membership of the organization (organization may be too strong a word). Seventeen were hanged – three for shooting Horsfall, convicted on the word of an accomplice who turned king's evidence, and fourteen for the attack at Cartwright's mill and associated crimes including robbery. That had a sobering effect, as did the presence of troops, the draconian legislation and mill owners' warnings that breaking machinery would only serve to drive employment away altogether. More importantly, that year's harvest was good, food prices fell, and trade and imports resumed following the ending of the continental and American blockades, so work picked up and grievances were reduced. Ned Ludd retreated into the forest.

The Luddites were far from the capital and so were many of the demonstrations that accompanied the passage of the Corn Laws in 1815. Suddenly, following the war, trade was contracting and unemployment was rising, just as troops were being discharged and sent home to go onto the jobs market. Now the most basic of food was becoming both scarce, following the poor harvest of 1816, and unaffordable, thanks to the protective tariff. Surely the government and parliament were acting not in the interests of the hard-working people of the country, but in defence of the profits and prosperity of the most affluent members of it – themselves and their sponsors among the land-owning and voting classes? To some of the demonstrators and their leaders the remedy seemed obvious: political reform to ensure a fairer representation of popular interests and a government more responsive to public needs.

At the end of 1816 there were disturbances following overtly political meetings in Spa Fields, in the middle of London, only a couple of miles and no marching time at all from Westminster and the City. The speechifying was fiery, polemical and subversive. The speaker Henry 'Orator' Hunt addressed a crowd of 10,000 people from the first-floor window of a pub with a French tricolour and a cap of liberty waving behind him. Much worse, after the second meeting, some of the crowd, juiced up on fervour and beer, marched towards the City, looting a gun-shop in Clerkenwell on the way before being seen off by troopers from the Tower of London. Some of the organizers had indeed planned an incendiary outcome in which the Bank of England would be seized; these included veteran revolutionaries such as the impoverished apothecary James Watson (so fervent that he had named his son James Camille Desmoulins Watson after the French revolutionary) and Arthur Thistlewood, who was also well known to the authorities.

One of the ringleaders, subsequently sentenced to hang, was an Irish former Royal Navy seaman called Cashman, who had been wounded several times in battle and petitioned the Admiralty, without success, for the five years' back pay he was owed. As he was strung up, before a crowd hugely sympathetic to his plight, he shouted out: 'Hurrah my hearties in the cause! Success! Cheer up! Now you buggers, give me three cheers when I trip!' The crowd did so and turned their anger on the execution party. The mob's cheers for an executed insurrectionist were not what the government wanted to hear. In truth, however, London might supply mobs but not a cohesive, organized crowd. There was no great industry to supply a coherent grievance; instead, there were lots of small businesses and individual firms, bustling and competing for work and for labour.

Respectable radicals steered well clear of such gatherings and none advocated insurrection or acting outside the law. There were very few MPs who described themselves as radicals – maybe thirty in total – and, following Whitbread's suicide, they lacked parliamentary leadership. Indeed, many of them were moving towards the Whig opposition, whose leader Lord Grey was as disturbed by the extra-parliamentary pressure as the government and believed that there were widespread revolutionary conspiracies as much as ministers did. Jeremy Bentham, the leading philosopher of the Utilitarian movement, and his followers such as James Mill, father of John Stuart Mill, were converts to the need for parliamentary reform as a means of improving the efficiency and effectiveness of the government of the country – and absolutely not because they believed in the idea that its citizens had any sort of natural right to participate in any sort of electoral process.* Bentham was writing about the need for reform of parliament during this period, because he believed its current condition made things worse and inevitably caused repression and the loss of liberty. Universal male suffrage and secret ballots, for instance, would improve the diligence of MPs and their responsiveness to their electors and reduce corruption and the number of government placemen. But he was extremely cautious about publishing his thoughts for fear of being prosecuted for sedition. His 320-page *Catechism of Parliamentary Reform* was written in 1809, but he did not dare publish it, nor could he find a publisher willing to do so, until 1817. This was not a philosophy, however, that would have much traction with the crowds attending reform meetings such as those at Spa Fields. The idea of violence was anathema to him: it was not of utility.

The men whom the government really feared were those capable of firing up the mob. Such people were dangerous and they mainly came not from among the artisans, but from renegade members of

---

* Bentham thought the idea of natural rights was 'nonsense on stilts'.

the landed classes themselves: educated, literate, articulate men. With their oratory and their pamphlets they gave a degree of shape and a political dimension to the protests. There was a maelstrom of political ideas on the excluded, radical fringes of politics, which had been circulating for decades without having the spark of economic hardship to ignite them. The most famous of such writers was Thomas Paine, author of *The Rights of Man*, who had died in 1809, but closer to revolution, so far as the authorities were concerned, were the Spenceans, followers of the bookseller and pamphleteer Thomas Spence, who died in 1814: men such as Thistlewood and James Watson and his son, also named James, who had argued the heretical notion that all land should be held in common and rented out to everyone, not annexed and owned solely by the wealthy.

Then there was the elderly Major John Cartwright, who was the brother of the man who invented the power loom. He had served in the navy and the army and had become radicalized by the American War of Independence. Now in his mid-seventies, Cartwright spent his life writing polemics and tramping round the country speaking at meetings and calling for universal manhood suffrage and political reform. When the authorities questioned what he was doing, he retorted: 'English gentlemen are perpetually travelling. Some go to see the lakes and mountains. Were it not as allowable to travel for seeing the actual condition of a starving people?' Cartwright was still energetic enough to address thirty-five public meetings in a thirty-day tour stretching from Taunton to Manchester in 1814 – and capable of getting himself arrested, even though he advocated entirely consti-tutional means of gaining reform. He was a venerable patriot in the eyes of the young Lancashire radical Samuel Bamford: 'rather above the common stature, straight for his age, thin, pale and with an expression of countenance in which firmness and benignity were most predominant. I see him, as it were, in his long brown surtout and plain brown wig, walking up the room and seating himself placidly in the head seat.' He was not an insurrectionist – he called only for legal protests: 'Hold fast to the law!' – but that did not stop the authorities harassing and periodically arresting him.

Cartwright and his generation had had a lifetime of disappointed ambitions, official disapproval and not a little ridicule. By 1815 they were being joined and overtaken by younger, more radical men. Perhaps the richest and most aristocratic of them was Sir Francis Burdett, who had married into the Coutts banking family, but found himself an ardent campaigner for constitutional parliamentary reform.* 'The best part of my character is a strong feeling of indignation at injustice and oppression and a lively sympathy with the oppression of my fellows,' he remarked. His outspoken opposition to the conduct of the war had led him to be briefly committed to the Tower by a vote of parliament in 1810, but his patrician demeanour made him an uncomfortable leader of the working classes and he was far happier to associate with Lord Byron. Bamford, who met Burdett in London, wrote years later: 'He was a fine-looking man on the whole, of lofty stature, with a proud but not forbidding carriage of the head. His manner was dignified and civilly familiar; submitting to rather than seeking conversation with men of our class.' Burdett was not the man to lead a popular insurrection: he was already in the Commons, sitting for what was then, thanks to its populous artisan electorate, the radical constituency of Westminster. His periodic attempts to promote parliamentary reform were easily seen off, and he was reluctant to associate himself with extra-parliamentary pres-

---

* Burdett's daughter, Angela Burdett-Coutts, would be one of the great social philanthropists of the nineteenth century.

sure or anything that smacked of insurrection. He was, said William Cobbett scornfully, 'a democrat in words but an aristocrat in feeling'.

Cobbett was the leading pamphleteer of the extra-parliamentary democratic movement. A large, red-faced farmer himself – 'the perfect representation of what he always wished to be: an English gentleman farmer,' wrote Bamford – he boasted that he had started out as a ploughboy, albeit on his father's farm. By 1815, however, polemics had firmly supplanted agriculture. His *Political Register* was originally founded in 1802 to report debates in parliament, but newspaper tax made it too expensive for the ordinary people who he wanted to read it, and so in 1815 he abandoned the reporting of news and turned the *Register* into a weekly pamphlet, which avoided the tax and allowed it to be sold for twopence. When political opponents derided it as trash, he gleefully accepted the insult and the *Register* became known informally as the *Tuppenny Trash*. As such it quickly reached a circulation of 40,000 copies every week and was said to be read by schoolmasters and parish clerks, artisans and innkeepers across the breadth of the country. It certainly campaigned vociferously for parliamentary reform, but Cobbett himself was no radical – he was, rather, a conservative romantic – and however rumbustious and even unpleasant some of its opinions, the *Register* never advocated violence.* He campaigned for reform to restore what he saw as the ancient, rustic traditions of the olden times, which had been supplanted by the corruption and venality of the political system: the rotten boroughs and the speculators and financiers of the Great Wen, as he called London, who were buying up second homes in the countryside. Cobbett created a populist climate for political reform

---

* A robust little Englander, Cobbett opposed the abolition of bull- and bear-baiting and thought the anti-slavery campaign in defence of 'fat and lazy and laughing and singing negroes' a waste of time.

and gave his readers the arguments and opinions to campaign for it, but when he was threatened by the authorities with a charge of seditious libel in 1817, he fled to America. Cobbett may have been the most prolific journalist of all time – it is estimated that he composed 30 million words in a lifetime of publication – and was certainly a pioneer of editorial commentary, but he was not an organizer of protest or a leader of it.

That was left to 'Orator' Hunt, a brass-lunged man who was not afraid to incite the crowds. Henry Hunt was himself a Wiltshire gentleman farmer who had inherited 3,000 prime agricultural acres in the West Country, but felt ostracized and isolated by the local farming fraternity after he eloped with a friend's wife. A man with a flamboyant rhetorical style, a stentorian voice and a disputatious manner, he had become radicalized by his concern for the abuses of the parliamentary system (under which he had so far failed to be elected) and was touring the country by 1816 calling for annual parliaments and universal suffrage. Easily recognized, both by his followers and by the authorities whom he baited, because of the white top hat he customarily wore. Hunt trod a narrow path between calling for mass extra-parliamentary pressure and advocating physical force. He generally managed to avoid directly advocating violence and he certainly did not want his meetings hijacked by more revolutionary agitators. He told the first Spa Fields gathering that 'before physical force was applied to, it was their duty to petition for reformation… but if the fatal day should be destined to arrive, he himself would not be found sheltering in the rear'. It was probably not surprising that his audience missed some of the nuances, and his willingness to appear flanked by men waving tricolours made him an object of fear and suspicion to the authorities. Bamford left a vivid picture of him:

His eyes were blue or light grey, not very clear nor quick, but rather heavy except… when he was excited in speaking; at which times they seemed to distend and protrude; and if he worked himself furious, as he sometimes would, they became blood-streaked and almost started from their sockets. The kind smile was exchanged for the curl of scorn, or the curse of indignation. His voice was bellowing; his face swollen and flushed; his griped [*sic*] hand beat as if it were to pulverize; and his whole manner gave token of a painful energy, struggling for utterance.

Bamford wrote this twenty years later when he had grown disillusioned with radicalism, but he added understandingly: 'He was constantly, perhaps through good but misapplied intentions, placing himself in most arduous situations. No repose – no tranquillity for him. He was always beating against a tempest of his own or others' creating.' Such a man found it easy to fall out with his colleagues.

Francis Place, a London breeches-maker, had a long history of peaceful radicalism, from 1790s Jacobinism to 1840s Chartism. He was scornful of men such as Hunt and Cobbett, who incited the uneducated but failed to direct them constructively. Cobbett, he said, was 'too ignorant… to see that the common people must ever be imbecile in this respect [he meant they were ignorant of political organization] when not encouraged and supported by others who have money and influence'. Place added: 'Hunt says his mode of acting is to dash at good points and to care for no one; that he will mix with no committee, or any party; he will act by himself, that he does not intend to affront anyone, but cares not who is offended.' This did not make for a coherent campaign, a well-directed and coordinated organization, or an effective leadership.

Men like Place and Bamford were neither ignorant nor illiterate;

their radicalism was informed by the associations they joined, such as the Hampden Clubs,* formed in cities and towns at the instigation of Cartwright from 1812 to discuss and campaign for parliamentary reform. The clubs, successors to the old corresponding societies of the eighteenth century, were places where working men and sympathetic middle-class supporters could meet, listen to talks and articles being read aloud, and debate politics. They were not secret – members paid a penny a week – and they usually met in local pubs. The mass meetings that Bamford and the others attended were similar, too, to the open-air gatherings of the nonconformist and particularly Methodist sects that many of them supported on Sundays. Even these religious gatherings could be seen as subversive by the authorities, preaching as they did a Christian creed that showed no respect for the complacent routines of the established church. The Duke of Wellington would not allow Methodist chaplains in his army for fear that they might subvert the troops. It was from this sort of background that many of those involved in campaigning for parliamentary reform sprang.

In January 1817, a month after the Spa Fields disturbance, representatives of the clubs attended a meeting at the Crown and Anchor Tavern in London's Strand to discuss their demands, and it was here that their divisions emerged and with it a sense of betrayal. Burdett, who had been expected to attend, backed out, but Cartwright and Cobbett, who were present, put forward a motion that the baronet had indicated he could support, which went no further than calling for the vote at elections to be extended to householders, not for the universal suffrage that most of the meeting had expected. Such a reform would have left most of them still disenfranchised.

---

* Named after John Hampden, the seventeenth-century parliamentary leader at the outbreak of the Civil War.

The motion was defeated amid angry scenes, and Hunt accompanied by the other delegates and a large huzzaing crowd carried their petition to parliament, where it was summarily rejected. The Hampden Clubs were legal and so had been their delegate meeting, which was held in public and reported by the press, so the government's response was to introduce a crackdown in the shape of the Seditious Meetings Act to stop such gatherings in future. Ministers also went further and suspended habeas corpus so that the authorities could arrest and detain indefinitely those suspected of political activism. Over the coming months the clubs would be harried out of existence, pub landlords intimidated into not allowing their rooms to be used, and their members threatened, harassed and arrested. Nevertheless, in March 1817 as far as ministers were concerned, the threat of insurrection seemed to be spreading. Several hundred unemployed and starving Lancashire mill workers started marching towards London from Manchester; their aim was to get relief by delivering a petition to the Prince Regent. Their protest was orderly if naïve; they carried blankets for the journey, earning themselves the name of Blanketeers. They were seen off from St Peter's Fields by Samuel Bamford, who had opposed the march for tactical reasons:

> The appearance of these misdirected people was calculated to excite in considerate minds pity rather than resentment... A few were decently clothed and well appointed for the journey; many were covered only by rags which admitted the cold wind and were already damped by a gentle but chilling rain. Some appeared young, with health in their cheeks, every care behind and hope alone before; the thoughts of others were probably reverting to their homes in the hill sides, or in the sombre alleys

of the town, where wives and children had resigned them for a time, in hopes of the return with plenty.

They were not doing anything illegal, but they presented a pathetic spectacle, rather than a terrifying one. Even the money they had raised to pay for accommodation on the journey went missing when their treasurer, trusted to go ahead and make the bookings, disappeared with the cash. At the outset, the Manchester magistrates ordered them to disperse and many peeled off; the yeomanry saw off more by the time they got to Stockport, and still more melted away overnight. They had been promised that by the time they got to Birmingham there would be 100,000 others with them, but in the event only one man got beyond Leek in Staffordshire. It did not stop the authorities rounding up the ringleaders and even trawling in Bamford, who had stayed at home. The spectacle that the local magistrates and ministers had in mind was not the bedraggled Blanketeers, but the Paris mob that had marched on Versailles at the start of the French Revolution.

Bamford's opposition to the Blanketeers did not do him much good. He was too smart to be seduced by the unknown man who sought him out with a plan to set fire to Manchester, but he was soon rounded up by the magistrates in Middleton anyway, on suspicion of the potentially capital crime of high treason, and sent down to London in irons with a group of others to be interrogated by members of the Privy Council, no less, in Whitehall. The main questioner was Lord Sidmouth, the home secretary, the man chiefly responsible for the panic-stricken crackdown. Surprisingly, they got on rather well: 'His manner was affable and much more encouraging to freedom of speech than I had expected,' Bamford wrote in his memoirs twenty years later. Over the next few weeks, he was interrogated five times and by his own account responded to the allegations of treason with spirit and openness. They eventually let him go.

Bamford had avoided falling victim to one of the spies the government was now sending to infiltrate the Hampden Clubs and other sources of what it took to be potential sedition. Local magistrates, too, had their informers, but the most systematic undercover men were fanning out across the country and reporting back directly to Sidmouth. Of these, the most notorious was a man whose name was probably Richard Richards, but who became known as Oliver the Spy because of his cover name of William Oliver. Richards, 'a person of genteel appearance and good address, nearly six feet high and marked by smallpox', was a carpenter in his forties who had recently been released from debtors' prison. He had had some peripheral connection with the Spenceans and knew men who had been involved in the Spa Fields riots. In the spring of 1817 Oliver offered his services to the government. He evidently had a plausible manner and was sent off on a tour of the disaffected industrial districts of the Midlands and the north to find out whether trouble was planned. He was not the only spy doing the rounds; there were undercover missions of similar men genuinely wandering the country seeing whether a general uprising could indeed be provoked. In such times, with unknown men from London and elsewhere turning up unannounced and murmuring about imminent revolution, it was difficult to know who to trust. But some of the government's agents were undoubtedly also becoming *agents provocateurs*.

In June 1817 there was a new, more violent but equally pathetic, attempt to stir up unrest in the so-called Pentrich Revolution in a village in Derbyshire, which seems to have been at least partly provoked by Oliver. On his tour of the east Midlands and Yorkshire during the previous few weeks he apparently told those he met that there would shortly be a general uprising in which they should play a part; but how far he was following Sidmouth's instructions, or whether he was acting on his own initiative, cannot be known. He was, however, plausible enough to have convinced an unemployed and starving stockinger named Jeremiah Brandreth, later known as the Nottingham Captain, that he should lead a local part of the rising. Brandreth, a large, fearsome-looking figure with a black beard, was the stuff of respectable folks' nightmares, but he was more delusional than revolutionary. He nevertheless managed to persuade a couple of hundred men from the villages around Pentrich to join him in a march on Nottingham fourteen miles away. His followers were either stockingers or iron-ore miners – both trades badly hit by the post-war economic depression – and they were promised bread, rum and a hundred guineas each when they seized the local castle, as well as a boat trip on the River Trent. They were also told they were part of a national uprising that would take control of the country and set up a provisional government, which at least one of the crowd took to mean that they would be given provisions. The new government would apparently wipe out the national debt. One of Brandreth's lieutenants was said to have told their followers that 'he believed the day and hour were fixed when the whole nation was expected to rise and before the middle of the week… there would be hundreds of thousands in arms… there were men appointed from all over the nation'. An army would sweep down from Yorkshire 'like a cloud'.

None of this was true – a separate putative rising near Huddersfield the same night scarcely left the pub – so the Pentrich men were on their own. The group, lightly armed with pikes, bill-hooks and a few muskets, set off haphazardly from the nearby village of South Wingfield, led by Brandreth, who succeeded in shooting and killing a recalcitrant servant at one of the farmhouses on the way. Soon it was raining hard and most of his followers disappeared into the night, pursued by shouts from Brandreth that he would shoot them too if they did not come back. Finally the bedraggled remainder were rounded up by a detachment of local dragoons. In the end, eighty of the crowd were arrested and thirty-five were subsequently put on trial for high treason, though only twenty-three were eventually sentenced, three of them to transportation. The three ringleaders most involved, including Brandreth, were hanged and their bodies then decapitated in Derby, the due punishment for treason;* the traditional penalty of quartering while still alive had been graciously remitted by the Prince Regent. One conspirator, Thomas Bacon, was not tried at all for fear he would disclose the role of the *agent provocateur*, with whom he had been the chief contact. The government, however, was determined to make a terrifying example to deter anyone else.

By the time the Pentrich revolutionaries marched, Oliver was already heading south to report to Sidmouth, but his cover was blown within weeks when smart journalism by the *Leeds Mercury* exposed his activities and named him as a spy. This revelation seriously compromised the government's activities and had the effect of nullifying some of the trials it had embarked upon to teach the insurgents and their potential supporters a lesson. Not only could they not try Bacon and others like him for treason for fear of having their agents' provocations uncovered, but they discovered that juries were unwilling to convict some of those who had been arraigned. Among

---

* In his last letter, Brandreth left his wife Ann all his worldly possessions. They were pathetically few: 'one work bag, two balls of worsted and one of cotton and a handkerchief, an old pair of stockings and a shirt and the letter I received from my beloved sister.'

those acquitted at this time were Arthur Thistlewood and James Watson, following their trial for treason arising out of the Spa Fields riot, and while Watson would later espouse constitutional politics, Thistlewood would go on to attempt genuine terrorism.

The 1817 clampdown nevertheless took the wind out of the radical campaigns: some of their leaders were held in jail following the lifting of habeas corpus, others were cowed, and others still, like Cobbett and Watson's son, had fled abroad. The harvest that year was better, as the after-effects of Tambora waned, and the price of wheat fell. There were strikes in the north by jenny-spinners and power-loom weavers, but these were settled peacefully.

But the harvest of 1818 was poor and by the following summer the parliamentary reform campaign had begun again. It culminated in a mass meeting called at St Peter's Fields in the middle of Manchester on 16 August 1819. Despite its burgeoning size Manchester at this time did not have an MP of its own in the unreformed Commons. The meeting, which would culminate in the worst violence ever seen at a British political gathering, was intended to be peaceful and was responsibly conducted. Those attending were called upon by the organizers to be respectably dressed: 'cleanliness, sobriety, order and peace' were to be the watchwords. The rally's purpose could not have been more moderate: to consider 'the propriety of adopting the most legal and effectual means of obtaining Reform of the Commons House of Parliament'. There was nothing revolutionary about this: the meeting was held to call for parliamentary reform, not the overthrow of the state or the monarchy, and was quite legal, even under the Seditious Meetings legislation. The revolutionaries of Spa Fields were not present, the weather was sunny and the atmosphere was relaxed and orderly: many men brought their wives and families to listen to the bands patriotically playing 'Rule Britannia' and to hear the speechifying. 'Orator' Hunt was to be the star attraction. By the early afternoon there were an estimated 60,000 people crammed into the space – 'a chasm of human beings', in Bamford's words – which, if true, would have been the equivalent of half the population of the city and its outlying towns at that time. They were listening to the national anthem being played by a band and waiting for Hunt to appear in his barouche. The local magistrates were also waiting, watching the crowd from a nearby building and ready to arrest Hunt if he said anything incendiary. They did not try to stop him making his way into the middle of the crowd, but then they seem to have lost their nerve and belatedly decided he must be stopped from speaking and arrested. To do this they sent in the local Manchester and Salford Yeomanry, a newly formed unit made up of young, uniformed local tradesmen mounted on horseback. Some of these weekend soldiers may have been drunk; certainly neither they nor their commanders had any experience or understanding of crowd-control. Samuel Bamford, who was present, gave a graphic account of what happened next:

> The cavalry were in confusion; they evidently could not, with all the weight of man and horse, penetrate that compact mass of human beings; and their sabres were plied to hew a way through naked, held-up hands and defenceless heads; and then chopped limbs and wound-gaping skulls were seen; and the groans and cries were mingled with the din of that horrid confusion. 'Ah! ah!' 'for shame! for shame!' was shouted. Then, 'Break! break! They are killing them in front and they cannot get away'... For a moment the crowd held back as in a pause; then there was a rush, heavy and resistless as a headlong sea; and a sound like low

thunder, with screams, prayers and imprecations from the crowd-moiled and sabre-doomed who could not escape.'

The horsemen were, wrote the *Manchester Observer* afterwards, 'the stupid boobies of yeomanry cavalry, fawning dependents of the great with a few fools and a greater proportion of coxcombs, who imagine they acquire considerable importance by wearing regimentals'. They barged their way through the tightly packed crowd and arrested Hunt, their horses kicking and bucking in the crush, but then found themselves surrounded and hemmed in by jeering people and started lashing out with their sabres. At this point, seeing the mêlée, the magistrates called up a detachment of the regular army, the 15th Hussars, which they had also summoned to be ready in reserve, and sent them too into the crowd to rescue the yeomanry. These men, some Waterloo veterans, laid about them with their swords too, sending the crowd fleeing in packed disorder, tripping over each other and running for dear life. Some found their way out blocked by more troops, increasing the panic and the crush. Within minutes the field was empty, but hundreds had been injured and at least eleven, including women and children, were dead. Bamford again:

The hustings remained with a few broken and hewed flag-staves erect and a torn or gashed banner or two... whilst over the whole field were strewed caps, bonnets, hats, shawls and shoes and other parts of male and female dress, trampled, torn and bloody. The yeomanry had dismounted... some were wiping their sabres. Several mounds of human beings still remained where they had fallen, crushed down and smothered. Some of these still groaning... others would never breathe more. All was silent

save those low sounds and the occasional snorting and pawing
of steeds.

The exact number of casualties is not known because some of the
wounded disguised their injuries for fear of losing their jobs at
the hands of employers who were members of the yeomanry, and
others were denied treatment for taking part in such a meeting. The
violence shocked many. Far away in Florence, Percy Bysshe Shelley
was appalled by the news when the English papers sent him by
Thomas Love Peacock arrived three weeks later: 'the torrent of my
indignation has not yet done boiling in my veins,' he wrote back the
following day. 'I await anxiously to find how the country will react to
this bloody oppression of its destroyers. Something must be done…
what yet I know not.' His own contribution was the ninety-one
stanzas of *The Mask of Anarchy*, probably the most savage political
poem ever written in English, which he composed in high passion
over the following fortnight. It starts with a remorseless satire of the
members of the government: Castlereagh – 'very smooth he looked,
yet grim' – accompanied by seven bloodhounds, Eldon, the Lord
Chancellor, whose tears turn to millstones, and Sidmouth riding
on a crocodile. It then builds remorselessly to a stirring crescendo
calling on the people of England to overthrow their bloodthirsty
oppressors:

> Rise like lions after slumber
> In unvanquishable number –
> Shake your chains to earth like dew
> Which in sleep had fallen on you –
> Ye are many – they are few.

But there was no widespread revolt. The government commended the magistrates and the troops for doing their duty. The Prince Regent also sent his thanks, which only added to the bitterness of some survivors. Hunt and the organizers of the meeting were subsequently jailed for sedition, and the *Manchester Observer*, which had first coined the phrase 'Peterloo' to describe the massacre, was closed down – to be succeeded shortly by the *Manchester Guardian*, predecessor of the modern *Guardian*. Bamford, too, was arrested and sentenced to a year's imprisonment on a charge of inciting a riot, which, since he had been a silent bystander, was ludicrous. By the end of 1819 the government had passed more repressive measures: the six acts, which included restricting further the right to attend meetings, increasing taxation on newspapers, extending powers of search, and making it increasingly difficult to obtain bail.

Now desperate, some radicals were prepared to go further. Arthur Thistlewood, the man acquitted after the Spa Fields riot, organized a hopeless plan to assassinate the entire cabinet in February 1820. He hoped by doing so to foment a general uprising, but the government had sent a spy named George Edwards to infiltrate the conspiracy and knew all about it: indeed, the ministers' dinner which the plotters were intending to turn into a bloodbath was actually a decoy – it was never going to happen. That night when they gathered at a loft in Cato Street, off London's Edgware Road, to finalize their plans, Thistlewood and his colleagues were surprised by a contingent of Bow Street Runners and a detachment of troops and arrested. Charged with high treason, Thistlewood and four others were convicted at the Old Bailey (five others were transported), executed and beheaded, as Brandreth had been.

Four years after the battle of Waterloo, Britain had not yet become a peaceful nation at ease with itself. Although the insurrections which so frightened ministers and magistrates were actually small, disorganized and piecemeal, they still represented the visible tips of a more general, subterranean discontent which was becoming focused on a series of demands for political reform. The changes that protesters wanted were not in the least revolutionary and most would eventually be implemented, but they panicked a government and a political class of tired and frightened men, most of whom had been in office through war and its aftermath for many years. Peterloo was in this sense a culmination of the period that had started with Waterloo. There was nothing like it again. Economic conditions improved, harvests returned to normal in the 1820s, and the causes of immediate discontent were eased.

Nevertheless, even nearly 200 years on, the Peterloo massacre still has a resonance. The coining of the name in counterpoint to the earlier battle was journalistically brilliant and it has never been forgotten as an injustice perpetrated against respectable, unarmed demonstrators campaigning for their democratic rights. As recently as 2006 a *Guardian* newspaper poll named Peterloo as the second-most important event in British political history and one that deserved a permanent memorial. Worse assaults are perpetrated regularly on peaceful protesters across the world today, but not in Britain, where the shadow of the yeomanry and the hussars lashing out with their sabres remains a folk memory even when the causes of the St Peter's Fields demonstration are forgotten.

One of those killed was a Waterloo veteran called John Lees, who was sabred and died three weeks later from his wounds. He told a relative poignantly: 'At Waterloo there was man to man, but here it was downright murder.'

Not everyone chose politics to remedy their ills; many more members of the working classes turned to God and in particular to the millenarian prophesying of itinerant preachers and prophets. In an age when many countryfolk still believed in green men and devils and sprites in the absence of more rational explanations for happenings they could not understand, there was a simple incredulity. Looking back on his career, a Cornish vicar named Polwhele wrote in 1826:

> Within my remembrance, there were conjuring parsons and cunning clerks, every blacksmith was a doctor, every old woman was a witch. In short, all nature seemed to be united: its wells, its plants, its birds, its beasts, its reptiles, and even inanimate things in sympathising with human credulity; in predicting or in averting, in relieving or in aggravating misfortune.

No one was more accomplished at offering guidance for the inexplicable than a dumpy, middle-aged farmer's daughter from Devon named Joanna Southcott. In the first decade of the nineteenth century she may have had as many as 100,000 followers, rather more than ever took part in political demonstrations and comparable with the 190,000 that the Methodists claimed at this time.

Joanna's proselytizing took place in pamphlets blending her personal experiences with warnings of the apocalypse to come. Written in vivid prose and occasionally bursting into verse, they demonstrated a simple solipsism, for God spoke through her, His unlikely vessel. He enabled her to prophesy the future, generally somewhat like Nostradamus in terms so general as to be meaningless except through the eye of faith, or so obvious – Napoleon was naturally the Beast of Revelation – as to be commonplace; but she sealed the predictions away when she did not share them with her followers. Her God was a fierce and vengeful deity too, but there was a way of avoiding His wrath and that was by signing up for one of Joanna's seals, a piece of paper with a circle drawn on it which was signed both by the believer and by Southcott herself and then closed up. The token would save the bearer from the coming Day of Judgement and, better still, allow them to 'inherit the Tree of Life to be made Heirs of God and joint-heirs with Jesus Christ'. It helped if they also purchased one of Southcott's books of prophesy such as *Sound an Alarm in My Holy Mountain.*

Southcott was not the only such prophetess. Another, called Mary Bateman, exhibited millennial eggs obtained from a miraculous hen, defrauded her followers and was eventually hanged for poisoning one of them. Bearded Southcottian prophets infested the West Riding of Yorkshire and Joanna herself was taken up and apparently treated seriously by some nonconformist clergymen, but her powers and influence were waning by 1814. Perhaps too many predictions of the Day of Judgement had passed unapocalyptically. There was a need for a new revelation and that summer she announced that she was pregnant, though a virgin and aged sixty-four – and not just with any child, but Shiloh, the new son of God. She announced the event, inevitably, in new pamphlets for her followers, and even allowed her tummy to be inspected by doctors. To counteract any hint of public scandal, she married a family friend who was allowed to become her Joseph. The impending immaculate birth was greeted with some ridicule by profane non-believers, including Thomas Rowlandson whose cartoon of the event was entitled: 'Miracles will never cease.'

And then, on Boxing Day 1814, Joanna Southcott died. She was not pregnant but she did bequeath her box of secret prophesies to her followers, to be opened at a time of national crisis, but only by the archbishop of Canterbury in the presence of twenty-four bishops of the Church of England. Sadly, the episcopate has never yet got round to doing so.*

---

* The box eventually devolved to an Anglican clergyman's wife named Mabel Barltrop in the 1920s. She founded the Panacea Society, which sold small linen squares soaked in tap-water to those who believed they would cure them of their ailments. The profits of the prophet went into buying property in Bedford, which by the early twenty-first century was valued at £14 million and attracted the Charity Commissioners, who wondered what charitable purposes the society was actually serving since it never gave any of its funds away to good causes. The last, elderly Southcottian follower reportedly died in 2012.

14

'The bravest and most fortunate nation in the world'

— NAPOLEON BONAPARTE, 1815

When Napoleon returned to Paris three days after the defeat at Waterloo, it was quickly borne in on him by his advisers that there would be no more armies raised and no more battles. They – and France – would not stand for it. His only option was to abdicate and maybe escape to the United States. Within a few days he and a small entourage of loyalists had made their way to the port of Rochefort on the Atlantic coast. The British knew he was coming and posted a warship, the seventy-four-gun ship of the line HMS *Bellerophon*, offshore to make sure he did not escape again.* He might have done so, in a fast cutter under cover of darkness, but the lassitude that had affected him during the Belgian campaign seems to have overwhelmed him again, and on 15 July 1815, four weeks after the battle, he surrendered to Captain Frederick Maitland, the *Bellerophon*'s commander, and threw himself on the mercy of his former enemies.

On board the ship, he sought asylum in England and wrote to the Prince Regent: 'I come like Themistocles to throw myself upon the hospitality of the British people. I put myself under the protection

---

* *Bellerophon* was known as *Billy Ruffian* to her crew, who found the Greek hero's name too difficult to pronounce.

of their laws, which I claim from your Royal Highness as the most powerful, the most constant and the most generous of my enemies.' He charmed everyone on the ship, flattering the crew and their officers – 'Well gentlemen,' he said, 'you have the honour of belonging to the bravest and most fortunate nation in the world.' He wandered amiably around the deck every day asking questions about why the Royal Navy was superior to the French: 'What I admire most is the extreme silence and orderly conduct of your men: on board a French ship everyone calls and gives orders and they gabble like so many geese.' Napoleon seemed quite happy with what he had convinced himself would be the prospect of living in retirement in a cottage in the West Country.

That was never going to happen, of course, but while the government decided what to do with him, the *Bellerophon* anchored off the Devon coast and Napoleon made genial daily appearances to the crowds of sightseers who rowed out to surround the ship in order to catch a glimpse of a man who for twenty years most of them had regarded as a devil incarnate. *The Times*'s correspondent reported: 'We anchored… amidst thousands of boats etc. Bonaparte repeatedly appeared at a cabin window which was wide open; he appears rather stout, very full in the face, but very stern and thoughtful in his manner.' Perhaps it was just as well that the reporter did not realize that the former emperor was appraising the female tourists as they waved and smiled up at him: 'What charming girls! What beautiful women!' There were calls for him to be put on trial and executed, not least by *The Times*, for the years in which he had 'deluged Europe in blood' – but, perhaps surprisingly to modern eyes, that does not seem to have been seriously considered by the British government. Wellington himself was horrified by the very idea. They decided to put him instead on St Helena, a remote island in the South Atlantic from which he could never escape again, and appear to have reached the decision unilaterally without consulting any of the European allies – including the Prussians, who were very keen to see him hanged. But he was, after all, a British prisoner. After nearly a month stuck on the *Bellerophon*, denied his wish for the chance to meet the Prince Regent, Napoleon was transferred to another warship, the *Northumberland*, and, complaining loudly, shipped off to his rocky exile. Once he had gone, Captain Maitland asked a member of the crew what they had thought of the emperor, to be told that if the people of England had known him as well as they had come to do, they would not have hurt a hair on his head. Or as Admiral Lord Keith, in charge of the Channel Fleet, observed: 'Damn the fellow: if he had obtained an interview with His Royal Highness, in half an hour they would have been the best of friends in England.'

Napoleon's adversary, the Duke of Wellington, returned to his post as the British ambassador in Paris, where he was showered with medals and honours by various allied heads of state: the Order of the Holy Ghost by Louis XVIII, the Order of the Black Eagle from Prussia, the Order of the Elephant from Denmark, the Order of St Andrew from Russia and the Royal Hanoverian Guelphic Order from the Prince Regent. He was also created Prince of Waterloo by the king of the Netherlands. These were added to his previous Spanish honours and the Order of the Garter. A grateful nation granted him £200,000 to buy Stratfield Saye House and estate near Basingstoke – nowhere near as grand as Blenheim Palace, bought for the Duke of Marlborough a century earlier, whose extravagant costs had run out of control – but at 5,000 acres more than adequate for his needs. The French were less magnanimous: a Napoleon loyalist who took a pot-shot at Wellington in Paris was acquitted in court and bequeathed 10,000 francs by the emperor in his will.

Battlefield tours at Waterloo started even before the bodies were buried. Sir Walter Scott was an early visitor that summer, as were William and Dorothy Wordsworth. A group of affluent young tourists from Brentford armed themselves with three pints of brandy and some snuff to disguise the smell when they visited that August, spotting a leg in the stubble and cutting fingers off a hand sticking out of the ground to take home with them. Lord Byron toured the following summer and wrote his name in the visitors' book at Hougoumont's chapel. He did not think the site compared with the battlefields of ancient Greece and sneered at 'the cause & the victors – & the victory – including Blücher and the Bourbons'. But he could not resist buying souvenirs including a brass cuirass, a helmet with plume and a sword to send back to his publisher John Murray in London.

Lord Liverpool's government ploughed on through the 1820s. Castlereagh, though, worn down by overwork and public attacks, and perhaps fearing accusations of homosexuality, had a breakdown and killed himself in 1822, and Liverpool eventually had a stroke and left office in 1827 – both men reviled, their role in the conduct of the war and its aftermath dismissed and overshadowed by the domestic repression that succeeded it. Byron's savage little verse on hearing of Castlereagh's death was characteristic of the *bien-pensants*:

> Posterity will ne'er survey
> A nobler grave than this:
> Here lie the bones of Castlereagh;
> Stop, traveller, and piss.

Perhaps fortunately for the long-serving prime minister, both Byron and Shelley died before Lord Liverpool did.

The battle of Waterloo was celebrated even at the time as one of the great days of British history. The engineer John Rennie's new bridge over the Thames, originally called the Strand Bridge and described by Canova as the noblest in the world – 'worth a visit from the remotest corner of the earth' – was renamed after Waterloo and formally opened by the Prince Regent amidst great celebrations on the second anniversary of the battle. The railway station built on the South Bank next to the bridge was also named after the battle in 1848. The resonances of the name continue to reverberate for the British: when Queen Elizabeth II entertained the French president Jacques Chirac at a state dinner at Windsor Castle in November 2004, it was no coincidence that she chose that the post-prandial entertainment – excerpts from the musical *Les Misérables* – should take place in the Waterloo Chamber.

The battle stood as a great punctuation mark for Britons alive at the time. Those who could remember when Britain had previously been at prolonged peace were into their middle age.* Henry Thomas Cockburn, the Scottish Whig lawyer, wrote in the 1820s that the end of the war 'separated the lives and the recollections of that generation into two great and marked parts. From this moment the appearance of everything was changed': dress, habits, hopes and attitudes were transformed; older people had only a dim memory of peace, while younger people knew peace for the first time. 'The change in all things, in all ideas, conversation and objects, was as complete as it is in a town that has at last been liberated from a strict and tedious siege.' This was an exaggeration: the changes were under way before 1815 and continued after it. The costumes and wigs of the

---

* Any who could remember the period before the American War of Independence (1775–83) or the Seven Years' War which preceded it between 1754 and 1763 were into their sixties and already past the average contemporary lifespan.

1790s were already old-fashioned and the Palladian architecture was already being superseded by the gothic. The pressure for parliamentary reform had rumbled on since the time of the French Revolution, but it was given new impetus and urgency by the economic downturn that followed the war. Waterloo was seen at home – erroneously – as a largely British triumph. It gave the country a sense of martial success and self-worth, just as the maritime triumph at Trafalgar a decade earlier had meant that it ruled the waves. These were feelings – the sense that Britain *mattered* in Europe and the world as a result of its military victory – that have persisted ever since. The peace that Waterloo inaugurated in Europe lasted, as far as Britain was concerned, until 1914 – and the military self-confidence lasted that long too. For the countries of the continent, the Concert of Europe – the balance of power inaugurated by the Congress of Vienna – lasted into mid-century until the Crimean War of 1854–6 and the brief wars which resulted in the reunification of Italy and Germany. But the European powers, too, grew used to peace and prosperity and complacent that they would last, until the guns of August 1914 taught them differently.

At Christmas 1815 a new, young actress was welcomed to the London stage: Mrs Barnes of Exeter was playing Juliet at the Drury Lane Theatre. *The Times* critic was not entirely impressed, as he made clear in the paper's last edition of the year, on Saturday 30 December:

> The lady is on a very small scale as to figure… her profile is by no means good, the contour of her face is void of dignity, but the eye has considerable expression. Mrs Barnes may boast of a voice rather strong than melodious – she manages this organ however

with superior skill and never fails to articulate with force and clearness; her manner seems to indicate no slight acquaintance with the walks of tragedy.

The critic was trying to do his best:

In the scene where she addresses him from the balcony (the most trying in the whole play) her conception of the feelings and demeanour of Juliet may be regarded as nearly faultless… she dwelt upon the horrors of their separation with successful energy and of no contemptible talents and if she will correct a certain provincial peculiarity of utterance she will make a valuable acquisition to the London stage.

At least she did better than Romeo:

Mr Rae gave spirit enough to the lover of Juliet but was wholly deficient in softness and elegance. The still carriage of this respected performer and his unfortunate habit of throwing away his voice towards the close of every sentence are seldom productive of more unfavourable impressions on the audience than in his attempts to personate the love inspiring Romeo.

One wonders what became of Mrs Barnes's and Mr Rae's careers? Did they hasten back to Exeter? The anonymous reporter also had harsh words for another quarter:

Before we conclude this article we think it right to say that the very foolish person who wished to bribe our good opinion on a late occasion by sending a bank note may have his note again

whenever he chuses [*sic*] to call for it and identifies the letter…
we are willing to ascribe this insult to ignorance of the true
character of London Journals and shall therefore take no severer
notice of it.

Such an attempt at bribery – of course – would be as shocking now
as it evidently was then. Some things never change.

Source notes

INTRODUCTION: 'A CHANGE IN LIFE ITSELF'

The general histories of Britain in the early nineteenth-century include notably Boyd Hilton's *A Mad, Bad and Dangerous People? England 1783–1846* in OUP's British history series; Linda Colley's *Britons: Forging the Nation, 1707–1837*; and from an earlier era, Asa Briggs's *Age of Improvement*. Now somewhat dated, R. J. White's *Waterloo to Peterloo* remains an engaging read. Roy and Lesley Adkins have recently published an entertaining and informative account of life in Jane Austen's England (*Eavesdropping on Jane Austen's England*), while William Darter's reminiscences, originally published in the 1880s (*Reminiscences of Reading, by an Octogenarian*), are a nostalgic evocation especially for those such as this author who were born in Reading.

The *Times* Waterloo despatch was printed in its edition of 22 June 1815; the paper's obituary of George IV was published on 16 July 1830. *Black Dwarf*'s editorial was published on 10 December 1817.

Jane Austen's letters are taken from her *Collected Letters* and references to her correspondence with the royal librarian are in the Austen biographies by Claire Tomalin and Lord David Cecil. The account of George III's health at this time is in John Brooke's biography.

1. 'A BURLESQUE UPON WAR'

There are many accounts of the battle of New Orleans, especially by American historians, though it has received more attention on the

British side in recent years. Accounts of the war – *The War of 1812 in the Age of Napoleon* by Jeremy Black and, most recently, Jon Latimer's *1812: War with America* – offer fresh perspectives from British historians, while Alan Taylor's *The Civil War of 1812* is a particularly interesting American account of the war's effects. Remini's *Battle for New Orleans* offers an old-fashioned pro-Jackson perspective in which the British are the villains as well as incompetents.

2. THE PEACE OF EUROPE

John Bew's recent biography of Castlereagh is not only an outstanding and sympathetic account of that tortured statesman and his achievements but also contains a lively description of the Congress of Vienna. Two recent studies of the congress – the American author David King's *Vienna 1814* and Adam Zamoyski's *Rites of Peace* – are both thorough and hugely entertaining, not to say exhaustive, accounts of the shenanigans that happened in the Hapsburg capital that autumn. Elizabeth Longford's classic biography, *Wellington: The Years of the Sword*, relates the duke's arrival at the congress to replace Castlereagh and what happened when news of Napoleon's escape from Elba broke to the delegations. Georges Lefebvre's biography of Napoleon tells the story of the start of the Hundred Days from a French perspective.

3. 'A FEARFUL INTERVAL'

Norman Gash's *Lord Liverpool* is the only modern biography of the Regency prime minister and Michael Brock's study of *The Great Reform Bill* remains academically outstanding on the nature of the pre-reform parliament. There are fine biographies of some of the leading personalities of the period: Bew's *Castlereagh*, Wendy Hinde's *George Canning*, Fintan O'Toole's *A Traitor's Kiss*, on Sheridan. The biographies of other politicians such as Samuel Whitbread can be found on the History of Parliament website, as can the *Hansard* account of the pre-war debate on 28 April 1815. The papers of the Whig Thomas Creevey and the Tory John Wilson Croker offer gossipy insider accounts of the period and its personalities. There are two outstanding recent accounts of how Britain organized the war against Napoleon: Rory Muir's *Britain and the Defeat of Napoleon* and Roger Knight's *Britain against Napoleon*, which shows how victory was a triumph as much for the organizational abilities of the nascent civil service in Whitehall as it was for the armies in the field.

4. 'THE DAMNEDEST MILLSTONE'

Apart from Brooke's *King George III*, Saul David's *Prince of Pleasure* complements Christopher Hibbert's standard biography of the Prince Regent: *The Rebel Who Would Be King*. Kenneth Baker's pictorial history of the cartoons of the period – *George IV: A Life in Caricature* – is an enthusiastic politician's evocation, while *Mirza Abul Hassan Khan's Journal* is a relatively recently discovered and fascinating outsider's account of what the royal court was like. Graham Robb's *Strangers* contains an account of homosexuality in the period.

5. 'AN IDEA OF THE REGIONS OF PLUTO'

Barrie Trinder is the doyen of Industrial Revolution studies, and his books, *The Making of the Industrial Landscape* and *Britain's Industrial Revolution*, written thirty years apart, form the backbone of the accounts of industrial development in early nineteenth-century Britain given here. For wider economic perspectives, Briggs's *Age of Improvement* and particularly Boyd Hilton's more recent general history of the period, *A Mad, Bad and Dangerous People?*, are most helpful. Faraday's probable role in the development of the Davy safety lamp is outlined in James Hamilton's biography *Faraday*. A spirited account of the career of Patrick Colquhoun is contained in Ben Wilson's hugely impressive, entertaining and original study *Decency and Disorder*. Hadcock and Millson's *History of Newbury* gives details of the making of the Newbury Coat; the Adkins' *Eavesdropping on Jane Austen's England* offers wide-ranging and striking contemporary accounts of many aspects of early nineteenth-century English society. Harry Hopkins's *Long Affray* is the definitive history of the long-running poaching wars. J.J. Tobias wrote perhaps the only biography that will ever be needed on Ikey Solomon, *The Prince of Fences*.

6. 'THE GREAT WEN'

The Zythophile website (see page 307) has a full account of the great beer explosion of 1814 and the Greater London Authority website has population statistics for the capital. There are numerous histories of London: I made most use of Roy Porter's *London*, Judith Flanders's excellent *The Victorian City*, and Weightman and Humphries's *Making of Modern London*. Judith Flanders's *The Invention of Murder* and Vic Gatrell's *The Hanging Tree* have full accounts of the sad case of Eliza Fenning. McConnell Stott's biography of Joey Grimaldi, *The Pantomime Life*, is poignant. On the architecture of the period, *Pevsner's Guide to Sussex* details the Royal Pavilion in Brighton; Gillian Darley's biography of *John Soane: An Accidental Romantic* is excellent; but for John Nash you have to go to John Summerson's biography *John Nash: Architect to George IV*, which dates back to the 1930s. *The Times*'s edition of 22 June 1815, which carries the news of the battle of Waterloo, has been reproduced many times but, as so often, some of its most interesting contents are the other notices it contains, such as that week's theatrical shows; my facsimile is taken from the Jackdaw history folder about Waterloo that I collected as a boy in the 1960s.

7. 'THE AGE OF SURFACE'

Ian Kelly has written the definitive biography of *Beau Brummell: The Ultimate Dandy*, but there are several lively memoirs by dandies and their associates, including those of Captain Gronow and Harriette Wilson (she also has an entertaining biography by Angela Thirkell, *The Fortunes of Harriette*, published in the 1930s). Scrope Davies's papers only came to light when a trunk he had left with a bank for safe-keeping was opened in the 1970s, and in Burnett's *The Rise and Fall of a Regency Dandy* they give a direct, contemporary insight into the life and debts of a hanger-on about town. Ben Wilson, in *Decency and Disorder*, writes about the dandies' milieu, as does Fergus Linnane in his *Lives of the English Rakes*. Boyd Hilton's *A Mad, Bad and Dangerous People?* draws attention to the numerous women novelists and philanthropists of the time, and their careers can be followed up through the *Dictionary of National Biography*.

8. 'LOMBARD STREET TO A CHINA ORANGE'

Captain Barclay's sporting life is entertainingly related in Peter Radford's biography *The Celebrated Captain Barclay*. The best of Pierce Egan's journalism is included in his *Boxiana* anthology, first printed during his life and regularly republished ever since; other boxing monographs include Dennis Brailsford's *Bareknuckles: A Social History of Prize-fighting* and Jon Hurley's biography *Tom Cribb: The Life of the Black Diamond* – though Hurley is no Egan. There is a huge history of cricket, also covering the Regency period, dating back to John Nyren's *Young Cricketer's Tutor* and including Sir Pelham Warner's devotional history of *Lord's 1787–1945*. Derek

Birley's *A Social History of English Cricket* has placed the game in its rightful social and economic context, as has – following in his footsteps – John Major's *More than a Game*. On racing, Professor Wray Vamplew's *The Turf: A Social and Economic History* is essential. For vermin hunts and animal-baiting, there is Henry Mayhew's Victorian journalism, *London Labour and the London Poor*, and the entertaining *Tales of a Rat-hunting Man* by D. Brian Plummer, the man who organized the rat hunt that the author once attended.

9. 'BARDS THAT ERST SUBLIMELY TOLD'

There are excellent, copious and exhaustive recent biographies of the romantic poets and their contemporaries, including their love lives: Fiona MacCarthy's *Byron: Life and Legend*, Andrew Motion's *Keats*, and Professor Richard Holmes's definitive studies *Coleridge: Darker Reflections*, *Shelley: The Pursuit* and *The Age of Wonder*. Hunter Davies's biography of his fellow Cumbrian William Wordsworth is much more readable than some of his subject's poetry. John Buchan's biography *The Life of Sir Walter Scott* is still valuable and acute after seventy years, as are more modern studies, such as Stuart Kelly's fascinating and innovative *Scott-land* and John Prebble's *The King's Jaunt* about Scott's organization of George IV's visit to Scotland in 1822. Martin Gayford's *Constable in Love* beautifully evokes the painter's long-running courtship of Maria Bicknell.

10. 'HEARTS BEAT HIGH TO TREAD THE PATHS OF GLORY'

The historian Kevin Linch has published a pioneering analysis of membership and recruitment to the British army during the latter stages of the Napoleonic wars in *Britain and Wellington's Army*. The doyen of military historians, Richard Holmes was the author of brilliant accounts of military life in *Redcoat* and latterly, sadly his last book, *Soldiers*, from which many of the anecdotes in this chapter are taken – proof that acute analysis does not have to be devoid of human sympathy or dully written. Several veterans who survived the war later wrote their memoirs (or had them written for them) including, used here: *The Letters of Private Wheeler*, *The Recollections of Rifleman Harris* and the intriguingly named *Jottings from my Sabretach*, written by a Chelsea Pensioner. Sir John Fortescue's magisterial *History of the British Army* is still valuable; volume 10, first published in 1920, applies to the American war and the Waterloo campaign. Elizabeth Longford's biography *Wellington: The Years of the Sword* remains excellent, as do Holmes's much briefer *Wellington* and Christopher Hibbert's *Wellington: A Personal History*. There are striking accounts of civilian life in Brussels in the summer of 1815 in Fanny Burney's *Journals* and especially in Thomas Creevey's *Papers*.

11. 'A DAMNED NICE THING'

There are very many British accounts of the battle of Waterloo, most quoting from the graphic memoirs of troops, such as Gronow and Wheeler, who were present. The best concise modern account is Andrew Roberts's *Waterloo: Napoleon's Last Gamble*, but earlier books – John Naylor's *Waterloo* and particularly David Howarth's *Waterloo: A Near Run Thing*, told largely from the eyewitness accounts of those who took part – must have thrilled and inspired many young would-be historians. John Keegan's ground-breaking *Face of Battle* similarly will have given very many readers a vivid feeling of what Waterloo was really like. David Hamilton-Williams's *Waterloo: New Perspectives* is a revisionist view of the battle, drawn partly from the letters survivors sent to Captain William Siborne to help him construct a model of the battlefield. A plethora of new books about the battle was published too late to be consulted for this study.

12. 'COMPLETE DARKNESS COVERED THE FACE OF THE DAY'

Accounts of the Tambora explosion and its effects have been few. Sir Stamford Raffles published eyewitness accounts of the disaster that he received from British district residents and sea captains as an interesting aside in his daughter Sophia's memoir of his life, which drew on his papers; these are the only contemporary reports in English of what the explosion was like. Until recently the only modern Western study was the Stommels' 1983 *Volcano Weather*, but a new study – *Tambora: The Eruption that Changed the World* by American professor Gillen D'Arcy Wood, published in 2014 – has offered a more detailed perspective. In 1816, the Year without a Summer, the press reported on the bad harvest without knowing why it had occurred; the stories of the effect on British agriculture are taken from *The Times*. Richard Holmes's biography of Shelley contains an account of how Mary Shelley came to write *Frankenstein* at the Villa Diodati as a result of the bad weather.

13. 'EMOTIONS BOTH OF RAGE AND FEAR'

E. P. Thompson's magisterial study of *The Making of the English Working Class* is a key romantic text for the working-class movements of the Industrial Revolution, though more recent historians have questioned his belief in the revolutionary and coordinated nature of the post-Waterloo protests. Different, more conservative perspectives are provided by F. O. Darvall's pioneering 1930s study *Popular Disturbances and Public Order in Regency England* and R. J. White's more populist, wry 1950s account *Waterloo to Peterloo* – both studies (and indeed Thompson's) now showing their age. Samuel Bamford's *Passages in the Life of a Radical*, written in the 1840s when he had long grown disillusioned with radicalism (he even became a special constable against the Chartists), is nevertheless the most direct and compelling account of what the post-war period in England was like for young men campaigning for political reform. Jeremy Bentham's *Parliamentary Reform Catechism* can be read online. The *Dictionary of National Biography* has useful short biographies of many of the radical campaigners of this period – and of Oliver the Spy. The Cornish clergyman Richard Polwhele's thoughts about rural incredulity are in John Rule's *Albion's People*. Shelley's furious composition of *The Mask of Anarchy* is fully described in Richard Holmes's biography of the poet.

14. 'THE BRAVEST AND MOST FORTUNATE NATION IN THE WORLD'

The story of Napoleon's surrender to the British and his time aboard the *Bellerophon* is told in Patrick Cordingly's *Billy Ruffian*. Brian Unwin's *Terrible Exile* is the most recent retelling of Napoleon's life on St Helena. Christopher Hibbert's biography of Wellington contains the details of the duke's medals and decorations, and Elizabeth Longford's second volume, *Wellington: Pillar of State*, magisterially takes the story on from the battle of Waterloo. Fiona MacCarthy's biography describes Byron's 1816 visit to the battlefield. Cockburn's quote about everything changing in 1815 is to be found in Michael J. Turner's *The Age of Unease*. *The Times* online archive (subscription required) for 30 December 1815 has the devastating review of the Drury Lane Theatre's production of *Romeo and Juliet*.

Bibliography

Adkins, Roy and Lesley, *Eavesdropping on Jane Austen's England* (Little Brown, 2013)

Ackroyd, Peter, *Blake* (Minerva, 1995)

Ackroyd, Peter, *London* (Chatto & Windus, 2000)

Austen, Jane, *Emma* (Penguin, 1976)

Austen, Jane, *Mansfield Park* (Penguin, 1975)

Austen, Jane, *Persuasion* (Penguin, 1981)

Austen-Leigh, James, *Memoir of Jane Austen* (Century, 1987)

Baker, Kenneth, *George IV: A Life in Caricature* (Thames & Hudson, 2005)

Bamford, Samuel, *Passages in the Life of a Radical* (OUP, 1984)

Barley, Nigel, *The Duke of Puddle Dock: In the Footsteps of Stamford Raffles* (Penguin, 1993)

Bates, William, *George Cruikshank: The Artist, the Humourist and the Man* (Houghton and Hammond, 1878)

Bentham, Jeremy, *Parliamentary Reform Catechism* (T. J. Wooler, 1818; available online)

Bew, John, *Castlereagh: Enlightenment, War and Tyranny* (Quercus, 2011)

Birley, Derek, *A Social History of English Cricket* (Aurum, 1999)

Birley, Derek, *The Willow Wand: Some Cricket Myths Explored* (Simon & Schuster, 1979)

Black, Jeremy, *The War of 1812 in the Age of Napoleon* (Continuum, 2009)

Bowen, Rowland, *Cricket: A History of its Growth and Development throughout the World* (Eyre & Spottiswoode, 1970)

Brailsford, Dennis, *Bareknuckles: A Social History of Prize-fighting* (Lutterworth, 1988)

Brewer, John, *The Pleasures of Imagination: English Culture in the Eighteenth Century* (HarperCollins, 1997)

Briggs, Asa, *The Age of Improvement, 1783–1867* (Longman, 1971)

Brock, Michael, *The Great Reform Act* (Hutchinson, 1973)

Brooke, John, *King George III* (Panther, 1974)

Buchan, John, *The Life of Sir Walter Scott* (Cassell, 1961)

Burnett, T. A. J., *The Rise and Fall of a Regency Dandy: The Life and Times of Scrope Berdmore Davies* (OUP, 1983)

Burney, Frances, *Journals and Letters* (Penguin Classics, 2001)

Byron, Lord, *The Major Works* (Oxford World Classics, 2008)

Campbell-Johnston, Rachel, *Mysterious Wisdom: The Life and Work of Samuel Palmer* (Bloomsbury, 2011)

Cecil, David, *A Portrait of Jane Austen* (Penguin, 1986)

Chesney, Kellow, *The Victorian Underworld* (History Book Club, 1970)

Clark, J. C. D., *English Society, 1688–1832* (CUP, 1985)

Cobbett, William, *Rural Rides* (Penguin, 1967)

Coles, Harry, *The War of* 1812 (University of Chicago Press, 1965)

Colley, Linda, *Britons: Forging the Nation, 1707–1837* (Pimlico, 1992)

Cordingly, Patrick, *Billy Ruffian: The* Bellerophon *and the Downfall of Napoleon* (Bloomsbury, 2004)

Creevey, Thomas, *The Creevey Papers* (Dutton & Co., 1904)

Cronin, Vincent, *Napoleon* (HarperCollins, 1994)

Dallas, Gregor, 1815: *The Roads to Waterloo* (Pimlico, 1996)

D'Arcy Wood, Gillen, *Tambora: The Eruption that Changed the World* (Princeton University Press, 2014)

Darley, Gillian, *John Soane: An Accidental Romantic* (Yale, 1999)

Darter, William, *Reminiscences of Reading, by an Octogenarian* (British Library Historical Collections, reprint of 1889 edition)

Darvall, F. O., *Popular Disturbances and Public Order in Regency England* (OUP, 1934)

David, Saul, *Prince of Pleasure: The Prince of Wales and the Making of the Regency* (Abacus, 1999)

Davies, Hunter, *William Wordsworth* (Frances Lincoln, 2009)

Davis, Terence, *John Nash: The Prince Regent's Architect* (Country Life, 1966)

Dickens, Charles, *Memoirs of Joseph Grimaldi* (Pushkin Press, 2008)

Dickens, Charles, *The Pickwick Papers* (Penguin, 1974)

Egan, Pierce, *Boxiana, or Sketches of Ancient and Modern Pugilism* (Elibron Classics, 2006)

Flanders, Judith, *The Invention of Murder* (HarperPress, 2011)

Flanders, Judith, *The Victorian City* (Atlantic, 2012)

Fortescue, J. W., *A History of the British Army*, vol. 10, *1814–1815* (Macmillan, 1920)

Foster, R. F., *Modern Ireland, 1600–1972* (Penguin, 1988)

Frith, David, *Pageant of Cricket* (Macmillan, 1987)

Gash, Norman, *Lord Liverpool* (Weidenfeld & Nicolson, 1984)

Gatrell, Vic, *City of Laughter: Sex and Satire in Eighteenth Century London* (Atlantic, 2006)

Gatrell, Vic, *The Hanging Tree: Execution and the English People, 1770–1868* (OUP, 1994)

Gayford, Martin, *Constable in Love* (Penguin, 2009)

Gittings, Robert, *John Keats* (Pelican, 1971)

Goff, Moira, Goldfinch, John, Limper-Herz, Karen and Peden, Helen, *Georgians Revealed: Life, Style and the Making of Modern Britain* (British Library, 2013)

Gillen, Mollie, *Assassination of the Prime Minister: The Shocking Death of Spencer Perceval* (Sidgwick & Jackson, 1972)

Griffin, Emma, *Liberty's Dawn: A People's History of the European Union* (Yale, 2013)

Gronow, H. R., *The Reminiscences and Recollections of Captain Gronow* (Surtees Society edition, 1984)

Hadcock, Neville and Millson, Cecilia, *The Story of Newbury* (Countryside Books, 1990)

Hamilton, James, *Faraday* (HarperCollins, 2002)

Hamilton, James, *Turner: A Life* (Sceptre, 1997)

Hamilton-Williams, David, *Waterloo – New Perspectives: The Great Battle Reappraised* (Arms and Armour Press, 1994)

Harvey, A. D., *Collision of Empires: Britain in Three World Wars, 1793–1945* (Hambledon Press, 1992)

Hay, Daisy, *Young Romantics: The Shelleys, Byron and Other Tangled Lives* (Bloomsbury, 2010)

Hibbert, Christopher, *The Recollections of Rifleman Harris* (Windrush Press, 1999)

Hibbert, Christopher, *George IV: The Rebel Who Would Be King* (Palgrave Macmillan, 2007)

Hibbert, Christopher, *King Mob* (Sutton, 2004)

Hibbert, Christopher, *Wellington: A Personal History* (HarperCollins, 1997)

Hilton, Boyd, *A Mad, Bad and Dangerous People? England, 1783–1846* (OUP, 2006)

Hinde, Wendy, *George Canning* (Purnell, 1973)

Hobsbawm, E. J., and Rudé, George, *Captain Swing* (Penguin, 1969)

Hochschild, Adam, *Bury the Chains: The British Struggle to Abolish Slavery* (Pan, 2005)

Holmes, Richard, *The Age of Wonder: How the Romantic Generation Discovered the Beauty and Terror of Science* (HarperPress, 2008)

Holmes, Richard, *Coleridge: Darker Reflections* (Harper Perennial, 1998)

Holmes, Richard, *Shelley: The Pursuit* (Harper Perennial, 2005)

Holmes, Richard, *Redcoat: The British Soldier in the Age of Horse and Musket* (HarperCollins, 2001)

Holmes, Richard, *Soldiers* (HarperPress, 2011)

Holmes, Richard, *Wellington: The Iron Duke* (HarperCollins, 2003)

Holt, Richard, *Sport and the British: A Modern History* (OUP, 1990)

Hopkins, Harry, *The Long Affray: The Poaching Wars in Britain* (Papermac, 1985)

Howarth, David, *Waterloo: A Near Run Thing* (Collins, 1968)

Howarth, David, *Waterloo: A Guide to the Battlefield* (Pitkin, 1980)

Hurley, Jon, *Tom Cribb: The Life of the Black Diamond* (History Press, 2009)

Jackson, Graham and Ludlow, Cate, *A Grim Almanac of Georgian London* (History Press, 2011)

James, Lawrence, *Aristocrats: Power, Grace and Decadence* (Abacus, 2009)

James, Lawrence, *The Middle Class: A History* (Little Brown, 2006)

Khan, Mirza Abul Hassan, *A Persian at the Court of King George, 1809–10* (Barrie & Jenkins, 1988)

Keegan, John, *The Face of Battle* (Penguin, 1976)

Kelly, Ian, *Beau Brummell: The Ultimate Dandy* (Hodder, 2005)

Kelly, Stuart, *Scott-Land: The Man Who Invented a Nation* (Polygon, 2011)

King, David, *Vienna 1814* (Broadway, 2008)

Knight, Roger, *Britain against Napoleon: The Organisation of Victory, 1793–1815* (Allen Lane, 2013)

Laski, Marghanita, *Jane Austen and Her World* (Thames & Hudson, 1969)

Latimer, Jon, *1812: War with America* (Belknap Press, Harvard University Press, 2007)

Le Faye, Deirdre, *Jane Austen's Letters* (Folio Society, 2003)

Le Faye, Deirdre, *Jane Austen: The World of Her Novels* (Frances Lincoln, 2002)

Lefebvre, Georges, *Napoleon* (Folio Society, 2009)

Liddell Hart, B. H. (ed.), *The Letters of Private Wheeler, 1809–1828* (Windrush Press, 1999)

Linch, Kevin, *Britain and Wellington's Army: Recruitment, Society and Tradition, 1807–15* (Palgrave Macmillan, 2011)

Linnane, Fergus, *The Lives of the English Rakes* (Portrait, 2002)

Longford, Elizabeth, *Victoria* (Abacus, 2011)

Longford, Elizabeth, *Wellington: The Years of the Sword* (Weidenfeld & Nicolson, 1969)

Longford, Elizabeth, *Wellington: Pillar of the State* (Panther, 1972)

Macalpine, Ida and Hunter, Richard, *George III and the Mad Business* (Allen Lane, Penguin Press, 1969)

MacCarthy, Fiona, *Byron: Life and Legend* (John Murray, 2002)

Major, John, *More than a Game: The Story of Cricket's Early Years* (Harper Perennial, 2007)

Marchand, Leslie A., *Wedlock's the Devil: Byron's Letters and Journals*, vol. 4, *1814–15* (John Murray, 1975)

McConnell Stott, Andrew, *The Pantomime Life of Joseph Grimaldi* (Canongate, 2009)

Mayhew, Henry, *London Labour and the London Poor* (OUP, 2010)

Meacham, Jon, *American Lion: Andrew Jackson in the White House* (Random House, 2009)

Mitford, Mary Russell, *Our Village* (OUP, 1982)

Motion, Andrew, *Keats* (Faber and Faber, 1997)

Muir, Rory, *Britain and the Defeat of Napoleon, 1807–1815* (Yale, 1996)

Nairn, Ian and Pevsner, Nikolaus, *The Buildings of England: Sussex* (Yale, 1965)

Naylor, John, *Waterloo* (Pan, 1960)

Nyren, John, *The Young Cricketer's Tutor* (Gay and Bird edition, 1902)

O'Toole, Fintan, *A Traitor's Kiss: The Life of Richard Brinsley Sheridan* (Granta, 1997)

Palmer, Alan, *Metternich* (History Book Club, 1972)

Peacock, Thomas Love, *Headlong Hall* (Wordworth Classics, 1995)

Plummer, D. Brian, *Tales of a Rat-hunting Man* (Boydell Press, 1978)

Pool, Bernard (ed.), *The Croker Papers, 1808–1857* (Batsford, 1967)

Porter, Bernard, *Plots and Paranoia: A History of Political Espionage in Britain, 1790–1988* (Unwin Hyman, 1989)

Porter, Roy, *London: A Social History* (Hamish Hamilton, 1994)

Prebble, John, *The King's Jaunt: George IV in Scotland* (Fontana Collins, 1988)

Quayle, Eric, *The Ruin of Sir Walter Scott* (Rupert Hart-Davis, 1968)

Radford, Peter, *The Celebrated Captain Barclay: Sport, Gambling and Adventure in Regency Times* (Headline, 2001)

Raffles, Sophia, *Memoir of the Life and Public Services of Sir Thomas Stamford Raffles, Particularly in the Government of Java, 1811–1816*, vol. 1 (James Duncan, 1835)

Reilly, Paul, *An Introduction to Regency Architecture* (Arts & Technics, 1948)

Remini, Robert V., *The Battle of New Orleans: Andrew Jackson and America's First Military Victory* (Penguin, 1999)

Richardson, John, *The Annals of London* (Cassell, 2000)

Robb, Graham, *Strangers: Homosexual Love in the Nineteenth Century* (Picador, 2003)

Roberts, Andrew, *Waterloo: Napoleon's Last Gamble* (HarperCollins, 2005)

Rodger, N.A.M., *The Wooden World: An Anatomy of the Georgian Navy* (Fontana, 1986)

Rosenthal, Michael, *Constable* (Thames & Hudson, 1987)

Rule, John, *Albion's People: English Society, 1714–1815* (Longman, 1992)

Schlesinger, Arthur M., Jnr, *The Age of Jackson* (Little Brown, 1953)

Scott, Sir Walter, *Waverley* (Penguin Classics, 2011 edition)

Stagg, J.C.A., *The War of 1812: Conflict for a Continent* (Cambridge University Press, 2012)

Stanhope, John, *The Cato Street Conspiracy* (Jonathan Cape, 1962)

Stommel, Henry and Elizabeth, *Volcano Weather: The Story of the Year without a Summer* (Seven Seas Press, 1983)

Summerson, John, *John Nash: Architect to George IV* (Allen & Unwin, 1935)

Taylor, Alan, *The Civil War of 1812: American Citizens, British Subjects, Irish Rebels and Indian Allies* (Vintage Books, 2010)

Thirkell, Angela, *The Fortunes of Harriette: The Surprising Career of Harriette Wilson* (Hamish Hamilton, 1936)

Thomas, Hugh, *The Slave Trade* (Papermac, 1997)

Thompson, E. P., *The Making of the English Working Class* (Penguin, 1968)

Tillyard, Stella, *Aristocrats* (Vintage, 1994)

The History of the Times: 'The Thunderer' in the Making, 1785–1841 (The Times, 1935)

Tobias, J. J., *Prince of Fences: The Life and Crimes of Ikey Solomons* (Vallentine Mitchell, 1974)

Tomalin, Claire, *Jane Austen: A Life* (Penguin, 1997)

Trinder, Barrie, *Britain's Industrial Revolution: The Making of a Manufacturing People, 1700–1870* (Carnegie, 2013)

Trinder, Barrie, *The Making of the Industrial Landscape* (J. M. Dent, 1982)

Turner, Michael J., *The Age of Unease: Government and Reform in Britain, 1782–1832* (Sutton, 2000)

Uglow, Jenny, *In These Times: Living in Britain through Napoleon's Wars: 1795–1815* (Faber and Faber, 2014)

Underdown, David, *Start of Play: Cricket and Culture in Eighteenth-Century England* (Penguin, 2000)

Unwin, Brian, *Terrible Exile: The Last Days of Napoleon on St. Helena* (I. B. Tauris, 2010)

Vamplew, Wray, *The Turf: A Social and Economic History of Horse Racing* (Allen Lane, 1976)

Vickery, Amanda, *Behind Closed Doors: At Home in Georgian England* (Yale, 2009)

Wardroper, John, *Kings, Lords and Wicked Libellers: Satire and Protest, 1760–1837* (History Book Club, 1973)

Warner, Pelham, *Lord's 1787–1945* (Harrap, 1946)

Weightman, Gavin and Humphries, Steve, *The Making of Modern London, 1815–1914* (Sidgwick & Jackson, 1983)

White, Jerry, *London in the Nineteenth Century* (Vintage, 2007)

White, R. J., *Waterloo to Peterloo* (Penguin, 1968)

Wilson, Ben, *Decency and Disorder: The Age of Cant, 1789–1837* (Faber and Faber, 2007)

Wilson, Harriette, *Memoirs: The Greatest Courtesan of Her Age* (Phoenix, 2003)

Zamoyski, Adam, *Rites of Peace: The Fall of Napoleon and the Congress of Vienna* (HarperCollins, 2008)

WEBSITES

www.ambervalley.gov.uk (Pentrich Rising)

www.hansard.millbanksystems.com (Parliamentary debates)

www.historyofparliamentonline.org

www.london.gov.uk (population statistics)

www.newlanark.org

www.oxforddnb.com (*Dictionary of National Biography*)

www.regencyhistory.net

www.spartacus-educational.com

www.thetimes.co.uk

www.walterscott.lib.ed.ac.uk

www.zythophile.wordpress.com

Acknowledgements

I wish to thank Richard Milbank and the staff at Head of Zeus for commissioning me to write this book as a sort of prequel to my previous contribution to their series on significant years in British history – *Two Nations: Britain in 1846* – which dealt with the denouement of the Corn Laws crisis which scarred the country's politics for thirty-six years. This book was the idea of my agent Charlie Viney and once again it was skilfully edited by Ben Dupré.

For nearly five years in the late 1990s I was the *Guardian*'s European Affairs Editor, based in Brussels mainly to cover the European Union, but I regularly escaped the longueurs of discussions on the Common Fisheries Policy or monetary union to walk in the countryside south of Brussels, tramping frequently over the battlefield of Waterloo. It is still possible to stand with one's back to the large mound built to commemorate the Prince of Orange's stand at the battle and the circular building housing the ancient diorama and get a good sense of what the land was like on 18 June 1815: the wide, open fields and the gentle incline up which the French cavalry and infantry laboured all afternoon to attack the allied army. When we had visitors from England, we often dragged them to the battlefield too, until my daughter, then aged ten or eleven, moaned how boring it was getting. If she gets round to reading this book now, as an adult, I hope she might glean something of its enduring fascination for her father.

My thanks for putting up with this go, as always, to my wife Alice, daughter Helena and sons Timothy and Philip. This book is dedicated to my older brother Chris Bates, a former colonel of the Royal Engineers who *was* interested in the battlefield of Waterloo, and my older sister Felicity Rickard, who worked for many years to help preserve the water meadows from which John Constable painted Salisbury Cathedral in 1831.

Stephen Bates
Deal, August 2014

Index

Abul Hassan Khan, Mirza 73–4
actors 124–6
Adams, John Quincy 28
Addington, Henry *see* Sidmouth, Viscount
adultery 156
agricultural workers 106–7
  wages 109–10
agriculture 8
  and enclosures 8, 106
  impact of Tambora eruption on 249–50
Aislabie, Ben 174
Albuera, battle of 5
Alexander I, Tsar 39, 42, 52
Allen, General Charles 226
Allen, John 109
Allen, William 101
Almack's club (King Street) 148–9
Alvanley, Lord 140, 150
Amelia, Princess 15
American War of Independence 27, 31, 33, 141, 209, 260, 285
animal cruelty 175–7
Apsley, Lord 37
aristocracy 4, 59, 99, 107, 156, 172, 206
army, British 197–210
  bounties and wages 200, 201
  fate of dead and wounded soldiers 207–8
  foreign troops and mercenaries 198

numbers in 5, 197
officer class and buying of commissions 4, 204–7
punishment of soldiers 203
reasons for joining 199–200
recruitment of soldiers 4, 197–9, 202–3
training 203–4
volunteer units raised 202
Astley's Royal Amphitheatre 127
Austen, Henry 187
Austen, Jane 5, 6, 16, 75, 153, 187–90
  Emma 187, 188–9
  Mansfield Park 6, 11, 187
  Persuasion 6, 187, 190
Austria 39, 40
Ayton, Richard 100–1

Bacon, Thomas 270
Baillie, Joanna 154
balls 148
Bamford, Samuel 93, 260, 261, 263–4, 266–8, 272–4, 275
Bank of England 137
Barbauld, Anna Laetitia
  'Eighteen Hundred and Eleven' 152–3
Barclay, Captain 161–3, 168, 170, 171, 177–8, 179
Barltrop, Mabel 279
Barrymore, 7th Earl of 163
Barrymore family 145
Bateman, Mary 278

311

Picture credits

1. George IV, by Sir Thomas Lawrence; The Art Archive/Private Collection/Philip Mould.
2. George Cruikshank, 'the Prince of Whales'; Leeds Museums and Art Galleries (Temple Newsam House) UK/Bridgeman Images.
3. The battle of New Orleans; The Art Archive/Kharbine-Tapabor/Coll. Jonas.
4. The Congress of Vienna; Mary Evans/INTERFOTO/Sammlung Rauch.
5. The Barton aqueduct; Oxford Science Archive/Print Collector/Getty Images.
6. The Red Rover stagecoach; Ann Ronan Pictures/Print Collector/Getty Images.
7. The 'Newbury Coat'; SSPL/Getty Images.
8. New Lanark; Oxford Science Archive/Print Collector/Getty Images.
9. Regent Street; The Print Collector/Print Collector/Getty Images.
10. 'Gay Moments of Logic'; The Art Archive/John Meek.
11. Joey Grimaldi; Mander and Mitchenson University of Bristol/ArenaPAL/Topfoto.
12. George Wilson; Guildhall Library & Art Gallery/Heritage Images/Getty Images.
13. Lord Alvanley; Look and Learn/Peter Jackson Collection/Bridgeman Images.
14. Elizabeth Fry; The Granger Collection/Topfoto.
15. Harriette Wilson; British Museum.
16. Cribb vs Molineaux; Mary Evans Picture Library.

17. Women's cricket match by Thomas Rowlandson; Derbyshire Record Office.

18. French cavalry attack an infantry square at Waterloo; Topfoto.

19 Viscount Castlereagh, by Sir Thomas Lawrence; The Granger Collection/Topfoto.

20. Viscount Sidmouth; Hulton Archive/Getty Images.

21. Napoleon is transferred from the *Bellerophon*; Fine Art Images/ HIP/Topfoto.

22. The caldera of Mount Tambora; NASA/JSC.

Note on the typeface

This book is typeset in Fairfield Light, designed by Czechoslovakian engraver, book designer and typographer Rudolph Ruziska. Released by Linotype in 1940, it is a contemporary typeface with roots in the Old Style tradition. The elegant variation of the strokes and the fine serifs of Fairfield reflect the philosophy of an artist dedicated to simplicity and clarity in typeface design.